Contextualizing Gender in Early Christian Discourse

Contextualizing Gender in Early Christian Discourse

Thinking beyond Thecla

Caroline Vander Stichele
and Todd Penner

t&t clark

Published by T&T Clark International
A Continuum Imprint

The Tower Building, 11 York Road, London SE1 7NX
80 Maiden Lane, Suite 704, New York, NY 10038

www.continuumbooks.com

British Library Cataloguing-in-Publication Data
A catalogue record for this book is available from the British Library

ISBN: 978-0-567-03035-1 (Hardback)
       978-0-567-03036-8 (Paperback)

Typeset by Newgen Imaging Systems Pvt Ltd, Chennai, India
Printed and bound in Great Britain by CPI Antony Rowe Ltd,
Chippenham, Wiltshire

For our parents

In gratitude

Bernadette and Robert Vander Stichele—De Waele

Pauline and Charles Penner—Rempel

Contents

Acknowledgments

This book has a long history, and with that comes an even longer list of people and organizations to thank. To begin with, this volume would not likely have been conceived if it had not been for the invitation by Mary Grey, almost ten years ago, to write a volume for the *Introducing* series. This volume never found its way into that series, as its scope shifted over time, but we are grateful to Mary for being the catalyst that got the proverbial ball rolling.

Our respective institutions (Austin College and the University of Amsterdam) have been of enormous help in terms of providing opportunities for travel to conferences, which allowed at least a good portion of the material in this book to receive initial scrutiny by colleagues and peers. The following papers ended up forming the backbone of this book: "Le territoire corinthien: Point de vue et poétique dans les Actes des Apôtres," presented in "Le point de vue entre Historie et Poétique" seminar at the third international colloquium of the Réseau de recherche en narrativité biblique (RRENAB) conference (Paris, June 2006); "Tracing the Pauline Corpus in and out of the Canon," presented at the Society of Biblical Literature Annual Meeting (Washington, November 2006); "Canonized Bodies: Gender and the Formation of Early Christianity," presented at the "Rhetorics of Social Formation" conference (University of Redlands, January 2007); "Knowing Gender Then and Now: Positioning Feminist and Gender-Critical Engagements of Historical Criticism," presented at the Amsterdam School for Cultural Analysis International Workshop "Inside Knowledge: (Un)doing Methodologies, Imagining Alternatives" (University of Amsterdam, March 2007); "Response to Mikeal Parson's *Body and Character in Luke and Acts*," presented in the "Biblical Scholarship and Disability Consultation" at the International Society of Biblical Literature Annual Meeting (Vienna, July 2007); "Read It as a Woman—Write It Like a Man: Gender and the Production of Knowledge," presented at the Society of Biblical Literature Annual Meeting (San Diego, November 2007); "Teaching with, against, and to Faith," sponsored by the American Academy of Religion Committee on Teaching and Learning, presented at the American Academy of Religion Annual Meeting (San Diego, November 2007); "Gender and Biblical Scholarship," presented at the Canadian Society of Biblical Studies Annual Meeting (University of British Columbia, June 2008); and "Confessions of a

Boundary-Crosser: The Eschatological Edge of Teaching, Research, and Practice," presented at the Center for Jewish Studies conference "On the Boundary—HoweverWhereverWhomever" (Baylor University, October 2008). We are most appreciative to the organizers of these various conferences and sessions for including our papers in their forums, and for the various responses and feedback we received on those occasions, with special appreciation going to Claire Clivaz, David and Jim Hester, and Marc Ellis for their critical engagement and spectacular hospitality. Special thanks also to Halvor Moxnes and Marianne Bjelland Kartzow for the invitation for Caroline to present the outline of this project at the Program Seminar on Intersectionality for the Norwegian Research Council project "Jesus in Cultural Complexity" (University of Oslo, October 2008). Similarly, we are grateful to Davina Lopez for extending an invitation to Todd to engage some of this material in the "Power, Gender, and Sexuality" working group at the "New Testament and Roman Empire: Resistance and Reimagination" conference (Union Theological Seminary, April 2008). Halvor, Marianne, and Davina proved to be most welcoming hosts and model examples of how scholarship and life can be mutually enriched when combined.

We are also indebted to the Netherlands Organization for Scientific Research (NWO) for a Replacement Grant for Caroline's teaching at the University of Amsterdam in 2007. This project would likely not have been completed without that support. Special thanks also to Jan Willem van Henten, who submitted the grant, and to Magda Misset-van de Weg, who was so kind to serve as a term replacement in the department. The funding provided to Todd from the Woodrow Wilson National Fellowship Foundation through a Millicent C. McIntosh Fellowship in 2006–2007 also proved vital for freeing up time to work on this project.

The Austin College "Gender and Early Christianity" students in the fall of 2007 proved most valuable as "guinea pigs" for the first few chapters of the book. They were most willing to provide feedback and identify particular points of interest along the way. That group of students definitely shaped the final outcome of the book by asking the crucial question: "why does any of this 'old stuff' matter?" Special thanks go to Kathryn Aken, Kelli Cook, and Elizabeth Ford for their extra labors and sharp insight. As always, special recognition goes to Bernice Melvin for her unbounded enthusiasm, encouragement, and support as the (now former) dean of the humanities at Austin College. We are also most grateful to Susanne Scholz, Tricia Sheffield, Joe Marchal, Laura Copier, Jan Jans, Michele Kennerly, and Kyle Poff, all of whom read some or all of the manuscript for this book and offered invaluable feedback and criticism. We are also appreciative of the efforts of Jaisy Joseph of Austin College, who, in her capacity as a Lilly Intern in the Department of Religious Studies, worked on the indices for this book. The final product has definitely been improved as a result of their labors. Thanks as well to Faith Kirkham Hawkins for some last minute critical engagement over "critical pedagogy." Further, we want to recognize all of those who gently encouraged us in the writing of this book: Bridgette Saladino, Mark Monroe, Andra Troncalli, Osman Umurhan, Gillian Townsley, Kimberly Stratton, Chris Freeman, Emily Searle, and Uma Shah. Appreciation also goes to Faith, Glenda, and Shiloh, whose hospitality and friendship made the final hours of this project both relaxing and enjoyable, and to the remarkable people at the Wabash Center for Teaching and Learning in Theology and Religion, who extended, once again, their welcoming hand, making the final hour of this project seem like the first. In terms of dialogue partners for this project, especially with respect to Gender Studies issues and theories, no two were more engaging and challenging than Tricia Sheffield and Joe Marchal. We are indebted to them both for their time, energy, creativity, and, on occasion, patience—and, last but not least, friendship. Joe also deserves recognition for his continuing desire to be a part of the agenda behind our work and to be a friend and comrade in scholarly endeavors, even as he is ever so sure he is deeply suspicious of our scholarship and us. What better friend than this (Plutarch would have loved him)! Joe has been a constant source of encouragement ("How's the book coming?"; "Are we there yet?"), and his deep and abiding commitment to the ethics and politics of scholarship has been an inspiration to us throughout the writing process.

The long prehistory of this book entails that we have had numerous contacts at Continuum, UK, over that time. Rebecca Mulhearn and Georgina Brindley deserve special note, as both of them were a pleasure to work with early on in the process. Haaris Naqvi was the editor when this project finally got wings, and his constant encouragement (and patience) has been most appreciated. In the fall of 2008, Dominic Mattos took over editorial responsibilities for the book. We are grateful to him for his work on the publication end and the gentle pressure to get this project completed. Special thanks also to the people at Newgen Imaging Systems, especially Murali, (whose patience has been most valued, as has his exceptional work on the difficult task of typesetting this manuscript). Anna Turton was also a key player in the final stages of production.

We also express our deepest appreciation to our partners, Jan Jans and Jacqueline Klassen, without whose support and encouragement this book could not have been written. They have truly been in this endeavor for the long haul and have been most gracious along the way. Lastly, we cannot leave out our countless cats—those who were there when this project started (Ishtar, Buzz, Ramona), those who arrived while it was in process (Thomasch, Dixie, Biba, Socks, Shiva, Lilith, Isis, Achilles, Adonis, Kali, Hercules, Pluto, and Freia), and those who died before it was completed (Effi, Eli, Hank)—all of whom have made us a little fonder for Thecla's feral ways.

InterseXions

And Thecla rose and told Paul: "I'm going to Iconium." And Paul said: "Go and teach the word of God."

—Acts of Paul and Thecla 3.41

The preceding quote appears at the end of an early Christian text from the second century CE, entitled the *Acts of Paul and Thecla*. This text offers a fascinating account about the encounter between Paul, the apostle, well known to us from both the canonical Acts of the Apostles and from his letters in the New Testament, and a young woman named Thecla who, after hearing Paul preach in her hometown of Iconium, decides to follow him. Unfortunately for her, abandoning her life as part of the social elite in Iconium appears to be not as simple as it may seem. Not only does she meet opposition from both her mother, Theoclia, and her fiancé, Thamyris, she is, more seriously, put on trial and condemned to be burned alive in the arena for her refusal to marry. Thecla is, however, miraculously saved and released. She then goes searching for Paul and finds him fasting in an open tomb on the road from Iconium to Daphne. He rejoices when he sees her, taking her with him to Antioch, but there Thecla is confronted with another problem. She is harassed by Alexander, an elite resident of the city and, when she resists his advances, she is once again sentenced to death, this time to fight wild animals in the arena. Again, she is saved and leaves to find Paul, who has gone to Myra. After they meet, she decides to go back to Iconium and Paul commissions her to preach the word of God. Back in Iconium, Thecla visits her mother, but continues her journey to Seleucia, where she stays and dies after having enlightened many people there with the "word of God."

As this plot summary makes clear, the roads that both Paul and Thecla travel in this story intersect at several points: first, when he visits Iconium, she hears him preaching there, then she meets him again on the road to Daphne after her first trial, and a third time in Myra, after her second trial. These various moments of meeting between Thecla and Paul are momentary points of interconnection, which are then followed by separation and differentiation. As such, they are symbolic for us of larger intersections both within the text, but also between the text and its world, and between these ancient texts and our contemporary reading of them. In the following five chapters of this book, we address in a variety of ways this phenomenon of multiple intersections in ancient texts and modern interpretations. We are interested in intersections between gender, sex, and sexuality to begin with, but also between gender and other markers of identity such as ethnicity/race and class, between past and present perceptions of gender, as well as interconnections between early Christian and Greco-Roman rhetoric and sociocultural discourses. As far as the approach that we develop in this book is concerned, we also see intersections between our own gender-critical approach and other ideology-critical approaches to biblical texts (such as feminist, queer, postcolonial), but also between Europe and America, where our respective institutions are situated, and thus also our social locations for interpretation.

Before explaining the title and subtitle of this volume, and providing a short overview of the chapters to follow, we offer a few words regarding the prehistory of this project. It is always easier to see in retrospect how earlier publications have led up to this current book. In our case, alongside numerous coauthored essays, there were three coedited collections in particular that map well our journey towards this present volume. All of these edited collections originated in sessions we cochaired at the International Meetings of the Society of Biblical Literature. These sessions operate under the umbrella of the title "Whence and Whither?: Methodology and the Future of Biblical Studies" (2001–present), and are devoted, in one way or another, to the exploration of methodological issues in the field of Biblical Studies, emphasizing newer ways of reading and interpreting the Bible in conversation with more conventional methodologies. The first volume thus conceived (*Contextualizing Acts*, 2003), focused on situating the Acts of the Apostles in the context of Greco-Roman discourse, from ancient rhetoric and historiography to the Greek novels and epics. The second volume (*Her Master's Tools?*, 2005) treated the reception of historical criticism in feminist and postcolonial biblical studies. The third (*Mapping Gender in Ancient Religious Discourses*, 2007) sought to engage issues related to gender at the intersection of religious discourses in antiquity.

This present volume has features in common with all three of these previous projects. Most explicit are our concerns to situate early Christian literature in the broader context of ancient literary and religious traditions, to focus on discourse as a constituent aspect of identity formation, to foster an appreciation for gender issues, to continue to value a historical approach (even if reconfigured), to stress the role of ideology in the formation of the worlds of the text as well as ancient and modern readers, and to highlight the colonizing nature of empire. All of these elements represent aspects of the gender-critical approach we lay out in this book, an approach that has evolved and developed in conversation with diverse fields and, especially, the various contributors to the aforementioned collections, without whose scholarly engagements and intellectual intersections we would not as likely have ended up methodologically and ideologically where we are at present. Further, as a result of all of this interaction and growth, our own approach and analysis has become increasingly interdisciplinary in focus.

This present volume also evidences two important shifts from our previous work. First, this book is consciously self-reflexive, in that we seek to reveal and foreground concepts and approaches used in our earlier work. In other words, our own selections, choices, and ideological biases are explicitly fronted, so as to delineate more clearly how the gender-critical approach we employ is decidedly our own version of such an approach. Further, we hope such self-reflexive interpretative practices aid in interdisciplinary and transdisciplinary conversations, and help foster interaction with other more traditional approaches in the discipline of Biblical Studies (i.e., we may not agree on how to read the past, but by foregrounding our implicit assumptions and values we can have a conversation about why our readings are different and why that matters). A second major shift is that this book is written with our students in mind rather than our peers, although we hope of course that it will be of interest to both audiences. We understand that the study of early Christian texts is not an end in itself, but, rather, it is, as we think it should be within the field of the Humanities, a stepping stone for political, cultural, and social engagement in our own time period and locales. Our hope is to offer a book that would indicate the importance of the politics of scholarship for us, and, conversely, to lay out a gender-critical methodology that would situate the study of texts, in this case early Christian writings, within a framework that would encourage readers to engage gendered and sexed politics in their own spheres of influence. Thus, with our students in view, we also want to push the edge of critical interaction with early Christian texts, making clear throughout that there is no critical thinking that does not bear a marked relevance for our own time and place, for our own thinking, in this instance, about gender, sex, and sexuality. In the end, then, this book is not about the ancient world; it is, rather, about rethinking our own world and our place in it through interaction with texts from long ago, including also the engagement of our own interpretative practices and disciplines. Thus, for us the challenge is to use the ancient world as a foil for interacting with our own, and, in the process, challenging our assumptions, values, and social-political identities.

In this respect, then, the title of this book—*Contextualizing Gender in Early Christian Discourse: Thinking beyond Thecla*—entails both the components of our own disciplinary, professional, and personal journeys, as well as this focus on a praxis-oriented, critical-thinking engagement of the material from the context of our own time period and reading location. Each component of the title is thus reflective of an aspect of our particular approach. To begin with, *contextualizing*, which already played a role in our earlier edited collection on the Acts of the Apostles, reappears here as we situate the views on gender, sex, and sexuality present in the early Christian documents within the larger context of the ancient Greco-Roman world, including attention to the contextualization of our own assumptions and values in historical research. Further, apart from this larger sociocultural and political contextualization, we also find it important to investigate the unique contours of these conceptions in the context of early Christian history itself, as well as to analyze how gender, sex, and sexuality intersect with other facets of identity such as ethnicity and class.

With respect to the use of the term *gender*, we understand "gender" to be a distinct but congenial category to the related concepts of sex and sexuality—it is most definitely not to be framed as an isolated phenomenon. Thus, we define "gender" as referring to the performative aspect of being a "man" or a "woman," the cultural role models one adopts to act as one or the other. The second term, "sex," is understood here to refer to the physical aspects of being identified as "male" or "female," while "sexuality" refers to one's sexual orientation, if one is heterosexual, homosexual, or bisexual. In the gender-critical approach that we develop in this volume, we address these three components of one's identity by exploring how gender "works" in early Christian texts. More specifically, we do so by using three major forms of analysis. The first one is historical, in that we approach early Christian texts as historical documents to be situated within their ancient contexts. The second analytical tool is literary, in that we understand these texts as being rhetorical in character. By this designation, we imply that we do not see them as passive recipients of meaning, but as discursive or communicative interactions between the author of a text and its readers, both past and present. Third, we undertake an ideology-critical analysis both of the texts under discussion and also of their interpretations, insofar as we look for the values, prejudices, and worldviews embedded in them. Through these three primary modes of analysis, our aim is to explicate contextually the integrated and complex nature of gendered, sexed, and sexual identities, both ancient and modern.

Besides the issue of gender, the term *discourse* provides another link with our previous work related to mapping gender in ancient religious discourses, but it is also meant to indicate that we are discussing textual material in this book, rather than archeological remains or visual representations from antiquity, which are no less relevant. Our use of the term "discourse" rather than "writings" or "literature" signals that we intend to stress the link between those texts and the power structures in which they are situated and with which they intersect. As we will explain in our first chapter, the work of Michel Foucault has been a major source of influence in why we have chosen this term. One of our main assumptions in this study is that language shapes the way we perceive the world, and contributes to how we then act in it. Thus, in our view, by far the most critical element in historical investigation is gaining an appreciation for the *function* of language within the historical and sociocultural contexts in which it occurs. The very act of scholarly historical analysis is already a language-act, since our methods, analyses, and results are all framed discursively. Thus, whether we look at the ancient material or at ourselves examining the ancient material, in both cases we are analyzing the operation of language. Discourse therefore forms a critical component of our approach in the ensuing chapters.

Moreover, the focus of this analytical work is *early Christian* discourse in particular. By "early Christian" we refer not just to the canonical writings of the New Testament, but also to the so-called apocryphal texts of the first few centuries CE, including the *Acts of Paul and Thecla*, to which we have given a significant presence in this book. In what follows, we limit our scope mostly to texts that deal with the apostles and the early Christian communities, in order to provide our argument with more focus. More specifically, we discuss the Acts of the Apostles, the Pauline correspondence (with a particular emphasis on 1 Corinthians), and the *Acts of Paul and Thecla*. Not only does this latter text relate to both the canonical book of Acts in dealing with the spread of the gospel, and to Paul, in that he is one of the main characters in this apocryphal book, but it is also an intriguing text from the perspective of gender. It is, moreover, a liminal text of sorts, contested as it was in antiquity and beyond, because it represents a different cultural expression of Christianity, not in the least because it offers us one of the most famous examples of an "active female" in early Christian narrative. While male characters feature prominently in the Acts of the Apostles and in Paul, the *Acts of Paul and Thecla* presents us with a female on the "stage," and it is precisely the unusual nature of having a woman in the public forum that allows us to rethink our concepts of gender, sex, and sexuality and to reengage traditional categories and methods. Thus, the *Acts of Paul and Thecla* is essential for us as a source of difference, of alterity, and, as we demonstrate later in this study, the history of scholarship on the *Acts of Paul and Thecla* attests to this difference.

Finally, the subtitle of the book, *Thinking beyond Thecla*, reveals elements of our larger agenda. The phrase represents a play on the title of Shelly Matthews's article "Thinking of Thecla: Issues in Feminist Historiography." In that article, which we discuss briefly in chapter one, Matthews is concerned about the modern scholarly focus on ancient discourse related to women and the tendency to "forget" about "real" historical early Christian women in the process. In our title, we refer more specifically to the feminist effort to reconstruct the history of women embedded in the texts, in this case Thecla. While we do not take explicit issue with this task per se, thinking *of* Thecla is not the focus of our approach in this book. Along these same lines, we distance ourselves from another approach, one that could be called "thinking *with* Thecla," a formulation taken from Daniel Boyarin's chapter title "Thinking with Virgins: Engendering Judeo-Christian Difference" (*Dying for God*). Here Boyarin explores how both rabbis and church fathers used the figure of the virgin as a tool to think with in late antiquity, a move entailing that this female figure is used (by men) as a means to communicate about matters between men.

Instead of thinking *of* or *with* Thecla, then, we prefer to designate our approach as thinking *beyond* Thecla. The Thecla story forms a continuous thread throughout this book, as every chapter opens with a quote from and subsequent reflection on that early Christian text. The selections chosen serve more specifically as a starting point for the issues under discussion that move *beyond* the story of Thecla to broader matters of gender, sex, and sexuality in antiquity and the relevance thereof for our own time period. This focus also links up with the political agenda of our approach: we are less invested in recovering "dead" women/people from the past than in exploring how our own world might be more engaged and enlivened by these ancient texts, insofar as our own understandings of power, gender, ideology and such might be challenged and transformed as a result. We thus seek to move "beyond" the historical past, as much as we are also interested in that same past, but largely as a tool "to think about" the present. This reconfigured paradigm means, for us, that we have one foot in the past and another in the present, trying to keep that balance, as delicate a balancing act as it may be.

Following from the earlier discussion, a further way in which we move "beyond Thecla" is, from a gender-critical perspective, questioning the focus on her as a "female" and "woman," thereby opening up the possibility for broader views and practices of gendered, sexed, and sexual identities (ancient and modern) within our framework. This move also explains why we chose the term "gender-critical" for designating our approach, since it denotes that we are studying texts with a focus on reading (for) gender critically and contextually. In an essay on women's history, Joan Scott indicates the problematic use of "woman" as a stable and univocal signifier, often also tacitly understood to refer to white, middle-class, heterosexual women. As she further notes, however, the use of "gender" as a critical category to conceptualize sexual difference has in turn been criticized for being apolitical, because it does not allow for activism based on an appeal to shared experience as the category "woman" has done in the past. Caught in the same dilemma is another controversy, which is framed as a choice of "theory" over "politics," which centers on the debate over the utility of critical theory for feminism, especially given the latter's traditional activist focus.

Our position is that these two potential dilemmas outlined by Scott and the proposed dichotomies are falsely construed, insofar as both critical theory and the category of "gender" have overt political significance. They certainly do so for us. The crucial question rather is what kind of political significance does the use of "gender" and "theory" entail? We also see no conflict between feminism and gender criticism, in that the two work in tandem, both functioning as destabilizing forces, in the academy and beyond, in their opposition to exclusionary ideologies and practices on the basis of discourses related to gender, sex, and sexuality. The main difference that we perceive between the two approaches is that feminism is a political advocacy movement centered around women, while gender criticism moves beyond women to conceptualize other forms of gendered and sexed difference, including as well intersections with other forms of difference, such as race/ethnicity, class, age, disability. Still, as Scott notes, some tension may continue to exist between the two approaches as "'gender' often (though not always) indicates a critique of identity-based politics, 'women' an endorsement of those politics"

("Women's History," 64). That said, as we develop our gender-critical approach in the following chapters, we take seriously Scott's feminist challenge: that "we can analyse the ambiguity of women's history and its potentially critical political force, a force that challenges and destabilizes established disciplinary premises but without offering synthesis or easy resolution" (51). We certainly consider this goal to be one of the main elements of our approach to gender, sex, and sexuality in historical contexts as well.

To that larger end, we have broken down the chapters in this book so as to better address the various facets we have raised in this introduction. In the first chapter, we introduce the theoretical insights that we draw on throughout the book, outlining the conceptual framework of our gender-critical approach. Here we present a number of authors who have had a major influence on the discussion of gender issues, followed by an application of their insights by scholars in the field of Biblical Studies. In this chapter, we focus on issues related to discourse and the social production of knowledge (Michel Foucault); sex, gender, and politics (Judith Butler, R.W. Connell); colonial contexts and gender (Edward Saïd, Franz Fanon, Homi Bhabha); and history and discourse (Hayden White). Far from being exhaustive, these theorists represent, for us, exemplary models that illustrate our gender-critical approach.

Because early Christian ideas on gender, sex, and sexuality have largely developed within an ancient context, in the second chapter we delineate the differences between our modern perceptions of these categories and earlier Greco-Roman perspectives. Herein we show how the concepts we use today are informed by modern discourses and how these differ from notions that were current in antiquity. In the third chapter, we focus on early Christianity and its boundaries in order to demonstrate that gender, sex, and sexuality are not just a matter of physical bodies but that these concepts also apply to other bodies as well, as boundaries are drawn to solidify the identity of individuals and communities. We thus conceptualize gendered and sexed discourses in the context of broader delineations of boundaries in early Christianity. In this chapter, we are invested in exploring the intersecting contexts of ancient life and thought with respect to gender, sex, and sexuality, examining the way in which individual and collective bodies are shaped at the border (and the crossings thereof) of diverse bodily worlds, real and imaginary. In particular, we look at canonical, conceptual, cultural, political, and social bodies and boundaries, analyzing the complexity and multiplicity that such diverse correlations offer for our interpretation of early Christian texts.

In chapter four, we shift our attention more overtly from the past to the present and from ancient texts to their modern interpreters, in order to demonstrate how biblical scholarship itself is gendered and sexed. Our main focus here is on the intersection between our own ideologies and those of the past. More specifically, we engage modern understandings of race and gender, which arose largely coterminous with the development of biblical scholarship in a European context, and which undoubtedly impacted the formation of modern biblical methodological categories and conceptions in that same time period. Finally, in the fifth and concluding chapter of this book, we apply the insights from the earlier chapters to the interpretation of specific biblical texts. We also situate our gender-critical approach in the larger framework of different ways of interpreting biblical texts when reading for gender, and revisit and restate some of our fundamental assumptions and reading strategies that surface in the earlier chapters.

We conclude this book with observations (disclosures) on the politics of the gender-critical approach we outline in this volume. Throughout, the politics of our approach, methods, and analyses are fronted, so the conclusion both summarizes these earlier emphases, and also more fully situates the assumptions, values, and ideologies we embrace (and endorse) in our book within the broader significance of the Humanities in a contemporary globalized world. Rather than seeking the "dead" past for its own sake, we aim to develop an approach to the ancient world that serves the interests and needs of the present. In some ways, then, this book represents our response to the situation we sketched four years ago in the conclusion to our introductory essay in *Her Master's Tools?*:

> An inherent ambiguity thus persists in the engagements over the past—there is both a contesting of the dominant discourses but also a degree of complicity as a result. The appeal to ethics and politics of interpretation therefore becomes particularly acute at this juncture. One can use the tools of traditional discourse, doing so uncritically, or one can reject them altogether . . . Finally, one can also engage the dominant discourses and create counter-discourses and communities, reconfiguring and reconstituting traditional tools, methods, and aims in alternative directions and contexts. In the latter case, voices within and without of the guild find each other, and those at the center and the margins can establish (some) common cause. Herein also lies the possibility and prospect for the creation of shifting identities and the development of subversive discourses amidst the employment of alternative ones. ("Mastering the Tools," 27–28)

Our hope with this book is that we have contributed, even if in some small way, to the task we identified earlier. In the end, the legacy of the past is contingent on what we make of that heritage today and to what use we employ it. Ultimately, in this endeavor, then, "thinking beyond Thecla" entails "being like Thecla," that is, "out of place." As Richard Walsh once noted (with a tip of the hat to Nietzsche), such being "out of place" requires us "'to become traitors' to our mythic enclosures and to become 'wanderers of the earth'" (*Mapping Myths*, 146)—much like, we might add, Thecla's own journey in the *Acts of Paul and Thecla*.

Bibliography

Boyarin, Daniel. *Dying for God: Martyrdom and the Making of Christianity and Judaism*. Figurae: Reading Medieval Culture. Stanford: Stanford University Press, 1999.

Matthews, Shelly. "Thinking of Thecla: Issues in Feminist Historiography." *Journal of Feminist Studies in Religion* 17 (2001): 39–55.

Penner, Todd, and Caroline Vander Stichele, eds. *Contextualizing Acts: Lukan Narrative and Greco-Roman Discourse*. Society of Biblical Literature Symposium Series 20. Atlanta: Society of Biblical Literature and Leiden: Brill, 2003.

—*Mapping Gender in Ancient Religious Discourses*. Biblical Interpretation Series 84. Leiden: Brill, 2007.

Scott, Joan. "Women's History." Pp. 43–70 in *New Perspectives in Historical Writing*. Edited by P. Burke. Second edn. University Park: Pennsylvania State University Press, 2001.

Vander Stichele, Caroline, and Todd Penner. "Mastering the Tools or Retooling the Masters? The Legacy of Historical-Critical Discourse." Pp. 1–29 in *Her Master's Tools? Feminist and Post-Colonial Engagements of Historical-Critical Discourse*. Edited by Vander Stichele and Penner.

Vander Stichele, Caroline, and Todd Penner, eds. *Her Master's Tools? Feminist and Post-Colonial Engagements of Historical-Critical Discourse*. Global Perspectives on the Bible 9. Atlanta: Society of Biblical Literature and Leiden: Brill, 2005.

Walsh, Richard G. *Mapping Myths of Biblical Interpretation*. Playing the Text 4. Sheffield: Sheffield Academic Press, 2001.

Introducing a Gender-Critical Approach

While Paul was saying these things in the middle of the meeting that was taking place at the house of Onesiphorus, a virgin named Thecla, whose mother was Theocleia and who was engaged to a man named Thamyris, was sitting at the closest window of her house and listened night and day to the word of God spoken by Paul about chastity, belief in Christ, and prayer. And she did not leave the window, but, rejoicing exceedingly, she was brought to belief. Moreover, seeing many women and virgins entering with Paul, she desired that she too would be deemed worthy to stand before the face of Paul and to hear the word of Christ, for she had not yet seen Paul's features, but only heard his word.

—Acts of Paul and Thecla 3.7[1]

The *Acts of Paul and Thecla,* from which these lines are taken, belongs to a group of early Christian texts not included in the New Testament. The literary landscape of early Christianity is full of such pieces of literature, which is a testament to the immense diversity and creativity of the early Christian movement in the pre-Constantinian period (prior to 330 CE). As we noted in the introduction to this book ("InterseXions"), in this particular story, Paul, the apostle, well-known from early Christian writings, arrives in Iconium to undertake what he is most often depicted as doing in the Acts of the Apostles and in his own letters: preaching the gospel. However, the specific message he delivers here—renouncing sound Roman mores—marriage, family—is not well received by the inhabitants of the city. He is shortly thereafter arrested and put on trial for disrupting the moral values of the city and thereby causing a civic disturbance.

Thecla, who is depicted as listening to Paul's words from her window, soon becomes his disciple, even visiting him in prison. Thus begins a tale of adventure as Paul and Thecla embark on a journey that takes them from the house of Onesiphorus to the public forum of Iconium. As the story unfolds, Thecla's adoration and devotion to Paul only grow in intensity. She follows in his footsteps and is thrown into the arena to undergo torture and death before angry rulers and citizens of the empire. We will return to particulars of this story throughout this book, but for the moment we want to explore not so much the content of this story but its interpretation in modern scholarship, which originated in the seventeenth century and developed into a scientific approach in the following centuries designated as "historical criticism."[2] This approach studies the Bible as a historical document and subjects it to the same critical questions prevalent in the study of history and literature in other fields. The immense changes in the study of early Christianity that have taken place over the last two centuries or so can be illustrated in an illuminating way through the interpretation of this text related to Paul and Thecla.

Because of the dramatic, exotic, adventurous, erotic, gendered, and supernatural elements in the narrative, the *Acts of Paul and Thecla* initially received little attention from the modern scholars who examined early Christian literature. For instance, Ferdinand Christian Baur (1792–1860), one of the founding "fathers" of the modern study of early Christian texts, relied heavily on the New Testament to reconstruct the development of and conflict in early Christianity. He was not invested in drawing on more fanciful tales of popular literature, such as he believed the *Acts of Paul and Thecla* to be, which were not included among the canonical writings of the New Testament. Baur's lack of interest in this type of literature is worth noting, because it is related to the fact that he adopted a model of historical study often associated with historians such as Leopold von Ranke (1795–1886), Johann Gustav Droysen (1808–1884), and Jacob Burckhardt (1818–1897), and applied it to the study of the Bible. These historians more specifically focused on seminal political and cultural moments of the past, especially the men and institutions that shaped those "great moments" of European history. Thus, as we discuss further in chapter four, European scholars tended to replicate their own political and cultural identity through their scholarship, particularly focusing on historical males in their connections to institutions.[3]

Scholars such as Baur, who were interested in approaching early Christian texts from the same "great men and institutions" perspective, looked to those early Christian materials that would most readily support such an enterprise. They were drawn to explore the development and evolution of Christian institutions, which, in their mind, were formed and solidified by the apostles, the great leaders of the early Christian churches as mapped out in the canonical writings of the New Testament. As a result, more entertaining, robust, embodied, and sometimes even bawdy narratives such as the *Acts of Paul and Thecla* were not deemed relevant to such a "high-minded" task. Not only were these materials generally considered to be nonhistorical, but such texts were also regarded as being too exotic. In their perspective, this literature was clearly intended for common people in antiquity, and thus not to be taken seriously by males of high elite culture. Not insignificantly, the resultant focus on canonical materials and their later tradents (especially the apostolic fathers of the late first and early second centuries) shaped in specific ways how Christianity was remembered and thought about in later time periods.

When the apocryphal Acts of the apostles—stories related to the apostles but not included in the New Testament canon—finally became a subject of study in their own right at the turn of the 1900s, they were analyzed mostly for their cultural motifs and connections to Greek and Roman novels, such as Heliodorus's *Ephesian Tale* or Achilles Tatius's *Leucippe and Clitophon*, rather than studied to reconstruct early Christianity itself. Still, these early Christian narratives did gain some initial legitimacy by being linked with the Greco-Roman novelistic tradition. In Germany, for instance, one of the first scholars to study the early Christian apocryphal Acts was Rosa Söder. In her 1932 study, she both gave attention to the "erotic-ascetic" components of the narrative, viewing these as literary qualities of the text, and focused on the parallels between the *Acts of Paul and Thecla* and other Greek and Roman novels. In this literary approach, the figure of Thecla is valued as a literary type or as a broader sociocultural motif, rather than for her own possibly unique contribution (as a historical figure) to early Christian history and theological development. Moreover, in line with scholarship at that time, Söder continued to separate out the apocryphal Acts from the canonical Acts of the Apostles with its more "sober" treatment of early Christian "history."

The history and role of the *Acts of Paul and Thecla*, however, does not stop here. As cultural values and social contexts continued to change, so did the fate of Thecla. She moved from relative obscurity to significant prominence in more recent treatments of early Christian history and literature. Instrumental in this shift was the emancipatory impulse of the nineteenth and early twentieth centuries. Inspired by Enlightenment ideals, a liberal movement of mostly upper class women in both North America and Europe claimed equal rights and opportunities to men in the public sphere, including access to education and suffrage. Over time, this political and social movement for change gradually became institutionalized insofar as the politics of "women's rights" became a constituent feature of educational, political, social, and cultural institutions. As a result of this process, women such as Rosa Söder started to make their entry into the academy.

Another dramatic shift was triggered in the 1960s and 1970s by a number of historical currents and intellectual trends, such as the liberal leftist political movements in Europe and the rise of post-structuralism, which challenged the stability of dominant social and cultural ideologies. A further development was the emergence of a socially and politically critical feminist movement, which critiqued the earlier feminist emancipation agenda for merely integrating women into existing power structures, while leaving these male dominated structures intact.[4] Therefore, in order to provoke change, women would have to unmask these structures as patriarchal, androcentric, and sexist, liberating themselves from the multiple forms of oppression these institutions brought about. Thus, when Thecla reemerges on the academic scene in the 1980s, it is a different world indeed that is reflected in the scholarly agendas and concerns that surround the study of the *Acts of Paul and Thecla*. Some of these changes are aptly illustrated in the major feminist analyses of the time.

For instance, in order to reconstruct Christian origins from a feminist theological perspective, Elisabeth Schüssler Fiorenza began to raise a new set of questions regarding the role of women in early Christianity. In her book *In Memory of Her* (1985), she refers to Thecla in passing as evidence for the diversity and fluidity of the churches in Asia Minor at the end of the first century CE and as proof of the disruptive effect that the conversion of women to Christianity had on pagan households (246). Also in the 1980s, scholars such as Stevan Davies, Dennis MacDonald, and Virginia Burrus reevaluated the purpose of the stories in the apocryphal Acts. They suggested, for instance, that these stories bore witness to the struggle of women to assert authority within the patriarchal structures of the early Christian communities in which these narratives were circulating. For the first time in modern scholarship, Thecla is perceived as being not just a literary trope or type, but as a female (even if still a literary) figure who challenges Roman patriarchal structures and those in early Christianity as well. Thecla now appears in her own right as a rather free-roaming individual, who rejects social standing and marital obligation in favor of an ascetic lifestyle. Her story is used to put into question the dominant picture of apostolic leadership and authority present in New Testament texts such as the Pastoral Epistles (1 and 2 Timothy, Titus), where male bishops are established in positions of dominance over Christian communities. She thereby becomes significant as a (real or fictional) female who bears witness to historical movements in the early church. Feminist interpretation clearly shaped the perspective taken on Thecla in these studies. Depicted as a revolutionary figure, Thecla in some ways also becomes a reflection of the positions espoused by late-twentieth-century feminist scholarship.

By the end of the twentieth century, however, the optimism of the earlier feminist movement was discarded as a romantic illusion. As we will note later in this chapter, various elements came into play in these changes, including the rethinking of categories such as gender, sex, and sexuality, as well as the role of power in the shaping and balancing of social institutions. Feminism was, moreover, criticized by women of color for its universalistic and imperialistic claims, as the former was perceived to serve largely white, Western middle class interests. As a result, modernist presuppositions gradually gave way to a more postmodern approach regarding issues of identity and subjectivity (as these two categories are inextricably linked). The idealistic Enlightenment notion of an autonomous, universal, and free subject was discarded in favor of an understanding of the subject as a cultural construct, one that was historically contingent as well as fragmented.

With these shifts, the treatment of Thecla changed as well. Kate Cooper, for instance, more recently suggests that Thecla should be viewed as a trope of male identity, wherein Paul's masculinity is staged over that of Thecla's fiancé, Thamyris, who loses *his* woman in the contest for *male* authority (*Virgin and the Bride*, 55). The role that Thecla comes to play in the male imagination is vital in this formulation. Indeed, in this reading, she no longer serves the ends of resistance to patriarchal structures, but reinforces them in fundamental ways.

Rather than identifying the female character with feminist concerns (as in past scholarship), it is no longer assumed that a female character will necessarily represent female or woman(ly) viewpoints or interests. Instead, it is acknowledged that she can be a figure used to negotiate male identity. Some scholars have sought to resist this trend, trying to find a middle ground between earlier feminist approaches and more recent ones. Shelly Matthews, for instance, seeks to mediate between the way in which Thecla is presented in the text and ancient female experience more generally ("Thinking of Thecla"). The importance of Thecla as an actual historical character is minimized while her critical role as providing a "countervoice" to the dominant, restrictive claims of the Pastoral Epistles is underscored. Although Thecla hereby represents a literary character, she nevertheless is understood to have served real historical ends in terms of challenging male authority figures in the early church. Feminist concerns are thus reasserted in a new framework, where the older ethical values are reconfigured in light of a more theoretically sophisticated literary approach to the text.

Even more pertinent for this present book is the shift revealed in the work of scholars who have been influenced by changes in the perception of gender and power. According to Willi Braun, for instance, Thecla undergoes a change from "female" to "male" in the course of the narrative: she becomes independent from men, operates in both the private and public spheres, and starts dressing like a man ("Physiotherapy of Femininity"). Far from having a stable gender identity, Thecla represents for Braun a transformative (and even transgressive) character. Another approach is offered by Virginia Burrus, who was one of the first scholars to offer a feminist rereading and recovery of the figure of Thecla (*Chastity as Autonomy*). In her recent work on Thecla ("Mimicking Virgins"), however, Burrus incorporates the work of postcolonial critics who analyze the effect of colonial power on subjects in/of empire. For Burrus, situating the story of Thecla within the context of Roman imperial power reveals the malleable nature of colonial power as it intersects with embodied subjects. For both Braun and Burrus, then, the meaning of Thecla's body is ultimately unstable, insofar as she is used as a site on which power structures are inscribed. As such, her body becomes subject to the scrutiny of the critic who seeks to find the various and often conflicting ways in which this phenomenon unfolds. Although Thecla is still important for what she represents rather than for any particular historical action per se, her representation becomes more convoluted and complex as a result. This view does not imply that Thecla no longer has any independent identity as such, but it does suggest that power structures have a significant effect on how her identity is played out in the narrative (even if they are not solely determinative).

The interpretative trajectory of Thecla briefly outlined above is representative of the interpretation of many other early Christian writings in the development of modern scholarship. It also makes clear that there is no *neutral* point of view, that is, a place outside of sociocultural and historical contexts from which we can read the literature of the past or even construct the meaning of the figures in these texts. Thus, all readings are contingent in time and within the local contexts of interpretation, both of which are shaped by sociocultural factors. The gender-critical perspective that we detail in this book is just as much a product of the kinds of questions and issues that have been raised more recently and that have influenced the academic methods and contexts in which we ourselves were trained and now find ourselves working. To understand a gender-critical approach to early Christian literature, then, it is important to delineate first and foremost its own historical and cultural genealogy within the larger framework of study in the humanities.

Discourse and the social production of knowledge

In setting forth an agenda for a gender-critical approach to early Christian literature, it is helpful to unravel some of the diverse threads that constitute our particular approach to ancient literature. While there are many "beginning points" one could choose, we select Michel Foucault (1926–1984) as the place to start, in large part because of his emphasis on how knowledge is produced by and within specific social contexts. Foucault, perhaps more than any other theorist of the twentieth century, focused a major portion of his research on the social production of knowledge. That is, for Foucault, ideas, while often taken as "givens" or "natural" in a particular society, are actually products of sociohistorical processes. They can only be understood within the context of the social, cultural, and linguistic elements of the specific societies and historical epochs with which knowledge is intrinsically interwoven. Against the tradition of the Enlightenment, Foucault both questioned so-called rationalistic conceptions and methods and sought to demonstrate that the fundamental constituent nature of "rationality" itself (as articulated within the Western tradition) is produced by that tradition rather than being a "given" universal human faculty. Moreover, in his view, systems of knowledge are self-regulating self-confirming. Once such a system arises, then everything that it produces makes sense precisely within or related to that system of meaning.

To this end, Foucault was interested in analyzing two interrelated concepts: genealogy and discourse. With the former, Foucault indicates that cultural and social ideas do not simply arise out of nothing. Rather, they have long, often convoluted histories or genealogies that account for a variety of elements that are reconfigured over time in diverse historical epochs. In other words, not only do we *inherit* various components that go into shaping our present ideas and perspectives, but they also evolve over time. There is "nothing new under the sun" in one sense, but then there is, too, in that every society contextualizes the "received tradition" within specific webs of interaction (running the gamut from acceptance to rejection) that give a unique shape to the inherited ideas. In some sense, Foucault himself could only reconstruct the social production of knowledge in continuity with the past, so his own understanding of knowledge itself has a genealogy.

Discourse, the other element in which Foucault was particularly invested, refers to the act of speaking and writing in a society. Discourse constructs and distributes the ideas that constitute the norms, values, concepts, and practices of that society. Ideas themselves are formulated through the discourse in the very act of talking and thinking about them. In Foucault's analysis, discourse forms the context of ideas and determines the language used to articulate/ construct them. Thus, specific forms of discourse are related to, for instance, the scientific, political, economic, or religious spheres. From this perspective, then, there is no absolute standpoint of objective knowledge, but everything is in some sense constructed from a particular angle and is always in flux. The term "gender" can serve here as a case in point. Originally used in the context of grammar to refer to male and female gendered words, from the 1960s onwards feminists started to use the term to refer to socially determined differences between men and women, reserving the term "sex" for (presumed) biological differences between the sexes. In this case, "sex" and "gender" are understood to refer to distinct realities. "Sex" corresponds with differences that are thought to be "natural" and "gender" with those that are culturally based (Nicholson, "Interpreting Gender," 40). More recently, however, scholars such as Judith Butler have argued that not only gender but also the category of sex itself is socially constructed. We will come back to this issue later in the chapter.

From this emphasis one can see how power could form one of the key elements in Foucault's analyses, as his discussions of genealogy and discourse were intended to uncover the bases of power. Power, in his view, is fluid, with a

variety of forces (complimentary and/or competing) acting on and influenc-
ing the social production of knowledge. There is, then, no specific "villain"
in knowledge production. Foucault's perceptions also allowed for the notion of
power as a force that is constantly operative but always hidden, able to maintain a hold precisely by not being manifestly evident for all to see. "Biopower,"
for instance, became an important concept for Foucault, as it delineated the
power of the sovereign state structure to regulate the bodies of entire groups
of people. As such, Foucault's understanding of institutional power differs
from Marxist understandings of institutions as explicitly state controlled and
used to manipulate the populace. Furthermore, discourses arise in action and
interaction, which implies, as well, that everything from social relationships to
the organization of space could potentially be produced by and also contribute
to the formation of discourse. These discourses in turn *discipline* the subject,
regulating patterns of thought and behavior of individuals. As Foucault's
studies on institutions and discourses related to madness and criminality
demonstrate, part of this disciplining implies the discrediting of certain
behavior as deviant and results in the creation of social institutions (such as
the mental hospital and the prison) and systems of knowledge necessary to
manage them. In this way, Foucault was in fact more interested in *practices*
than in the mere description of events or "facts." In his mind, it was in social
practice and discourse that we could understand how, say, the modern
system of imprisonment came to be the way it is. Rather than describing what
a prison or jail cell looked like, he focused on why people sought to imprison
people in this manner (with attention also to what kind of people were considered suitable for incarceration). However, this is not to suggest that power was
impenetrable or could not be resisted. Foucault argues that "discourse transmits and produces power; it reinforces it, but also undermines and exposes it,
renders it fragile and makes it possible to thwart it" (*History of Sexuality I*, 101).
Discourse is thus critical for both the analysis of and resistance to specific
power distributions and structures.

Alongside the numerous studies that Foucault produced in his lifetime,
his most relevant work for our approach here is a three-volume study on the
history of sexuality, which remained incomplete at his death. In that study,
Foucault sought to elaborate on the modern understanding of sexuality by
tracing out a history of the discourses that contributed to Western perceptions.
In the next chapter we will look more closely at some of the implications of
Foucault's research for a gender-critical engagement of early Christian literature, but here we simply note that Foucault was one of the first to dislodge in a

systematic manner the notion that sex and gender are fixed, natural categories. Rather, our conceptions of these entities are shaped by particular social and cultural contexts. Although the categories of sex and gender are claimed to be universal and normative, the "claim" itself masks the contextual nature of the discourses related to these very conceptions. In this way, Foucault's work has clearly encouraged contemporary scholars to reevaluate the manner in which they think about sex, sexuality, and gender as well as the link made between gender performance and sexuality, with the latter referring to outward sexual interaction, desire, and expression (often designated, somewhat narrowly, by "bisexuality," "heterosexuality," and "homosexuality"). There has been a proliferation of scholarship on this theme in the past decades, which has helped reshape our understanding of these categories.

With his focus on discourse and power, Foucault provides us with a useful theoretical framework for the analysis of early Christian texts. A specific example of such a study is Elizabeth Castelli's *Imitating Paul* (1991), in which she analyzes Paul's use of the concept of "imitation" (*mimesis*) and its function as a discourse of power in his letters. According to Castelli, Paul's notion of imitation "articulates and rationalizes as true and natural a particular set of power relations within the social formation of early Christian communities" (15). In 1 Corinthians 4.16, for instance, Paul exhorts his readers to become "imitators of me," after he presented himself in the previous verse as their "father." Rather than a gentle metaphor, in the sociocultural world of Paul's time this image evokes the absolute power of a father over his children. Paul thus sets up a hierarchical relationship within the community, in which he is the one who speaks with authority (even when he does not always appear to be doing so). This hierarchy is further strengthened later on in the letter, when he again summons the Corinthians to be imitators of him, but adding this time "as I am of Christ" (11.1). Here the hierarchy is expanded, putting Paul in a structural parallel with Christ.[5] This analogy strengthens his own position of power with respect to the Corinthian community. Moreover, in the context of a letter dealing with problems and issues that have arisen in his absence, the call for imitation also serves the purpose of aligning this community with Paul. His "pastoral power" is used to silence those holding a view that deviates from his own. The desired result is unity and sameness rather than difference and dissent. This outcome, however, is reached not through dialogue but is the consequence of the imposition of power from above. The power in question is rhetorical and ideological, both of which are situated on the level of discourse. Thus, Foucault's insights prove useful for assessing aspects of early Christian discourse that would otherwise go unnoticed. In particular, such insights help the interpreter to move beyond the overt theological argument of such texts and expose the power dynamics embedded therein. These are not innocuous texts, since they mediate power and authority, which, in our view, need to be analyzed and also scrutinized.

Sex, gender, and politics

If Foucault's work was fundamental for raising awareness of how knowledge is socially and historically constructed and produced, including emphasizing the decisive role that discourse performs in that operation, then in more recent scholarship it was the work of Judith Butler that served to advance and deepen numerous insights related to sex and gender that Foucault had initiated. There are obviously many different contemporary thinkers upon whom one could draw in this context, and we certainly are not attempting to give an overview of gender theory and practice in this chapter. Rather, we turn to Butler because of her systematic attempt to rethink our modern notions of *both* sex and gender. In her groundbreaking book *Gender Trouble* (1990), Butler builds on but also contests particular aspects of Foucault's *History of Sexuality*. Since Butler is more adamantly committed to breaking down the gender binary—the notion that sex and gender identity must exist as either "male" or "female"—she pushes Foucault's insights further. According to Butler, in their political search for equality, many feminist scholars simply assumed the stability of the existing categories of sex and gender, when in fact they should have challenged the binary system itself, since precisely *that* system sustained repressive social and cultural normativities. While Foucault sought to explain how the idea of sex as a system of regulation and control arose, Butler is more concerned to dismantle it. Naturally, one needs the explanation before one can go about deconstructing its framework, and therefore Foucault was essential in providing a groundwork for the critical discussion to follow. As a result, Butler's work lends itself much more readily to scholars with an ideology-critical and political edge in their academic inquiry, particularly in terms of her work on deconstructing a binary system of thinking about gender, sex, and sexuality.

Butler's contribution to our own assessment of "gender" lies in a number of insights that her work as a whole promotes. For one, more than any other scholar, Butler has challenged the fundamental notion of binary sex and gender categories. Building on the groundbreaking observations by

Simone de Beauvoir, Butler (and many feminist scholars before her) argued that how a society constructs and thinks about "sex" and "gender" is not natural, although most societies are in fact invested in presenting these categories as universal and innate, because it allows these formulations to stand as unquestioned sites for the regulation of human behavior. Arguments about the "naturalness" of heterosexual orientations, for instance, readily lend themselves to bolstering hetero-normative politics. Butler criticizes the earlier feminist distinction between sex and gender, in which "sex" refers to the presumed "natural" biological identification of an individual (female, male, or other) and "gender" denotes the corresponding culturally determined role (masculine, feminine, or other). For Butler *both* of these categories are socially and culturally constructed. How we classify and identify males and females simplifies more complex identity issues and creates societal uniformity, discipline, and control. The gendered, sexed, and sexualized body thus becomes a site on which culturally determined meanings are mapped out, providing a type of corporeal cartography. As these categories of gender and sex become integrally linked, so then do the configurations in one category determine the options available in the other (which in turn are then mapped onto the category of sexuality as well).

Two other elements that are especially important for our understanding of a gender-critical approach are Butler's use of the concepts of "performativity" and "queer" identity, which come to the forefront in her later work (*Undoing Gender*) that delineates the implications of her earlier assessments on gender. In contrast to mere performance (like an actor on a stage), performativity is a critical Butlerian concept because it relates to the playing out of a particular identity. Performativity is acting in a way that simultaneously transforms one's own subjectivity or sense of self. Thus, identities, for Butler, are socially constructed rather than given by nature. That is, this notion of performativity suggests that there is no absolute or inherent identity "behind" oneself that lines up with the external/outside/expressive character of the performative. What one sees, in this respect, does not represent a core identity as such.[6] A man who acts in a so-called masculine manner is performing that identity and, thereby, also reproducing that sense of being masculine (for himself and others), but that outward manifestation does not link up to anything absolute or essential in this man's "internal" personhood. Moreover, since social and cultural forces have already shaped our sense of selves before we even begin to act on them, one cannot clearly state the volitional nature of this performance—sometimes there is a certain element of choice involved, but quite often there is not. There is thus complexity in the notion of identity right from the start. Moreover, people frequently have multiple identities that issue forth in a variety of performative acts and situations, and often these can interact with and shape one another. The point, then, is that identity itself (and gender, sex, and sexuality in particular) is not fixed—it is, rather, fluid. It can shift and morph throughout one individual's lifetime or even during the course of one day, depending on the different social contexts one inhabits. Someone may, for instance, dominate people at work, thus displaying "masculine" behavior, but be a caring individual at home, which is a traditional "female" quality. Or someone may dress conventionally during the day or out in public and be a transvestite or cross-dresser at night or at home. Even at a more basic level, how we act (and dress) in a church setting will usually differ from a night out at the club or an afternoon in the park. Diverse social situations thus evoke particular gendered and sexed performances.

The other element that Butler has emphasized and that has proven highly influential is the concept of queer politics. In some sense, Butler, like feminist scholars before her, reclaimed the term "queer" and redeployed it as an academic and political concept. If one understands, as Butler does, that a gender analysis and interrogation of culture is a political act, then "to queer"/ "queering" means to destabilize the normative, hegemonic discourses and conceptions of a particular culture, in this case those related to gender, sex, and sexuality. It is not so much "acting out" as in queer identity politics (e.g., the gay pride parades in San Francisco and Amsterdam), but rather it is about making facets of socially acceptable practices appear strange and unfamiliar to (and from) the dominant perspective. For instance, to point out the homosocial character and practice of male bonding in a traditional college fraternity or the army is to queer the identity of such males, since one is taking an acknowledged practice but exploiting a particular feature of it so as to twist its usual meaning and make it appear unfamiliar and perhaps also transformative to the very members who are engaged in what is thought to be a normative activity. Moreover, a queer approach shifts depending on the positioning of the person using it and based on the end for which it is being used. In other words, "queer" is a term that is always in flux—it is unstable, reconfiguring itself, with the aim of destabilizing the binary system of thinking about gender, sex, and sexuality. Used in this sense, queer is ultimately, then, a *political* concept and action, one that seeks to open up possibilities rather than closing them down. Moreover, feminist gender scholars such as Teresa de Lauretis would also want to ensure that the term "queer" in this sense is kept distinct from a LGBTI (lesbian, gay, bisexual, transsexual, intersex) political agenda per se. In other words, while they may have some overlap in their respective transformative aims, they are separate and distinct agendas.

Given the delineations mentioned earlier, it is not surprising that Butler's insights are eminently useable for the study of early Christianity. In his book *A Radical Jew* (1994), for instance, Daniel Boyarin draws on the insights Butler developed in *Gender Trouble* for his analysis of Paul's views on gender. His starting point is more specifically Butler's observation that the traditional philosophical distinction between mind and body corresponds with the division between male and female, in that the universal mind is understood to be male and the body to be female. Boyarin notes that a similar dualism is present in Paul's distinction between the spirit and the flesh. For Paul, the spirit represents the universal human essence, while the flesh (including gender, sex, and sexuality) bears the marks of particularity and contingency. This value judgment also helps one to understand more clearly Paul's famous dictum that in Christ "there is no male and female" (Gal. 3.28). This egalitarian statement is often taken as contradicting Paul's restrictive stance elsewhere in his letters, more specifically in his first letter to the Corinthians where he defends a hierarchical relationship between the sexes (1 Cor. 11 and 14). Boyarin, however, argues that these apparently contradictory statements make sense when one takes into consideration that Paul maintains a dualistic value system in which the spirit is ranked higher than the body, and that Paul is engaged in different arguments in Galatians than in 1 Corinthians. In Galatians 3.27–28, Paul's concern is to stress the unity and equality between men and women in the spiritual realm as experienced at baptism. In 1 Corinthians he is invested in maintaining distinctions in the earthly/bodily realm within the community.

On this level, then, gender can be transcended, because in Paul's view sex distinction and gender performance are situated on the level of the body. In 1 Corinthians 11.2–16, for instance, where Paul seeks to regulate the actual behavior of men and women in relation to each other, he stresses that the hierarchical difference between the two sexes needs to be maintained: "every man's head is Christ, but a woman's head is the man, and Christ's head is God" (11.3; Boyarin's translation), and only "in the Lord is there neither woman without man nor man without woman" (11.11). For Paul, then, the former ideal state of gender transcendence cannot yet be fully realized on a social level, but only on a spiritual level "in the Lord," as experienced momentarily by all at baptism (Gal. 3.28) and perhaps more permanently by those who practice sexual renunciation (1 Cor. 7). In this dualistic framework, Paul's politics of gender appears firmly grounded in sexual difference and is thus relegated to the body, while the spirit avoids these contingencies. The founding binary for Paul's gender politics, then, is not the difference between sex and gender, but rather between spirit and body. Moreover, depending on the particular context in which he is seeking to be persuasive, he can redeploy these categories towards different ends, stressing unity in the spirit when addressing the Galatians and gender difference when writing to the Corinthians. Butler's insights thus provide a more complex understanding of gender in Paul's letters than would otherwise be possible.

This case study further demonstrates that scholars such as Butler have pushed analysis towards a more broadly conceived appreciation of the socially constructed and ideological nature of gender. Whereas feminist scholarship and Women's Studies tended to center on the analysis and recovery of women in the past and present, Gender Studies widened the focus to the broader sociocultural context and the political use of "sex" and "gender," emphasizing a more diverse range of gendered and sexed identities in the process. Although feminism also had these concerns (and Butler's own work is part of a feminist genealogy), gender criticism has broadened the scope. As a result, masculinity became included as an important component of gender-critical analysis. There is still continuity here with the feminist critique of patriarchal structures, but in the framework of Men's Studies, masculinity is more than just patriarchy. Rather, in line with Foucault, masculinity is understood as a sustained system of domination that is enacted by and on diverse individuals in a society, male and female alike.

In this sense, the *masculine* element here corresponds with Foucault's more general sense of *power*. R. W. Connell's analysis in his book *Masculinities* (1987) is illustrative of this approach. He argues that in the contemporary globalized world institutions and organizations tend to be structured along the lines of modern conceptions of human reproduction, so that men frequently are "on top." For Connell, what consolidates control in the "hands of men" are the shared gender assumptions sustained and nurtured by Western culture.[7] In other words, the language and concepts related to gender, sex, and sexuality tend to structure the world in specific ways, much to the advantage of the "male sex." Connell makes clear that these categories are cultural and that any appearance of biological foundationalism, which presumes that sexual differences are grounded in human biology, is a creation (and fiction) of the discourse itself. This observation does not imply that biological differences do not exist, but it does suggest that the way that the "male sex" is classified and valued (in an absolute sense) is misdirected. Even within this larger system, moreover, there are diverse forms of masculinity, which are produced by the local and varied discourses of specific classes and groups of people. Still, those local forms of masculinity replicate, albeit in differing ways, the larger gendered and sexed power structures of society. In the following chapters, our investigation of early Christian sources places a significant accent on the concept of masculinity, recognizing that, even though gender and sex are culturally constructed categories, in the development of Western culture "man" and "male" are still frequently situated at the center of discourses, institutions, and societies. Thus, power issues are central to our gender-critical investigation of ancient sources, which naturally expands, as well, to the broader notion of colonialism and imperial authority, which wields some of the most cutting masculine edges.

Tat-siong Benny Liew offers an analysis of early Christian texts along these lines. In his study on the image of Jesus in the Gospel of Mark ("Re-Mark-able Masculinities"), he draws attention to the way in which Jesus acts toward and relates to other characters, seeking to demonstrate that Jesus clearly displays behavior that is in line with the stereotype of masculinity that is dominant in the Greco-Roman world of the time. Jesus operates in the public sphere, where he is portrayed in competition with other men, especially through his conflicts with the authorities in Jerusalem, including Roman leaders. On several occasions, he displays mastery over others, be it his own disciples, women, or foreigners (such as Pilate). He appears as the *pater familias* (Roman head of family), who is in charge of a new household. But the picture is more convoluted than that. Jesus also displays characteristics of another, competing ideology of masculinity in antiquity, one put forward by ancient philosophers who stress the importance of self-mastery. In accordance with that image, Jesus manifests determination and self-discipline. He faces his own death with aplomb, enduring the pain and suffering associated with his passion until the very end. The tensions between these two images, of mastery over others and self-mastery, are never fully resolved. In the end, however, Jesus appears less a master than an obedient son of his Father and a person subservient to God, who is the driving force behind all these events. Jesus' masculinity is thus sanctioned by patriarchy and, as a result, "Mark's Jesus continues to pass on the destructive demands of patriarchy and masculinity to his disciples and, by extension, potentially to Mark's readers" (132–33).[8] We thus observe here again the interplay between sociocultural constructions of gender performance and broader issues related to power. Particularly noteworthy in this respect is the interface between gender construction and colonialism, as this intersection further demonstrates the point we have made earlier, that conceptions related to gender, sex, and sexuality intersect with a whole complex of other lived realities related to the construction of individual and community identity.

Colonial contexts and gender

If Foucault's legacy can be traced to gender critics such as Butler, it can equally be seen to influence the work of cultural and literary theorists such as Edward Said (1935–2003), who was one of the first scholars to explore thoroughly the way in which European colonial contexts shaped the portrayal of the "Oriental Other." Said was a literary scholar and thus focused on the representation of colonial subjects through and in the literature of European imperialist writers, such as the British novelists. He challenged the notion that there could be any objective portrayal of a "native" subject even in the most seemingly unbiased form of reporting. In his seminal work *Orientalism* (1991), Said questioned more specifically the connection of racism and classicism, especially as those concepts were bound up with European colonialism, which produced images of Orientals that served colonial interests. In *Culture and Imperialism* (1994), Said analyzed further the roots of imperialist agendas in European culture. Following Foucault, he understood that language is frequently used to support particular power structures but, more complexly, this support often happens in the most innocuous and seemingly harmless of ways. As far as the colonizer is concerned, Said also observed that Western historians have participated in a particular discourse of doing and writing history that has its basis in colonial perspectives. That is, the representation of the Other is based on presumed universal and innate categories of analysis that are actually socially constructed aspects of Western European history and culture. Although Said did not invent postcolonial studies, he was a major factor in bringing discussions of colonial power to the forefront of academic inquiry.

Much earlier in fact Franz Fanon (1925–1961), in his short life span, had already written two foundational texts. The first, *Black Skin, White Masks*, originally published in 1952, dealt with his experience of conceptualizing himself as "French" only to find out that systemic racism had constructed him as an Other set against the dominant culture. Fanon was particularly interested in exploring the psychological damage that is imposed on blacks in colonial conditions, where the expressed racism generates a bifurcated colonial subject.

In Fanon's analysis, the black man raised in French culture, like himself, spoke the language of the colonizer, producing a universal subject of "whiteness" that was predicated on its opposite, "blackness." The black male, in speaking this discourse, came also to don a "white mask," in a sense becoming a black man posing as a white male, looking on "blackness" as something abominable (here passing/crossing in racial terms produces a particularly negative effect on human subjectivity). Thus, from a psychological perspective, the black man is separated from his own physicality. This disjunction between dominant and colonized identities is brought on, in Fanon's view, through the colonizing process. Fanon's analysis was furthered in his final book, *The Wretched of the Earth* (1961), where he essentially revised the basic structure of the Marxist class struggle, arguing that most of the so-called revolutionary class movements tended to reproduce dominant structures rather than eradicating them. For Fanon, there needed to be a more totalizing revolutionary process that would result in a utopian society, where the class and race categories produced by colonialism would finally be eradicated.

Fanon's work is interesting from a historical standpoint, insofar as his insights were still relatively exploratory at a time when there was little reflection on the effects of European colonialism. It is not surprising, however, that at the very same time that we see feminism beginning to critique the patriarchal structures of society, we see other "minorities" also criticizing dominant cultural and political frameworks, such as racism and colonialism.[9] Fanon's work is thus in some sense in step with (or just a bit ahead of) his time. Moreover, his analysis of the way that language embodies culture is very much in line with the insights that Foucault would soon thereafter develop in terms of the power of discourse to shape not only our understanding of the world, but also one's actions in it.

The field of study that developed out of such engagements with colonialism became known as "postcolonialism," an interdisciplinary approach that has had a significant impact more recently on the study of early Christianity, in large part because Christianity arose in an imperial context and, from a certain angle, was most influential among people who were, at least initially, predominantly colonized subjects of the Roman Empire (although later Christianity would become Empire in its own right).[10] Outside of the study of early Christianity, critics have deepened postcolonial analysis by linking it with other modes of study. Homi Bhabha is probably one of the most oft-cited critics, being especially interested as he is in the way in which colonial powers inevitably destabilize themselves through their own discourses, which hints at the larger insecurities that even the most monstrous forms of domination could potentially embody. Along with other scholars of "third-world" postcolonial analysis, Bhabha was also interested in understanding the experience of the colonized subject, arguing that the simple binaries offered by earlier analysts such as Fanon were not adequate to explain both the combination of resistance (in diverse ways) to colonial powers and a certain degree of compliance and even collusion as well.

In terms of the earlier gender discussion, we would emphasize that categories of gender, sex, and sexuality have also played a role within this larger discourse and, as a result, have frequently been linked to colonial representations. An excellent example of a reading of an early Christian text that seeks to combine a postcolonial approach with a focus on gender is Musa Dube's analysis of the encounter between Jesus and the Canaanite woman in Matthew 15.21–28. In her book *Postcolonial Feminist Interpretation of the Bible* (2000), Dube both establishes the extent to which the narrative endorses or rejects imperialism and undertakes a decolonizing feminist reading in order to "illumine and problematize the power relations entailed in the construction of mission, empire, gender, and race" (144). To that end, she first analyzes the Gospel as a whole and concludes that, although it is written from the perspective of the colonized, it nevertheless supports imperialist views, which themselves correlate with the postcolonial concept of mimicry (which is a term that denotes that subjects of colonialism both reinscribe colonial discourses but also, in the process, destabilize those same discourses because repetition does not produce the identical discourse, but a distorted and impure form of the original). Moreover, the Matthean gospel also subscribes to the promised-land foundation myth of Israel, thus sanctioning the invasion of foreign territories by divinely authorized "travelers." These elements reoccur in Matthew 15.21–28, where Jesus travels abroad to the area of Tyre and Sidon. The woman who comes out to meet him there is explicitly identified as "Canaanite," thereby evoking the past conquest of the land by Israel. Moreover, the attitude of both Jesus and his disciples towards the woman is surprisingly negative, and Jesus' initial reply to the desperate woman's cry for help is dismissive: "It is not fair to take the children's food and throw it to the dogs" (15.26). A hierarchy is thus established in which the children of the house of Israel stand over those foreign "dogs." The woman in fact accepts this category when she argues that "even the dogs eat the crumbs that fall from their masters' table" (15.27), and in that acknowledges the superiority of both Jesus and Israel. Gendered images further strengthen this picture of domination and subordination of the foreigner. In Dube's view, these characteristics of the story in Matthew therefore support rather than subvert imperialist and patriarchal relationships between different people by affirming the superiority of some over others as opposed to fostering mutual interdependence.

Of particular importance for the gender-critical approach developed in this book is the exploration of how gender is linked up with issues of class, race, and sexuality in order to conceptualize and, ultimately, to construct other cultures and peoples.[11] In other words, gender is part of the larger sociocultural fabric. As such, it becomes a feature used by colonial powers in ruling territory and people. Even more so, notions of gender and sex are shaped in the crucible of power relations produced by colonial powers. Thus, gender, alongside race and class and various other means of creating and sustaining hierarchies, is mapped in a variety of ways within a colonial/imperial situation. The result is a complex and often convoluted construction of identity for both colonizer and colonized (and there is not always an easy separation between the two). The colonizer assumes their own identity to be "just as it is," in natural and essential terms, while the colonized is understood to be "constructing" an identity that is not universal and natural. Identity so conceived is contingent, a notion that relates back to Butler's paradigm of "male = universal" and "female = particular," thereby constructing the subject of colonization as "female." In the same vein, the identity of the colonized is also often fetishized from the vantage point of the dominant perspective, in term of its exotic, quaint, or even primitive state.[12] From within this framework, then, one can also see examples of how representatives of the imperial order classify and observe the Other through a particular colonizing gaze, often effeminizing the otherized culture or overdetermining its masculinity in the process. In the former case, the colonized subject is seen as a weaker and softer form of human over and against the more masculine and stable form of the Western colonizer. Often, as well, conquered territories are represented as "females," penetrated by the male invader. In the latter case, however, colonial subjects are constructed to the contrary, as over-masculine sexualized creatures, almost monstrous in their appetite and desire.

Gender thus plays into racial stereotyping to depict the (potential) danger of the other culture. These are just a few examples of how gender, race, class, and ethnicity play out in diverse power relations. For the moment, however, we wish to highlight two elements that arise out of this interrelation between postcolonial and gender criticisms. The first is that gender, sex, and sexuality are concepts that are inextricably linked with all other facets that constitute a societal system of classification and hierarchy, and they are just a few of the components in and through which power exerts its influence. These concepts must therefore always be studied within this broader network of identity construction and representation. Second, these concepts are also used in colonial resistance to imperial power, and thus are constantly shifting and morphing in particular historical and cultural contexts. Gender, sex, and sexuality thus function in a wide variety of (and sometimes even contradictory) ways depending on the diverse ends (and the manifold intersections made with other sociocultural aspects) that these conceptual categories serve in specific historical contexts. Thus, for instance, one needs to pay close attention to the intersection of race and class with gender, sex, and sexuality in hierarchical structures, which is why neo-Marxist approaches, like that of Connell on masculinity noted earlier, are useful for analyzing the intersection of gender with other facets of society. Following the work of Connell, the approach we are developing here appreciates that within a particular society a multiplicity of factors related to economics and social realities influence one's understanding of gender, sex, and sexuality. A correlation thus exists between lived realities and the production of knowledge related to these concepts. Elite classes will have a different gender conception than say economically struggling and politically marginalized groups in that same society. This divergence represents a critical feature to keep in mind when studying gender in historical perspective, because the kinds of social contexts that are created will in effect tend to "naturally" produce specific correlative gender identities.[13] But, as Said has demonstrated in his work on Orientalism, cultures are not uniform, but rather complex entities, and gendered and sexed facets can only be teased out with the most sophisticated and nuanced of analytic tools.

In many respects, then, this postcolonial emphasis links back with the political agenda of both feminism and gender studies, insofar as there is a significant challenge to hegemonic forms of the universal Western, white male, heterosexual subject. Moreover, in all of these fields of inquiry there is an awareness of the context of knowledge production related to the modern scholar her/himself. And this recognition then leads to an identification of intersecting elements that we have already at least implicitly delineated. That is, ideology plays a crucial role in terms of the ends gender, sex, and sexuality categories and concepts achieve, as ideologies create worlds of thought and action that shape the way we think and act, and, as such, are situated at the junction of discourse and power.[14] One of the key elements of a gender-critical approach in this respect is the deconstruction of the mechanisms that support hegemonic ideologies. In other words, we want to be critically attuned to the political, social, and cultural work that such conceptual categories achieve. Thus, already at the outset, there is a need for a "resistant" reader/interpreter. That is, one has to cultivate a "hermeneutics of suspicion" that always seeks to identify the power relations that are hidden and that create a compliant and sympathetic reader through rhetorical techniques and invention.[15] If a gender-critical approach is truly to engage its political genealogy, then the only way to accomplish this task is to deconstruct gendered and sexed categories, taking them apart in order to examine how they came into being, how they function, how they interrelate with other aspects of our sociocultural world, and how they sustain power over people individually as well as in community and society.

There is clearly an ideology-critical impulse in this political and moral endeavor, which links gender-critical approaches with earlier feminist and other liberationist movements. In particular, and shared with postcolonial analysis, one of the key features of a gender-critical approach is that it seeks to dismantle patriarchy, masculine domination, and other colonial systems of regulation and control by exposing the discourses in question and by analyzing how they function. This focus on discourse should not come at the cost of losing sight of the fact that there are very real world consequences to people's experiences of brute power—individuals die, countries are invaded, whole cultures are wiped out. Discourse analysis does not imply that it is all "word play" in the end. Rather, it seeks to understand human action and interaction within a linguistic framework, which means that humans act out of things they think, and that they can thus easily be persuaded (and perhaps manipulated) based on common cultural patterns of thinking. Therefore, although it can sometimes appear that way, the deconstructive task is no game—it is a serious enterprise that acknowledges that all cultures are sustained by a balance of power relationships based in diverse and competing communicative practices. Exploring both communication and the concepts that are thereby disseminated represents a key facet of our gender-critical approach. In the next section, we delineate further how this insight bears out in analyses of historical texts.

History and discourse

Since the gender-critical perspective we are developing in this book is meant to be employed in the study of early Christian literature and history, we conclude this chapter with some general considerations related to our approach to the past. In light of what we have suggested earlier, we consider our under-standing of history and historical study to be informed by our specific sociocultural context. Thus, a critical study of early Christian sources begins by reflecting on our own historical methods and assumptions.

If our aim, as stated in the earlier discussion of gender, is to examine the multiple ways in which gender can be used in a broader *discursive* framework, then the interrelation between rhetoric and ideology forms a fundamental aspect of this approach. Our method includes, then, the exploration of how images are constituted, how language persuades readers, how ideologies are operative in the construction and deployment of discourse, how readers are shaped by the representations of texts, and how readers might recognize and/or resist ideologies, dominant or otherwise. In the gender-critical approach we employ, as outlined in this chapter, we do not seek to erase *real* women and men from history, but we do emphasize the difficulty of making the move from discourse to reality. Moreover, we understand that any move between the two necessarily entails a whole web of knowledge production related to the scholar her/himself. At least one prong of the political aspect of a gender-critical approach to early Christian history is to challenge the presuppositions on which the modern discipline of historiography is based. Modern historians (of recent or ancient history) have often articulated their task and the subse-quent results of their analyses in universalistic terms, showing little awareness of the limited nature of their historical understanding and assessment. Another feature that often escapes notice is that the sources upon which we rely are them-selves *narrativized*, and that they are so from a perspective other than our own.

This dual problem of the modern historian has come into sharp relief in much the same context that gave rise to feminist historical challenges to *mas-ter* narratives in general. Hayden White was one of the scholars to champion the so-called "new historiography".[16] Critical for this new approach to the study of the historical past was the emphasis that our sources *represent* the past to us. They do not provide us with an objective description of "facts," but contextual-ize raw data for us in a variety of ways (even as they have the semblance of presenting "reality," "factuality," and "actuality"). There is, in short, no possible outside to narrative framing, no direct access to a "core" reality. As a result, the attempt by modern historians to develop a system of historical inquiry that was to parallel the scientific (positivistic) paradigm in the human sciences has fallen short, in part because the methods of verification in scientific inquiry cannot be applied to the past. Moreover, scholars such as White were keen to underscore that modern historians similarly had an interpretive framework into which they placed their data. This framework narrativizes the data and determines, at least in part, their meaning. Parallel to the developments in gender analysis, the critical turn in historical analysis hinged on the premise that all human conceptions of the past are linguistically constructed and therefore contextually determined.

In general, historians have long sought to reconstruct historical moments of the past, and thus tried to order, shape, and delineate the contours of the history that they are studying. The aim of the historian is not simply to study discrete data, but to trace out the threads of development from existing remains of the past, textual and otherwise. The major goal of this endeavor is to provide an *explanation* for why things happened in a particular way, to place the *human* subject in historical perspective, and, thereby, to gain some grand standpoint on the whole (even as it is generally understood that each historical epoch needs to be understood in its particularity). It is important to emphasize that the approach we develop here also seeks to explore the *human* subject in historical perspective. However, our understanding of how that is enacted differs significantly from more conventional tradents of modern historical scholarship. The meta-narrative of this conventional historical study, which details what it is that historians "ought" to be doing in their work, dramatically shapes what methods are employed and how information is understood, organized, assessed, and used.

Given these differences in vantage point with respect to historical methods and their application, we turn to a delineation of some of the broad contours of our own approach to ancient history. This outline helps to contextualize the interpretative framework of the gender-critical approach operative in the following chapters. Although in this book we focus mostly on textual history, much of what we write could also be applied to non-textual material (e.g., archaeological) history, which is an alternative "text" that is just as open to interpretation. With respect to texts, then, we understand that ancient narratives interconnect with the social, cultural, and political worlds that have informed the imagery and concepts embedded in a specific text. Following Foucault's approach outlined earlier regarding the importance of sociocultural conditions for the production of knowledge, ancient texts from the past can provide insight into the sociocultural conditions of the past and the present. The threads that can be traced out from any text are diverse and varied, because words and concepts from the past are often in themselves open to multiple signification, and, therefore, do not fit into a neat framework for interpretation. Ancient readers of these texts would not necessarily have followed the same threads that an author laid out, and they would not inevitably interpret even one thread in the way an author may have intended. Thus, even after admitting that texts are produced out of but also reflect particular sociocultural contexts, we cannot thereby assume that the same text would communicate that socio-cultural world in exactly the same way to two different receivers in antiquity. In fact, we are certain that almost every text opens itself up to a diversity of interpretations given the multitude of sociocultural threads that flow out of a text into the broader historical world of which it was a part. Yet, this observa-tion implies more than simply stating that different readers may read a text differently. Rather, it signals that even ancient authors, like their modern coun-terparts, open up meanings they may not have intended. Within this historical reconceptualization, we would also question the notion of "authorial intent" itself—writers have a degree of intention, but there are also unconscious and even random factors that make "intentionality" more complex when thinking about the expression of arguments and ideas. There is thus a creative power to language that defies and challenges simplistic renditions of historical inquiry.

Apart from these more general observations, an approach that has been useful to us in thinking about texts in their historical context is the one offered by *socio-rhetorical criticism,* a specific form of discourse analysis that exam-ines, among other things, the complex ways in which texts utilize the imagery of various modes of life and thought in the world to influence readers in and through textual argumentation. Vernon Robbins's work has been especially helpful in delineating the multifaceted nature of ancient discourses that are embodied in texts.[17] Robbins's socio-rhetorical approach is indebted to Aristo-tle's appreciation of rhetorical technique, wherein the practitioner of rhetoric is encouraged to draw on social and cultural *topics* that would prove to be the most persuasive in certain contexts. In his treatise *On Rhetoric,* Aristotle notes that rhetoric is "the ability to see in every situation the available means of com-munication" (1.2.1). Each particular social context thus demands a specific language and argumentation (for instance, one accuses or defends in a law court, but one [generally] praises the dead). Robbins has gone on in recent research to pin down in more detail how images and topics from the social and cultural sphere are blended together to form unique pictures and how those mental images often merge distinctive spheres of sociocultural interac-tion so as to produce a new way of being and thinking in the (ancient) world. In other words, while language, images, and forms of argumentation tend to be confined to particular social realms, those various realms can also be blended and reconfigured. So, for instance, when God is called "abba, father" by Jesus in the New Testament Gospels, this language blends the kind of speech a child might utter in the home with the language by which disciples are called on to address God, thus framing the concept of a kingly/imperial deity in language that evokes associations with the home and patriarchy. As a result, potentially innovative images arise out of these blendings of spaces through language. The importance of this observation is that we can more readily assess how early Christian discourses were both indebted to ancient cultures but also how they developed their own unique characteristics (and accents) in the ancient world. This process represents something of an evolutionary understanding of how discourses arise and differentiate themselves in specific historical contexts.[18]

Robbins's earlier commitment to analyzing the function of ideology in the socio-rhetorical analysis of a text is also important for our approach here. That is, for Robbins, textual rhetoric also promotes the particular ideology of the writer/community. In that light, ancient texts mediate specific ideas and concepts to people in a way that will shape their thinking and acting. Gayatri Chakravorty Spivak's understanding of the "subject-object effect" that surfaces in literature offers an even better framework for this broader notion we are developing here. The "object" in "subject-object effect" refers to how texts accomplish the dissemination of ideology, and "subject" to what characters in texts actually represent. This shift entails that characters in texts should not be viewed as "real" flesh and blood people. They are, rather, simulations (even if the characters are stand-ins for actual/real-life historical people) that give the impression of a conscious subject operating in the narrative ("Subaltern Studies," 213). In other words, there is no simple connection to the "real" historical world or personages behind the text. That said, however, the text nonetheless presents us with fragments of the historical context out of which it arose, and, as such, texts do reflect a rich and varied historical world, even if such a world is still difficult to reconstruct as a "real" and "ideal" entity.

Following from these observations, then, we draw out several points that we deem valuable for our own gender-critical reading strategy. To begin, we understand texts to embody multiple and diverse connections to their broader social and cultural contexts. There are intentional and unintentional connections, and the social production of knowledge relies on both. It is in this multifarious manner that we see gender, sex, and sexuality also playing a role in textual argumentation. As a critical element of both the social and cultural worlds of various local contexts in antiquity, these conceptions are employed throughout texts in both overt and more implicit ways to bolster argumentation and to build conceptual images. Moreover, many images from the ancient world are already gendered and sexed when they are taken over in order to create a textual-rhetorical world. For instance, drawing on the imagery of "father," as Paul does in 1 Corinthians 1–4 will not only pull that social relation into the argument, but it will also, intentionally or not, bring with it particular ideas about fatherhood that then play out later in the text. A term like "father" will also possibly be associated with other images, as the language of the family household easily spills over into other types of households, including more public images, such as the *oikoumene*, the universal "house" of the world/cosmos, wherein the emperor comes to be understood as "father of all."[19] Herein empire discourse is linked to domestic spaces, thereby enhancing the public presence of the private and constructing the emperor in the less brutish language of domesticity, which masks his power while at the same time transfiguring that power onto another plane of authority. Language and images are thus tied to specific social locations, but they also readily connect with concepts in other spheres, and tracing out these associations can prove fruitful for understanding the potency of certain linguistic images in the ancient world, including as well an appreciation for the "ideal" construction as it is conceived in a specific sociohistorical context.

In general, texts produce a narrative or story (often implicit) that interprets the outside world. This aspect becomes critical in the examination of early Christian literature. In what way, for instance, does a text reflect the "actual" reality of an early Christian community? To what degree and in what way does a text produce a world that corresponds to something "out there" and "beyond itself"? Moreover, we need to take into consideration that an author's own persona is involved in the act of narration—an author is situated *in* the text as much as he/she is outside of it as well. The author perhaps seeks to gain recognition and honor through story-telling, and the story, even if fictional, presumably connects with his or her own construction of identity. Further, authors are embedded in their texts in other ways as well. A Roman novel intended purely for entertainment, for instance, also reproduces the political and social values of its writer (e.g., Petronius's *Satyricon*). Thus, every text re-produces a series of values and ideologies. Complicating the picture is that for most of early Christian literature we have very little information about the authors and their social and cultural contexts. Even when we do, such as is the case with the Pauline letters, our evidence is still scanty and difficult to interpret. Thus, we are often left with puzzles to construct and piece together. Moves to real, actual historical communities and individuals must always, in our view, be made with caution. Since complex social processes are played out in ancient texts, we have to be critically astute in terms of the assumptions we impose on the connections between a text and its larger world.

In this approach to ancient texts, we recognize that our present models of ancient history and historical development provide the lens through which we perceive the data from the literature of the past. This observation brings us back to the contentious issue of the ideology of scholarship, with which we opened this section (see chapter four for further discussion). Even when using a gender-critical approach, different scholars with divergent understandings of the complex sociocultural and textual interactions in early Christianity will arrive at differing conclusions with respect to the same data. We will have multiple, diverse, and sometimes even competing readings/interpretations as a result. This situation is to be expected and in many respects also welcomed.

Further, as a way of coming back to the political aspect of the gender-critical approach outlined earlier, it is important to underscore again the ideological contours that all texts and readings possess. All texts make particular arguments—all texts seek to promote a specific worldview and ideology (and we understand that sometimes complex and even contradictory ideologies are present in a text). Within this larger rhetorical agenda, gendered and sexed concepts are used and thereby contribute to and often become a part of the larger ideological aim of a specific text. That aim, furthermore, relates not in small part to the creation and maintenance of specific identities. In other words, ideology here reflects the performance aspect of human interaction that Butler addresses in her work. Insofar as gender is taken up in this larger rhetorical framework, the latter promotes a gendered identity for the reader of these texts as well. That is, one is shaped by the literature one reads, and modern interpreters are not immune from the discursive pull and rhetorical effects of the ancient texts they read and study. In the end, finally, it bears noting that ideologies often operate as much on the basis of what is unstated as on what is explicitly articulated in the text. There are often referents that are absent but that nonetheless are critical players in the narrative. Perhaps the most obvious "player" like this in early Christian narration is *God*. Like all other concepts, the deity is intricately bound up with sociocultural webs of meaning in the broader world, including, we might add, categories of gender, sex, and sexuality. Thus, the examination of ideology in text and context, with special attention paid to the gendered and sexed nature of the discourse, requires careful analysis and close scrutiny of ancient texts, often reading them against what is the most obvious (to us) rendering of their meaning.

Concluding contextual observations

It seems appropriate to acknowledge at this point that we ourselves are not outside of the contextualized nature of knowledge we are promoting in this chapter. In fact, we have been, all along, arguing for a particular ideological perspective, seeking to persuade you, the reader, of the validity of our gender-critical approach to early Christian literature. Moreover, we have actually established a narrative that incorporates a sense of modern development in theory and practice, which in turn validates the historical framework of analysis we will follow in this book. This gender-critical approach, like any other method, is thus constructed in the very act of writing/talking about it. In other words, there is no outside to thinking about methodology as a whole. We are always on the inside, articulating an approach that in effect determines what historical elements come into focus (and which are left out) and how those features are then interpreted. Thus, we note at the outset that a gender-critical approach is one method alongside others, and it both opens up spaces for seeing things that other methods have occluded, but it overlooks elements as well, a phenomenon that is the limitation of all models and methods. This approach also has no universal pretensions—ancient interpreters did not work with this model in mind; scholars one hundred years ago did not either. This model exists precisely in and through the present modes of discourse and social institutions in which we, the authors, find ourselves. It is a product, in our estimation, of current contexts in the academy and institutions of higher learning in the United States and Western Europe, but also, to be fair, of larger issues such as class, race, and, of course, gender, sex, and sexuality as these have emerged in our own time period. These contexts and issues, as personally and collectively experienced by us, have influenced this blending of different methods and agendas. Finally, the approach we have outlined here is also politically motivated (see further the conclusion to this book, "[Dis]Closure"). For us, the object of studying the past is to better understand the present in which we are currently situated. To wit, understanding ancient conceptions of gender, sex, and sexuality, particularly in dialogue with the modern notions that have framed our thinking about the past, helps us to better appreciate the complexity (and ambiguity) of conceptions of gender, sex, and sexuality in our own time and location. The issue of ethics, as we understand it in the gender-critical paradigm we are developing in this discussion, is thus much more focused on our own world than fixated on evaluating the past as an end in itself. Through comparison with the past, we can see diversity better in our own context, we can more clearly assess the constructed nature of our own gendered and sexed identities by observing a similar constructive function of discourse in a context different from our own, and we can thereby open up spaces for changes in contemporary contexts.[20] Still, understanding, though necessary, is insufficient. We believe that study and analysis should aim to create critically engaged readers and practitioners who will be suspicious of and interrogate all forms of ideology, including the ones we formulate and promote in this book.

Notes

1 All translations from the *Acts of Paul and Thecla* are our own. Unless otherwise noted, translations from other ancient writings are either from the Loeb Classical Library (LCL) or from the New Revised Standard Version of the Bible.

2 See further, Klaus Scholder, *The Birth of Modern Critical Theology: Origins and Problems of Biblical Criticism in the Seventeenth Century* (trans. J. Bowden; London: SCM, 1990).

3 See our discussion of the context of these developments in Caroline Vander Stichele and Todd Penner, "Mastering the Tools or Retooling the Masters? The Legacy of Historical-Critical Discourse," in *Her Master's Tools? Feminist and Post-Colonial Engagements of Historical-Critical Discourse* (ed. C. Vander Stichele and T. Penner; Global Perspectives on the Bible 9; Atlanta: Society of Biblical Literature and Leiden: Brill, 2005), 1–29.

4 For further discussion of these developments and trends, see our "Mastering the Tools or Retooling the Masters?" where we detail both the separation of feminist scholarship from the male dominated constructions of the earlier era and the manner in which earlier feminism also tended to reinscribe some of these very same power structures, focusing particularly on issues of class and race.

5 A similar argument, but from a queer perspective, is formulated by Stephen Moore, in his book *God's Beauty Parlor: Queer Spaces in and around the Bible* (Contraversions; Stanford: Stanford University Press, 2001), chapter 3. Also see Joseph A. Marchal, *The Politics of Heaven: Women, Gender, and Empire in the Study of Paul* (Paul in Critical Contexts; Minneapolis: Fortress Press, 2008).

6 Reflecting on the classic line by Simone de Beauvoir—"one is not born, but, rather, *becomes* a woman"—Judith Butler argues that "gender is in no way a stable identity or locus of agency from which various acts proceed; rather, it is an identity tenuously constituted in time—an identity instituted through *stylized repetition of acts*" ("Performative Acts and Gender Constitution: An Essay in Phenomenology and Feminist Theory," *Theatre Journal* 40 [1988]: 519–531 [519; her emphasis]).

7 We also note that, while we are referring specifically to male forms of masculinity, there are also female performances of the masculine that have to be taken into consideration in such discussions. See especially Judith Halberstam, *Female Masculinity* (Durham: Duke University Press, 1998).

8 For a slightly different reading, which emphasizes the contested masculinity of Jesus in light of colonial ambivalence in the Markan text, whereby Jesus also exhibits feminine qualities alongside

more conventional masculine ones, see Eric Thurman, "Novel Men: Masculinity and Empire in Mark's Gospel and Xenophon's *An Ephesian Tale*," in *Mapping Gender in Ancient Religious Discourses* (ed. T. Penner and C. Vander Stichele; Biblical Interpretation Series 84; Leiden: Brill, 2007), 185–229. Also see Colleen Conway, *Behold the Man: Jesus and Greco-Roman Masculinity* (New York: Oxford University Press, 2008).

9　In the American context, one would think first and foremost of W. E. B. Dubois and his book *The Souls of Black Folk* (Chicago: McClurgt, 1903), in which he details the interconnection of racial disparity and the restructuring of the United States after the Civil War.

10　There is debate whether or not one can legitimately apply a postcolonial analysis to past (and particularly ancient) historical settings. Postcolonial methods were formulated in modern colonial contexts, and ancient and modern colonialisms, while they do have elements in common, are also quite distinct (see Ania Loomba, *Colonialism/Postcolonialism* [The New Critical Idiom; second edn; London: Routledge, 2005], 7–22). We would argue that the focus on discourse and its connection to race and ethnic otherization in conditions of coloniality can apply in the ancient context, even as one has to be attuned to the differences between the modern and ancient worlds in this respect (see the discussion in John Marshall, "Postcolonialism and the Practice of History," in Vander Stichele and Penner, *Her Master's Tools*, 93–108). Also see Stephen D. Moore, *Empire and Apocalypse: Postcolonialism and the New Testament* (The Bible in the Modern World 12; Sheffield: Sheffield Phoenix, 2006).

11　In this way, later postcolonial scholars would more tightly wed colonial formations to sexual constructions, arguing that one of the elements frequently neglected in earlier discussions of European colonial encounters was the way in which sex, gender, and sexuality were shaped, contested, and reconstituted in colonial interactions. In this connection, see especially Ann Laura Stoler, *Race and the Education of Desire: Foucault's* History of Sexuality *and the Colonial Order of Things* (Durham: Duke University Press, 1995); Robert J. C. Young, *Colonial Desire: Hybridity in Theory, Culture and Race* (London: Routledge, 1995); and Anne McClintock, *Imperial Leather: Race, Gender and Sexuality in the Colonial Context* (London: Routledge, 1995).

12　A particularly good example of this phenomenon is offered by George Steinmetz, *The Devil's Handwriting: Precoloniality and the German Colonial State in Qingdao, Samoa, and Southwest Africa* (Chicago Studies in Practices of Meaning; Chicago: University of Chicago Press, 2007), where he delineates the German colonial interaction with and appreciation for the Samoan culture.

13　One might note that the study of gender itself is something of a leisure activity, usually engaged in by elite cultural representatives (often university and college professors) who can afford to do so. This privileged position is too frequently overlooked in gender-critical analyses. We might also add that it is largely a Western gaze that is established in Gender Studies, which connects with criticisms of non-Western feminists on the application of Western feminist theories to other cultures (see especially Saba Mahmood, *Politics of Piety: The Islamic Revival and the Feminist Subject* [Princeton: Princeton University Press, 2005]; as well as Chandra Talpade Mohanty, *Feminism without Borders: Decolonizing Theory, Practicing Solidarity* [Durham: Duke University Press, 2003]). It is important to acknowledge these conditions and the limitations of one's perspective, but also to stress that this situation does not simply amount to an endorsement of the status quo, at least not when there is a critical engagement of these power issues in the interpretive process.

14 For a fuller discussion of this and other definitions of ideology, see T. Eagleton, *Ideology: An Introduction* (updated edn; London: Verso, 2007), esp. chapter 1.

15 The concept of a feminist "hermeneutics of suspicion" was substantively promoted in Biblical Studies by Elisabeth Schüssler Fiorenza. See, for instance, her essay "Remembering the Past in Creating the Future: Historical-Critical Scholarship and Feminist-Critical Interpretation," in her *Bread Not Stone: The Challenge of Feminist Biblical Interpretation* (Boston: Beacon Press, 1984), 93–115.

16 See especially his seminal work on modern historiography: Hayden White, *Metahistory: The Historical Imagination in Nineteenth-Century Europe* (Baltimore: Johns Hopkins University Press, 1973). Also see the excellent summary of this shift in historiographical theory and practice by Alun Munslow, *Deconstructing History* (second edn; London: Routledge, 2006); and Elizabeth Clark, *History, Theory, Text: Historians after the Linguistic Turn* (Cambridge, MA.: Harvard University Press, 2004). For a nuanced discussion of the material conditions of the "linguistic turn," including a mediation of traditional and postmodern methods, see William H. Sewell Jr., "The Political Unconscious of Social and Cultural History, or, Confessions of a Former Quantitative Historian," in *The Politics of Method in the Human Sciences: Positivism and Its Epistemological Others* (ed. G. Steinmetz; Politics, History and Culture; Durham: Duke University Press, 2005), 173–206.

17 See especially Vernon K. Robbins, *The Tapestry of Early Christian Discourse: Rhetoric, Society and Ideology* (London: Routledge, 1996); and *Exploring the Texture of Texts: A Guide to Socio-Rhetorical Interpretation* (Harrisburg, Pa.: Trinity Press International, 1996).

18 See further our discussion of these themes in Todd Penner and Caroline Vander Stichele, "Rhetorical Practice and Performance in Early Christianity," in *The Cambridge Companion to Ancient Rhetoric* (ed. E. Gunderson; Cambridge: Cambridge University Press, 2009), 245–60. Also see Vernon K. Robbins, *The Invention of Christian Discourse* (Rhetoric of Religious Antiquity; Blandford Forum, U.K.: DEO Publishing, 2009).

19 We are reliant here on the helpful studies by Eva Marie Lassen, "The Use of the Father Image in Imperial Propaganda and 1 Corinthians 4:14–21," *Tyndale Bulletin* 42 (1991): 127–36; and "The Roman Family: Ideal and Metaphor," in *Constructing Early Christian Families: Family as Social Reality and Metaphor* (ed. H. Moxnes; New York: Routledge, 1997), 103–20.

20 Trish Sheffield, in her recent article "Performing Jesus: A Queer Counternarrative of Embodied Transgression," in *Theology and Sexuality* 14 (2008): 233–58, aptly illustrates the way in which this goal can be accomplished. By employing a queer reading of the Chalcedonian Creed related to the relationship of Jesus to the Godhead, Sheffield explores how a transgendered reading of Jesus' body in traditional theology can open up spaces for transgendered individuals today.

Bibliography

Aristotle. *On Rhetoric: A Theory of Civic Discourse.* Translated by G. A. Kennedy. New York: Oxford University Press, 1991.

Boyarin, Daniel. *A Radical Jew: Paul and the Politics of Identity*. Berkeley: University of California Press, 1994.

Braun, Willi. "Physiotherapy of Femininity in the *Acts of Thecla*." Pp. 209–30 in *Text and Artifact in the Religions of Mediterranean Antiquity*. Edited by S. G. Wilson and M. Desjardins. Studies in Christianity and Judaism 9. Waterloo, Ontario: Wilfrid Laurier University Press, 2000.

Burrus, Virginia. *Chastity as Autonomy: Women in the Stories of the Apocryphal Acts*. Studies in Women and Religion 23. Lewiston: Edwin Mellen Press, 1987.

—"Mimicking Virgins: Colonial Ambivalence and the Ancient Romance." *Arethusa* 38 (2005): 49–88.

Butler, Judith. *Gender Trouble: Feminism and the Subversion of Identity*. New York: Routledge, 1990.

—*Undoing Gender*. New York: Routledge, 2004.

Castelli, Elizabeth A. *Imitating Paul: A Discourse of Power*. Louisville: Westminster John Knox Press, 1991.

Connell, Robert W. *Masculinities*. Berkeley: University of California Press, 1987.

Cooper, Kate. *The Virgin and the Bride: Idealized Womanhood in Late Antiquity*. Cambridge, MA.: Harvard University Press, 1996.

Davies, Stevan L. *The Revolt of the Widows: The Social World of the Apocryphal Acts*. Carbondale/Edwardsville: Southern Illinois University Press, 1980.

Dube, Musa W. *Postcolonial Feminist Interpretation of the Bible*. St. Louis: Chalice Press, 2000.

Fanon, Frantz. *Black Skin, White Masks*. London: Pluto Press, 1986.

—*The Wretched of the Earth*. New York: Grove Press, 2004.

Foucault, Michel. *The History of Sexuality I: An Introduction*. New York: Vintage Books, 1990.

—*The History of Sexuality II: The Use of Pleasure*. New York: Vintage Books, 1990.

—*The History of Sexuality III: The Care of the Self*. New York: Vintage Books, 1988.

Liew, Tat-siong Benny. "Re-Mark-able Masculinities: Jesus, the Son of Man, and the (Sad) Sum of Manhood?" Pp. 93–135 in *New Testament Masculinities*. Edited by S. D. Moore and J. Capel Anderson. Semeia Studies 45. Atlanta: Society of Biblical Literature, 2003.

MacDonald, Dennis R. *The Legend and the Apostle: The Battle for Paul in Story and Canon*. Philadelphia: Westminster Press, 1983.

Matthews, Shelly. "Thinking of Thecla: Issues in Feminist Historiography." *Journal of Feminist Studies in Religion* 17 (2001): 39–55.

Nicholson, Linda. "Interpreting Gender." Pp. 39–67 in *Social Postmodernism: Beyond Identity Politics*. Edited by L. Nicholson and S. Seidman. Cambridge: Cambridge University Press, 1995.

Petronius. *The Satyricon*. Translated by P. G. Walsh. New York: Oxford University Press, 1999.

Said, Edward W. *Orientalism*. London: Penguin Books, 1991.

—*Culture and Imperialism*. London: Vintage Books, 1994.

Schüssler Fiorenza, Elisabeth. *In Memory of Her: A Feminist Theological Reconstruction of Christian Origins*. New York: Crossroad, 1985.

Söder, Rosa. *Die apokryphen Apostelgeschichten und die romanhafte Literatur der Antike*. Stuttgart: Kohlhammer, 1932. Repr. Darmstadt: Wissenschaftliche Buchgesellschaft, 1969.

Spivak, Gayatri Chakravorty. "Subaltern Studies: Deconstructing Historiography." Pp. 202–35 in *The Spivak Reader*. Edited by D. Landry and G. Maclean. New York: Routledge, 1996.

2 Contextualizing Gender in the Greco-Roman World

A certain man called Onesiphorus, hearing that Paul was coming to Iconium, went out with his children Simias and Zeno and his wife Lectra to meet Paul in order to welcome him. For Titus had described what Paul looked like, as he did not know him in the flesh but only in the spirit. And he took the royal road to Lystra and stood there waiting for him, looking at the people passing by according to the instruction of Titus. And he saw Paul coming, a small man in posture, with a bald head, crooked legs, strong looking, his eyebrows meeting in the middle, a somewhat large nose, full of grace, for in one moment he appeared like a human being and in another he had the face of an angel.

—Acts of Paul and Thecla 3.2–3

Before we meet Thecla as a character in the *Acts of Paul and Thecla*, we encounter Paul on the road to Iconium. A description of his physical appearance is given as an "eye-witness" account by Onesiphorus, who ends up hosting Paul for his initial stay in the city. The description of Paul is a piece of compositional *ekphrasis*, which, in ancient rhetoric, was the exercise of describing a particular place, person, or event in vivid detail, so as to make it appear so real that one was able to visualize the subject of the description, thus prioritizing seeing/visualization. In this case, Paul's body is brought palpably before the reader's eyes, with the aim that "we" are transported there in person with Onesiphorus, witnessing Paul walk up the road. This passage is intriguing, not in small part because it is the only ancient depiction we have of Paul's appearance in antiquity. Paul is described as being short in stature, bald, having crooked legs, possessing a somewhat large nose, with eyebrows that meet in the middle. The twenty-first-century reader might well wonder if this is a positive or negative (or possibly neutral) description of Paul's physical features. Earlier interpreters of this text viewed the description of Paul as suggesting that he was rather homely or even ugly. That is, they understood this picture of Paul to reflect a historical remembrance or tradition of what Paul actually looked like, and in their view the image was rather unflattering. This observation, however, immediately raises the question: what made a body look beautiful or ugly in antiquity? Or, to phrase it differently, how are we to read bodies in the ancient world, or, in turn, gaze at/upon them? As we already noted in the first chapter, bodies and their representations and performances are a pivotal aspect of a gender-critical analysis, and certainly a major feature of ancient world discourses (as much as they are of our own), including early Christian discourses. Therefore, reading bodies in all their diverse interconnections is one of the main foci of this chapter.

It was precisely this question of reading bodies that led some modern scholars to reassess the above description of Paul in light of the ancient practice of "body reading," known as *physiognomy*. This practice was considered a "science" in antiquity, and has roots as far back as Aristotle, and probably even earlier. Ancient scholars, poets, and philosophers established a correlation between the outward appearance of an individual and her or his inner character. In other words, the way a person looked signaled something quintessential about their inner virtue, and, vice versa, a person's character was made visible on his or her outward body. In this way, virtuous people were expected to bear the physical features that marked such virtue; villainous individuals likewise bore evidence of their wicked character in their own flesh. Moreover, so-called handbooks existed in the ancient world that offered a taxonomy and classification of various features of the body, thereby helping to identify the specific correlation between outward appearance and inner character.[1] As is to be expected, it is especially in narrative and visual representations that we see these patterns emerge in a concrete and sustained manner. Still, these signs of the flesh are open to multiple interpretations, as becomes clear from the fact that, over the past twenty-five years, scholars have offered differing physiognomic readings of Paul's appearance in the *Acts of Paul and Thecla*. One of the first attempts to move beyond the seemingly non-ideal or even ugly description of Paul's body can be found in an article by Robert Grant ("Description of Paul"), who argued that this depiction of Paul, when read in light of the Greek poet Archilochus, yields a reading of the apostle as the ideal general: short, bow-legged, firm on his feet, and full of heart. This portrayal of Paul was intended to highlight the noble and courageous aspects of his character, and his bodily appearance signifies these aspects through its outward physical characteristics.

Somewhat later, Abraham Malherbe elaborated on Grant's approach, arguing that Paul was rather to be compared to Suetonius's description of Augustus (described as small, with a hooked nose and conjoined eyebrows) or to a similar image of Heracles offered by Philostratus, who noted that Heracles had bowed legs (*Paul and the Popular Philosophers*, 165–70). For Malherbe, then, Paul is not a general per se, but rather he is to be placed into a larger heroic paradigm that carries with it specific stereotypical descriptive features. More recently, Bruce Malina and Jerome Neyrey offer an extensive reading of Paul's appearance, using each element in the description to show how Paul is configured as the ideal male in terms of his physical representation (*Portraits of Paul*, 100–52). Malina and Neyrey go to great lengths to demonstrate that Paul's bodily features map his personal comportment in terms of the dominant norms of how males were ideally to look and act in the ancient world. Mikael Parsons, who provides the most thorough treatment to date on the role of physiognomy in early Christian literature, presents the various options offered by these previous scholars (*Body and Character*, 51–56), but chooses to view them in continuity with each other. In particular, Parsons notes that in each of these three positions—general, hero, and ideal male—Paul is portrayed in *positive* terms.

Largely unnoticed in these discussions, however, is that all of the suggested categories refer to ideal *masculine* images in the ancient world. In other words, the depiction of Paul as read by modern scholars through the ancient physiognomic lens reveals a highly *gendered* portrait of the apostle.[2] Moreover, none of these scholars pays attention to the potential intersection with other identity markers in the portrait of Paul, such as ethnicity, race, class, or religious identity. Overall, then, the focus on Paul's body as an ideal male representation is separated from other readings and classifications of bodies in the

Greco-Roman world. Yet, as we would argue, this larger cartography of bodies at the intersection of culture and society in the ancient world is essential for a fuller appreciation of the complexity of reading ancient gender, sex, and sexual identities in context.

Perhaps most striking in this "male assessment" by modern scholars is that they have largely tried to cultivate an image of Paul as being ideal or even attractive—at least attractive to an ancient audience (as such is constructed through a modern lens) in terms of his representing normative physical values. This approach, however, overlooks the possibility that, depending on the precise end of the argument, ugly bodies or non-normative bodies could actually achieve a rhetorical aim that ideal and normal bodies could not. The latter was one of the original insights of Maud Gleason's important study (*Making Men*), in which she related ancient physiognomy to the performance of the orator in public contests. In this competitive environment, manhood was constructed in the act of two orators exhibiting their rhetorical prowess before an audience. One of the strengths of Gleason's work is her demonstration that non-normative performances could in fact win audience approval—the public forum functioned, after all, as a stage! The famous orator Favorinus, for instance, often had the upper hand against his frequent opponent Polemo, even though the former was effeminate in many of his public performances, which clearly did not match the normative expectations of masculinity presumably held by the audience. Yet Favorinus was able to use effeminate body markers (e.g., pitch of voice, movement of the body, style of dress) to outperform his opponent and to obtain the overwhelming approval of the crowds in the process.

Ugliness may well have had a similar function in the portrait of Paul. Jan Bremmer, for instance, offers a divergent perspective from the previous readings of Paul's body in the *Acts of Paul and Thecla*. He suggests that the author of the text intended to have Paul appear less than physically ideal so as to make clear that Thecla falls in love with Paul's words rather than his beauty ("Magic, Martyrdom and Women's Liberation"). Since Paul is depicted as promoting an ascetic gospel and lifestyle, to bring in overt sexual desire would be problematic. For Bremmer, then, Paul's appearance functions rhetorically to signify that Thecla's attraction to Paul focused on his speech not his body. Here we see how it might be possible to assess an ugly portrait of Paul in terms of the rhetorical argument of the text, which still supports the ascetic portrayal of Paul (and Thecla).

Further, ugliness may also be used to make a specific philosophical point, as was the case, for instance, with the early representations of Socrates, which highlight his unattractive appearance in light of the normative expectations of male beauty in ancient Greek society. Such an image could have been used to subvert dominant values of normativity for male citizens: if Socrates, the wisest man who ever lived, can be ugly, what does that say about the importance of appearance itself?[3] The philosophical point being made in this case is that a fundamental gap exists between appearance and reality. The young male citizens of Athens ought to be drawn to the inner beauty of the ideal pedagogue, not to his external appearances, because Socrates, while ugly on the outside, represents truth and beauty within, which is (or ought to be) truly desirable. The male gaze, in this case, should be fixed on inward realities. In other words, ugliness can have a critical function both rhetorically and ideologically, and, as János Bollók argues, the portrayal of Paul may have a similar function ("Description of Paul"). The attempt to read all bodies based on their correlation with physiognomic handbooks may therefore be misleading, because such a move overlooks the contextual nature of how bodies are mapped and configured towards specific argumentative ends. Moreover, any analysis of physiognomic categories must consider the intersection of these categories with a whole range of other classifications related to gender, class, status, religion, race, and deformity in the ancient world. There exists a mutually interpretive interaction that goes on, so that these facets cannot be abstracted and studied in isolation. In other words, there is a complexity to how people are ordered and classified in this ancient context, with physical appearance being just one (albeit significant) element in the mix.

Finally, while we have been focusing here on the presentation of Paul's body in the *Acts of Paul and Thecla*, it is noteworthy that Thecla's body comes into play as well. We are not told what she looks like, but she is described as beautiful and men around her look on her body with desire.[4] Although in the opening sections of the *Acts of Paul and Thecla* she is clearly presented as the dutiful virgin, awaiting her marriage to Thamyris, the story that unfolds offers quite a different portrait of this female character, as she abandons her role as the virgin bride in order to follow Paul's call to remain a virgin. As Willi Braun argues, Thecla appears to transform from female to "male" after her baptism ("Physiotherapy of Femininity"). From her desire to have short hair to the wearing of identifiable male clothing, she increasingly emerges in a male guise throughout the story. This gendered and sexed transformation (or display of "female masculinity") parallels her growing desire to follow in Paul's footsteps with consequent escalating public conflict. Introduced as the object of male sexual desire, Thecla thus offers an intriguing counterpoint to the physical representation of Paul, whose own body disappears behind the message he delivers in the narrative. These observations reinforce the point that bodies in texts must be read contextually.

The preceding reflections on the physiognomic features in the *Acts of Paul and Thecla* offer a glimpse into the complex and oft times convoluted world of ancient gender, sex, and sexual identity. As is clear from the discussion so far, it is no easy matter to map bodies in the ancient world and to delineate how seemingly simple categories such as "male" and "female" were understood and also represented. Indeed, as already suggested in the first chapter, there are at least two issues at stake here: first, we must determine how people in the ancient Greek and Roman worlds read and viewed the body, including how they interpreted human performative acts, and, second, we need to engage the representation of bodies in narrative and visual display. In order to understand these representations we should acquire some sense of the underlying ancient historical and cultural perspectives that inform perceptions related to gender, sex, and sexuality. Yet to appreciate the historical and cultural foundations we largely have to rely on literature. The problem is, as noted in the first chapter, that representations (both textual and visual) do not necessarily provide full or direct access to the historical and cultural experiences of real people, both elite and nonelite (although, admittedly, we have better access to the former). And herein lies one of the many problems we encounter in the attempt to assess how ancient writers and readers thought about and mapped bodies in texts.

That said, one of the fundamental assumptions of our gender-critical approach to early Christian literature is that bodies mattered as much in the past as they do now—and particular bodies mattered more and embodied more power and authority than others. Moreover, as we also noted in the first chapter, a gender-critical assessment is committed to exploring the rhetorical and ideological facets of gender, sex, and sexual representations in antiquity and the present (and especially the interaction of these three facets). As mentioned already in the opening discussion of Paul's appearance in the *Acts of Paul and Thecla*, the body in the text can signify a wide array of meanings in both ancient and modern contexts. Following on this observation, in this chapter we delineate features that one should take into account when conceptualizing bodies in early Christianity in relation to its ancient context, such as Greco-Roman perspectives on sex-distinction, gender performance, and the larger (and more complex) intersection of the individual body and collective social and cultural bodily identities. However we understand how bodies are constructed and imagined in ancient texts, one of the arguments we make is that an interpreter needs to appreciate that there is *no simple* reading of gender, sex, sexuality, and desire. Rhetoric and ideology have a dramatic impact on how the same body will be read as contexts—textual, social, cultural, and historical—shift and change. Moreover, the range of options for how bodies are interpreted are multiple and diffuse—there is no straightforward model or paradigm that one can readily employ to make sense of all the data. Moreover, the mapping of bodies in antiquity, like in our own world, produces a complex and variegated topography. This observation points to the overarching difficulty of reading bodies in the ancient world, especially in light of the fact that our modern preconceptions about bodies and how they should be (re)presented constantly interfere with our reconstructions of the past.

Discourse and the meaning of sex

In the first chapter, we outlined some basic features of Michel Foucault's approach to discourse, highlighting the way in which Foucault understood discourses to arise from within discrete historical and cultural periods. While emergent discourse is always connected to what comes before, there are also unique facets to the discourses of a specific time period. Foucault was thus instrumental for articulating a framework that illustrated the way in which sex/gender categories were not natural and fixed but rather fluid and malleable. As we noted in the previous chapter, one of the more difficult notions for people of any time period to grasp is that our understandings of the world, including how we understand gender, sex, and sexuality, are not "natural" or "given" as we most often assume. Exploring this insight further in the following pages, we contextualize ancient discourses and images related to sex and sexuality, so as to better understand differences between this earlier world and our own.

Rather than starting with the past, however, we prefer to begin with a closer look at the contextualized nature of these categories in the present, taking as our point of departure Alice Domurat Dreger's study, *Hermaphrodites and the Medical Invention of Sex* (2000), since herein she illuminates some of the contours of the modern view of sexual difference. In her historical analysis, Dreger more specifically explores the manner in which the discovery and initial scientific investigation of hermaphroditic individuals (those people possessing both male and female genitalia, or at least substantial traces of both sex organs), particularly in France and England, gave rise over time to a full-blown discourse related to sex differentiation. Dreger suggests that a shift occurred during the eighteenth through nineteenth centuries in the conception of the hermaphrodite, especially with respect to what constitutes a "true" hermaphrodite. As she notes, the concern to maintain the societal and cultural boundaries of a dominant heterosexual orientation provided significant impetus in the later part of that time period to reexamine the "in-between" sexual category of the hermaphrodite, thereby defining the "fluid" state out of existence. In the process, the concept of "sexual dimorphism," a classification that maintains the existence of an absolute set of differences between the "male" and "female" sex, became the normative category of description and discourse. As a result, the "age of gonads" came into existence, with the difference between "male" and "female" centering on reproduction. Thus, a discourse of distinction between two sexes arose, which was then reified (and deified) in the scientific lab. Far from being the result of unbiased, detached, objective descriptions of reality, in this framework science functions as the assessment of observable phenomena in light of specific sociocultural concerns, assumptions, and values that regulate the manner in which the results are classified and interpreted. In other words, the way in which we currently conceptualize the differences between the sexes—based largely, even if often implicitly, on the ability to reproduce—is related not in small part to debates from the more recent past, which have dramatically shaped the way we think in our current context. Yet this developmental character of our viewpoints is often eclipsed (and masked) by the universal and natural language of science and religion, both of which make normative claims that stabilize and universalize the natural world, even if achieving that end in different ways (one projecting onto "nature" what the other projects onto "god").

Dreger's study offers just one avenue into the larger debate regarding the construction of sex and sexual differentiation in the modern world.[5] Her approach is useful, however, in order to appreciate the ways in which our assumed "natural" views of the world have their foundations in the sociohistorical contexts in which those discourses themselves emerged. It is critical to be aware of the relative nature of our own conceptions of sex and gender lest we construct the ancient world in our own image, projecting our normative and dominant categories onto something that may be quite foreign and different. Scholars (predominantly male) of the nineteenth and early twentieth centuries were not all that interested in a detailed exploration of gender, sex, and sexuality in the ancient world, largely because modern gender and sex characteristics were assumed to be normative and universal (and there thus appeared to be little reason to study them in history). However, as perspectives on gender and sex changed in society, so did scholarly inquiry. Thus, in so far as homosexuality became an issue of debate in the modern context, scholars also took an increasing interest in this subject in relation to the ancient world. The same can be said for roles of women, constructions of sex, and understandings of gender performance. Moreover, with the influx of female academics into research institutions, each of these areas of investigation grew in importance and, with this shift in the analytic lens, awareness of these very issues in our own modern context increased as well. As a result, more recent forms of scholarship (often influenced by the "linguistic turn" outlined in the previous chapter) challenged previous paradigms, showing how social-constructive views on knowledge make it possible to re-evaluate more traditional models of analysis.

One place where this shift can be observed is in the study of ancient Greek and Roman homosexual practices. In his 1978 ground-breaking work on ancient same sex sexual relations, *Greek Homosexuality*, Kenneth J. Dover changed in significant ways how scholars thought about this particular sexual classification in relation to its ancient context. More specifically, he achieved this end by altering our understanding of the *differences* between the modern practice of homosexuality and its ancient analogue. Dover drew attention to a wide array of visual images (vase paintings) as well as textual representations (particularly an extended "lawsuit" by the Greek orator Demosthenes) that depicted homosexuality in terms of the relationship between older male citizens (*erastes*) and younger boys (*eromenos*), the former of whom were to assume an active, the latter a passive, role in sexual relationships. After reaching the age of manhood himself, the young boy would in turn become an *erastes*, as it was considered shameful to continue to be an *eromenos* beyond one's youth, since the liminal status of adolescence (when one could be penetrated without shame) disappeared once one was an adult, a status that demanded of him to perform as a penetrator.

Dover's work still represents an earlier model of scholarship in that he assessed Greek homosexual activity as distorted or even disdainful. In her *Bisexuality in the Ancient World*, written ten years later, Eva Cantarella took a similar approach to these issues, arguing that ancient Greeks and Romans had a proclivity towards bisexual orientation, albeit not in identical ways. In her estimation, the Greeks had a more educational view of homosexuality as pederasty (sex between men and boys), while, in the Roman world, young boys were not deemed suitable subjects for penetration, although slaves, enemies, and prostitutes were. In Cantarella's study, like Dover's ten years earlier, the operative classifications are "homosexuality," "heterosexuality," and "bisexuality" as we conceptualize those categories today. In other words, both Dover and Cantarella studied ancient sexual behavior using our modern conceptions, but, precisely in light of our understandings of those categories, they were nevertheless able to demonstrate that ancient homosexual behavior was different from the corollary in the modern world. Thus, to these scholars, while the ancient world may be perceived to enact its "homosexuality" differently than the same practice in the modern world, the category of "homosexuality" remains their "natural" frame of reference.

The importance of this observation cannot be overstated, since how one conceives of and uses the terminology of analysis and investigation in effect shapes the results that one discovers using that same terminology. Difference in this framework is thus one of variance in practice but not divergence in fundamental conception. In other words, the underlying assumption is that same-sex relations between males were differently framed in the ancient world in comparison with our modern viewpoint, but that there was still a consistency in terms of a structural relation in which two males had some kind of "same sex" relationship and attraction, denoted by the term "homosexuality" (and extended to "bisexuality" when those same individuals also had sexual relations with females, of which the majority did, although this element receives much less emphasis in the sources). The question we raise, however, is whether these are even appropriate categories to think about sex in the ancient world. It is precisely at this juncture that Foucault's work has been particularly helpful for opening up new ways of thinking about the ancient material.

In his third volume of *The History of Sexuality* (*The Care of the Self*), Foucault begins his discussion of sexuality in the Roman period with an intriguing text. Foucault turns to Artemidorus's *The Interpretation of Dreams*, investigating the various sexual dreams that Artemidorus lays out and interprets in his handbook on dream analysis. Foucault notes that Artemidorus's guide to the interpretation of sexual dreams follows a peculiar pattern: in all cases of sexual activity between two individuals appearing in the dreams, the question that Artemidorus raises relates to the social relations between the people involved (*History of Sexuality III*, 26–36). In particular, the main issue for Artemidorus is *who penetrates whom* in the dream, since that distinguishes the socially dominant individual (the penetrator) from the socially inferior one (the penetrated). Alongside the social sphere, Artemidorus also interprets the sexual scenario in economic terms, in that a sexual act generates "profit" in the form of sexual pleasure and "expenditure" in the form of ejaculated semen, which stand for "real life" economic gains and losses in his analytic lens. Foucault concludes that, for Artemidorus, "the sexual dream uses the little drama of penetration and passivity, pleasure and expenditure, to tell the subject's mode of being, as destiny has arranged it" (33). Understood in this way, sexuality in dreams does not refer to particular personal desires that the subject may have in "real" life, but rather becomes predictive of specific social and economic transactions that lie before the subject in the near future (or did in the recent past).

Of special interest to us here is the way in which the sexual act is read: it is not about desire and passion, but about social and economic relations. Foucault considered this framework of ancient views of sex and sexuality to be critical for any full understanding of sex and gender in the ancient world, and it was this specific insight that dramatically shaped the scholarship that followed his model. In this framework, then, when Artemidorus relates a scenario in which a man dreams of having sex with his mother, a favorable omen is rendered, since, according to Artemidorus's interpretation, the "mother" figure represents a man's trade, and this in turn suggests future success in business (and is not, as in a modern Freudian framework, indicative of say oedipal fantasies related to the mother). Likewise, if a man dreams of being penetrated by someone older and richer, this is also a favorable omen, as the status of the penetrator is higher than that of the dreamer. It is ominous, however, if a man dreams of being penetrated by a slave, a younger man, or an economically depressed male. Thus, the critical elements in these scenarios are social categories and economic exchanges, with the *penis* of the male forming the symbolic center around which the whole system of meaning turns. As Foucault notes, "the penis thus appears at the intersection of all of these games of mastery: self-mastery, since its demands are likely to enslave us if we allow ourselves to be coerced by it; superiority over sexual partners, since it is by means of the penis that the penetration is carried out; status and privileges, since it signifies the whole field of kinship and social activity" (34).

Having delineated Foucault's perspective, it is important to note that feminist scholars have criticized the phallogocentric (the privileging of the *phallus* or male/masculine hegemony in constructing discourses and construing meanings) interpretation offered by Foucault.[6] Sandra Lee Bartky ("Foucault, Femininity") argues that Foucault simply lumped women and men together within a male-dominated institutional context of modernization, without realizing that women were related in different ways to these systems of meaning.

Lin Foxhall, more specifically, offers a harsh critique of Foucault's *History of Sexuality*, arguing that Foucault made the classic error of "confusing the part for the whole" ("Pandora Unbound," 123). Foxhall here intends to criticize Foucault for taking the elite male discourse of the ancient texts he used and applying the observations based on those texts to the whole of ancient Greek and Roman society, in all its varied manifestations. In this respect, she argues, Foucault essentially eliminated women from the map of ancient gender, sex, and sexual discourses (making them commodities of scholarship and memory).[7] Foxhall goes on to offer numerous examples from other ancient texts to demonstrate that women were not passive, but actually could be quite active in terms of their gendered and sexed performances. Of course, there is a complex dynamic here with respect to the kinds of women who could be active in the public sphere, insofar as they are typically elite females, being socially and economically advantaged. At the very least, however, Foxhall draws attention to the possibility that the ancient grid system has to be expanded to include a more complex view of the hierarchies that existed in the imperial contexts of antiquity (i.e., there is a strategically multifaceted structure regarding who tops whom in the ancient world for that).

While we acknowledge these critiques and the problematic exclusion of female subjectivities in typical discourse analysis of this sort, we still find Foucault's perspective helpful in analyzing the ancient data: sex was first and foremost about social and economic relations rather than desires and passions (applied to both men and women), which signals a critical divergence between the modern and the ancient worlds in terms of ideal and conscious constructions of sex. From this Foucauldian perspective, then, the views of Dover and Cantarella appear in a different light. It is true that there are some important similarities between Foucault on the one hand and Dover/Cantarella on the other, especially in terms of the focus on penetration as a social act that maps dominant and subordinate relationships in the ancient world. Foucault, however, has moved the discussion much more thoroughly into the social sphere of interpretation. Sexual interaction in this ancient context is not as we understand that conception today. As noted earlier, Foucault emphasized the critical function of *self-mastery*, the ability to control oneself as the first step towards the control of others. From this perspective, the matter of homosexuality versus heterosexuality fades into the background, as the main issue first and foremost is the regulation of desire and only secondarily (and then from a social angle) does the specific object of desire come into play. While seeming like a small shift over the positions of Dover and Cantarella, the implications are significant, because from this vantage point the contemporary notion of "homosexuality"—and how that discourse functions within the modern system of meaning—cannot be applied *carte blanche* to the ancient world. If Dover focused on differences in the object of desire for homosexuals between the ancient and modern worlds (while the nature of desire and sexual orientation was understood to be similar), Foucault rather triggered a conceptual change in the discourse of homosexuality itself and its related social power dynamics (i.e., we cannot use modern categories to interpret what was taking place in an ancient cultural environment—we need a different conceptual framework for that).

Foucault's trajectory was fleshed out more thoroughly by David Halperin in his book *One Hundred Years of Homosexuality* (1990), where he persuasively argues that conceptions of homosexuality are social and cultural constructs, and that we cannot simply apply our modern notion to this ancient phenomenon, as scholars have been doing in the past.[8] The framing act may look the same in both ancient and modern contexts, but it has radically different respective meanings. The example he offers illustrates this contrast well:

> To assimilate both the senior and the junior partner in a peaederastic relationship to the same "(homo)sexuality," for example, would have struck a classical Athenian as no less bizarre than to classify a burglar as an "active criminal," his victim as a "passive criminal," and the two of them alike as partners in crime . . . Each act of sex in classical Athens was no doubt an expression of real, personal desire on the part of the sexual actors involved, but their very desires had already been shaped by the shared cultural definition of sex as an activity that generally occurred only between a citizen and a non-citizen, between a person invested with full civic status and a statutory minor. (32)

Halperin aptly captures here the social and cultural (and even political) nature of sexual desire in ancient Athens. *What matters, then, is not only what sexual acts look like, but also what they mean.* And they will bear dramatically different meanings depending on the specific sociocultural context in which they are situated and interpreted.

Within this Foucauldian paradigm, then, meaning is determined by seeking the broad intersections of the sociocultural world with, in this case, the specific gender, sex, or sexual related facet being examined. This shift also helps explain one of the fundamental differences between Halperin's and Dover's presentations of ancient sexual relations among men. While Dover's observations were not incorrect, they nonetheless were based on discrete pieces of data separated from the larger sociocultural context that could have helped flesh out their meaning and aid in distinguishing that ancient phenomenon from our own sense of it today. This observation does not imply that ancient people did not have sexual feelings, desires, and emotions, just as we do today.[9] It means, however, that the way in which these human features are mapped and classified vary considerably, and this awareness represents *the* critical feature for understanding the particularity of human experience in any historical context. Thus, the most crucial aspect for our analysis is not what one feels per se, but how one understands that sexual desire within a broader social and cultural environment. In his study of ancient Roman homosexuality, Craig Williams carefully delineates such a focus in this way:

> Beyond mere physical encounters, men have desired to form lasting bonds with sexual partners both male and female, and the spectrum of emotional states involved in pursuing and maintaining those relationships seems to have remained basically the same. But what has changed, and indeed what generally varies over time and between cultures, is the way in which men have been encouraged by their cultural heritage to categorize and evaluate these acts and actors, relations and relationships. (*Roman Homosexuality*, 13)

In summary, then, we note that gender, sex, and sexuality are not essential or natural categories but are given meaning in specific sociocultural and historical contexts. Although it is difficult to avoid projecting our own concepts onto the past, it is crucial to recognize that while there is a certain continuity to human experience, the meaning of that experience (and the articulation of it) varies widely across time and space. We are dependent on the various threads of data from the ancient world (and our understanding and contextualization of that data) in order to reconstruct a meaning that is not readily accessible to us since it is simply taken for granted by people in antiquity (just as our understandings of gender, sex, and sexuality are also assumed to be "natural" and "universal" by us). It is therefore critical to read the data in nuanced ways, avoiding grand schemes of meaning and, in exchange, teasing out the more complicated and convoluted nature of the rhetorical and ideological character of these diverse categories. In this framework, then, there is significant diversity. Just as there are divergences between Greek and Roman views, there are also further variances within various cultures over time, region, class, and so on. Moreover, various individuals will map (and receive) the broader sociocultural understandings of sex and gender in differing ways depending on a range of factors such as gender, sexual orientation, social status, geographical location, political realities, personal experiences, and so on. The rhetorical end of argumentation plays a pivotal role too, insofar as we often rely on elite textual sources (and we have already noted in the previous chapter the difficulty of historical reconstruction based on textual sources). Finally, one must connect discourses related to gender, sex, and sexuality to the broader sociocultural fabric out of which they arise and in which they make sense in order to flesh out the whole, since that approach is the only way in which these conceptions can be more fully grasped and articulated in meaningful ways.

Models for understanding sex

One of the critical issues for reflection in any field of study is the way in which theoretical paradigms are employed, as they provide a framework both for making sense of the known data and for predicting unknowns from within the given assumptions of that specific paradigm, all of which is put towards the purpose of classifying, assessing, and interpreting data. We tend to take these paradigms as implicit features of our analysis, failing to recognize fully the crucial influence frames of reference have on the way we perceive evidence as well as interpret it. In the first chapter, we indicated that one of the important changes that took place in the academy in the twentieth century was precisely a shift from the earlier universal and "natural" models of criticism to approaches that emphasized the contextual nature of knowledge, the social location of the interpreter, and the role of ideology in shaping scientific forms of analysis. Indeed, models not only affect how evidence is studied and organized, they also determine what kind of evidence is taken into account (to the exclusion of other data). In other words, the model one selects to frame the data will inevitably contribute to and also in some sense produce the results one arrives at in research, an observation that cannot be stressed strongly enough. Models consist of the various methodological approaches we employ, the assumptions we adopt, as well as the frameworks of interpretation we put in place to help us to make sense of the data.

Historical inquiry, for instance, proceeds as if data are not random or haphazard; rather, it is assumed that, if arranged and then read through a particular lens, data will reveal significant information about the period under study. If, within that historical approach, one uses a sociological model (one that analyses interactions based on social organizations and principles) to examine a specific facet of imperial Roman elite culture, one has already delimited the approach by virtue of drawing on a specific method and also narrowed the field of inquiry to the sphere of social strata (which presumably has already been defined and interpreted as an "elite" phenomenon). Further, there are also different sociological methods that one could employ: for example, one could use a functionalist approach, examining how a specific social phenomenon functions in a society, or perhaps a Marxist one, deciphering how class structures and ways of thinking are produced and sustained by concrete social and economic processes. Thus, we stress that all study of the ancient world proceeds through a series of established models of interpretation that are chosen to help classify the data and then, in turn, refract that material through an interpretive grid, sustained by assumptions and embedded values that shape both what we observe and how we interpret the results. Frequently, moreover, historians tend to favor one model (or series of models) over others, and thus the emergent data and results from these approaches look different and may also, in some respects, appear to be mutually exclusive in terms of meaning.[10] It is therefore difficult to use competing and even contradictory models, even as the data itself may require being read from a variety of angles in order to be elucidated more fully.

Further, most conventional historians would argue that the ancient sphere of human interaction and culture is static and stable enough so that historical data can be derived from it and interpreted. In other words, in this perspective it is quite possible to make sense out of the ancient past and its textual and material remains. Many scholars would also insist that one can use either an inductive (moving from observable evidence to a larger conclusion that accounts for the evidence) or deductive (using a preexisting model to read the data) method for interpreting ancient data. However, the data considered worthy of investigation in any historical study have already been determined by a preexisting model, so even moments of presumed inductive reasoning are already based on a number of prior deductive operations. In our estimation, then, attention to the use of models—both to their strengths and limitations—is paramount for any historical investigation.

Turning to ancient gender, sex, and sexuality, then, one of the first elements to engage are the models that scholars use both to think about these conceptions in the ancient world and to differentiate this ancient context from our own. Two models are especially noteworthy here for their use by scholars in analyzing the ancient world. One relates to how the sex of bodies is conceived in Greco-Roman antiquity and the other to the more specific nature of ancient gender performance. The first model is articulated by Thomas Laqueur, who attempts to make sense of how body and gender were conceived in the past in comparison to the contemporary world. As we have already noted in the first chapter, there is a link between gender performance and bodily conception, and Laqueur's model seeks to account for the interrelation of the two. The second model was developed *in nuce* by Foucault, but has received further elaboration in the work of classicists such as Jonathan Walters and Holt N. Parker. This model considers gender (particularly the male dominator/ penetrator) performance to be an essential component of ancient conceptions of the body.

Looking first at Laqueur, in *Making Sex* (1990) he details the conceptual shift related to the category of "sex" that took place from the ancient Greeks through to the modern world. In particular, Laqueur argues that modern conceptions of the body are based on a "two-sex" model that originated in the Enlightenment period. In this model, humans are divided into "male" and "female" bodies based on biological (external and internal) differences (see Alice Domurat Dreger's discussion earlier in this chapter). Laqueur further argues, on the basis of Greek evidence starting with Aristotle, that the predominant model for conceptualizing the body in the ancient world was significantly different from our own. He argues for the existence of a "one-sex" model, wherein the male human body was perceived as perfect and females were considered to be a derivative thereof—they were, in essence, inferior males. Thus, both internally and externally, the female body represented an underdeveloped version of the normative male body. In Aristotle's understanding, females were produced as a result of a deficiency or imperfection in the father's effort or *dynamis* (literally, "power") during the sexual act. Physical weakness in the male thus translates into female offspring. Moreover, the anatomist Galen of Pergamum (ca. 130–200 CE) understood the female genitalia to be inverted male penises, the chief cause of this perceived deficiency being that females, contrary to men, did not produce enough heat to push their penis outside so that it would be external to the body.

Rather than being just a conceptual model that describes the abstract views of Greek philosophers and scientists, there is also a critical social implication to this "one-sex" model in so far as females are not only regarded as biologically deficient males, but their inferiority is also grounded in a natural order of being. Thus, as with ideologies in general, there is a "real life" ramification related to this conceptual system of thought. In all aspects, women are deemed to be inferior in status. And, indeed, the evidence of the ancient world would seem to bear this perception out. Laqueur's model may also help to explain some possible analogues in early Christianity, such as the reoccurring notion that women need to become males in order to receive salvation.[11] In other words, the "one-sex" model explains not only the broader social conditions of women in antiquity, but it also makes sense of specific ideas and practices in the ancient world, such as Thecla's crossing the boundary towards an increasing male performance in the *Acts of Paul and Thecla*, which itself may stand in for a host of other types of crossings in early Christian communities.

Alongside the "one-sex" model, the other prominent model of interest to us is the "teratogenic grid," formulated most clearly by Holt N. Parker and Jonathan Walters in a series of signal essays. If the "one-sex" model relates to conceptions of sex-distinction in antiquity, the "teratogenic grid" connects more closely with gender performance. In Parker's discussion of the grid system ("Teratogenic Grid"), which is based on the Roman division of sex differentiation, he notes that the ideal male is active and the model female is passive. That is, in its basic formulation, the male is the penetrator and the female is the one penetrated, offering a highly phallogocentric system of classification. The active male (*vir*) and the passive female (*femina/puella*) are counterbalanced by their deficient "opposites," the passive male (*cinaedus/pathicus*) and the active female (*virago/tribas/moecha*). In this system, homosexuality and heterosexuality do not enter into the picture. Rather, the Roman *vir* penetrates either passive males or females. The status of the person who is penetrated is the main concern, insofar as to be a passive female was considered "normal," while being a passive male was considered to be a deviation, abnormality, and a social deformity. As the ultimate penetrator, a Roman *vir* could penetrate any orifice of the passive recipient (mouth, vagina, anus), but was not to perform any sexual act that might indicate passivity (such as cunnilingus or fellatio). Thus, *penetration* becomes the normative feature of this grid system—all else is defined in relationship to the centrality of the male/phallus (the metaphorical representation of hegemonic male power). In this system, then, "real" men were to be "impenetrable penetrators" (Walters, "Invading the Roman Body," 30).

Both of these models (Laqueur's "one-sex" paradigm and Walters's/Parker's grid system) illuminate a variety of data, creating a framework for understanding how gender, sex, and sexuality were framed and understood within the ancient context. At the same time, one should also question the historical accuracy of these models. They are useful for forming a heuristic lens, but should they be taken as "factual" representations of the past? With respect to Laqueur's model, for instance, there are elements of a "two-sex" model even in the ancient world, and there is a complexity to each historical epoch that eludes his more general interpretive framework. Even more to the point, since Laqueur's results are largely drawn from observations based on literary sources (which do not intend to provide a "handbook" of knowledge), one might query just how widespread in the ancient world such conceptions in fact were. Moreover, to what degree are we looking at *elite* perspectives and how widely were these shared among the general populace (non-elites) of the specific time periods in question? Of course, since cultural elites generally composed the texts that come down to us, these texts presumably reflect (even if not as clearly as we might like) at least some of the conceptions that were shared by this small group of ancient writers. Further, with respect to the teratogenic grid, one might also question to what extent the ideal type was prevalent across the empire or even across diverse social classes among the Romans. For example, as noted earlier in this chapter, Maud Gleason has shown how an effeminate orator could employ a culturally shameful performance to his advantage, winning the audience's approval, an act that runs contrary to the normative expectations of the grid system. Thus, a complexity emerges in the act of reversing the normative patterns of masculinity, and these must also be taken into account in forming a larger picture of the ancient world.

In the final analysis, these models prove useful most of all for helping us appreciate just how different the ancient world is from our own in terms of thinking about gender, sex, and sexuality. Our categories of "homosexuality," "heterosexuality," and "bisexuality" are not useful for historical investigation and reconstruction as they transfer too many modern assumptions onto the ancient evidence. Thus, we require alternative models (and language) by which we can conceptualize the way that other historical time periods and cultural contexts may think about gender, sex, and sexuality differently than we do. That said, we also need to be cautious with these models, not forcing them in one direction or another or employing them rigidly. Moreover, as we have already noted, one has to bear in mind that these models are constructed from Greek and Roman sources and thus represent an elite culturally dominant discourse in the ancient world (and, for that matter, the models themselves are also articulated by intellectual elites—academics—in our world). Further, other conceptions (e.g., Jewish, Parthian, Egyptian, German, etc.) related to gender, sex, and sexuality may also have circulated in the ancient world. Our current models therefore tend to reflect the imperial center of empire, but do not take into account the fluidity of its margins (and its borders). Thus, while we have models and need to use them, we also must explore their suitability to the sociocultural particularities of the ancient world, contextualizing these models in specific texts and locales, paying careful attention to the intersection of rhetoric and ideology in the process.

From the politics of the body to the body politic

The shifting balance of political and social power in the ancient world was reconstituted (not in small part) in and through language and literature, and the literary remains bear witness to the fluidity of and competition in identity construction in this context. It is this broader system of rationality (through discourse) that we explore in the following discussion, as this structure relates the gendered body to society, embodying in the former the basic character of the latter. There are two specific features that are of interest to us here. First, as is already clear from the preceding section, we are invested in exploring normative conceptions of gender, sex, and sexuality. We do not take these conceptions to be normative in and of themselves, but rather as _perceived_ universal, natural categories of identity in the ancient world. Second, we are also interested in examining the abject "other," which does not fit within the normative framework, but, even more importantly, in many respects exists in order to sustain the normative. That is, abjection and deviation from dominant discourses are posited oppositionally with respect to normative identity markers. Thus, as we make clear in the following discussion, there is a politics of representation in effect, which is critical for the maintenance and inscription of imperial aspirations (Greek or Roman). Moreover, there is a sociocultural reservoir of themes and conceptions that aids in the accomplishment of that political aim. These are not necessarily conscious aspects of individual reflection in the ancient world. Rather, these facets are embedded in the patterns and paradigms that seemingly "naturally" emerge out of language and discourse. In this framework, just as the ideal body manifests _in nuce_ the politics of empire, it also reflects through its public display the aspirations and values of the body politic. In this way, the individual and the collective in the ancient world are inextricably linked. It is this connection that we explore here, elucidating the various intersections and interconnections between the body of the individual and the political body of empire.

Physiognomy as politics of the body

Ancient discourse on physiognomy, which we delineated at the outset of this chapter, is an important site for the basic relation of the body to society. While physiognomy as a practice of reading the body (viewing external features as a reflection of the inner character of an individual or people group) may have formed a specific elite discourse, it is evident that that practice reflects something of a broader cultural ethos (even if varied and perhaps not as formulaic as we sometimes imagine) with respect to how bodies were both read and constructed in antiquity. The body becomes the primary site by which to establish personal and corporate identity, either by mastering, constraining, or restraining one's own body and a larger body politic, or, conversely, by controlling, denigrating, or mutilating the body of another, one's enemy or subordinate. A correlation can also be noted between the control or ordering/ regulating of the individual body and the way in which society as a totality was understood to be regulated and structured. Indeed, from the household to the city-state, and from there to empire and even to the transcendent and/or sacred realm, the body could be perceived as a site of stability (even if illusory) for structuring society as a whole.[12] In denoting physical description and bodily comportment, then, one is looking at how the body is constructed, its relation to social order, and the manner in which control of the body reflects a broader pattern of social ordering. As Joy Connolly notes with reference to Cicero's conception of the intersection of rhetorical practice and the body politic, "the (speaking) body is the site of reflection and discipline, the object of intensive labor that anchors and sustains the community through performance and observation" (*State of Speech*, 155). This notion can be extended to broader relations between the body and society as well.

Thinking here of physiognomy in a larger sense, then, this society-body relationship can be conceptualized in a variety of different ways. For instance, Polemo, the second-century (Greek) physiognomist and rhetorician from Laodicea, states the following:

> Where you have noticed dampness in gently smiling eyes, and you observe that the whole face is open and that eyelids and forehead are smooth and relaxed, the possessor of such eyes tends more toward good than bad. You will find in consequence that his character is attractive and benevolent, and in that person you will find fairness, leniency, piety, and hospitality. You will find further that he is intelligent, prudent, quick to learn, and strongly sexed. (*Physiognomy*, trans. from Gleason, *Making Men*, 56)

Compare this statement with the much earlier and related characterization of the middle-aged man by Aristotle:

> At this age, men are neither over-confident . . . nor too fearful . . . neither trusting nor distrusting all, but judging rather in accordance with the facts . . . Speaking

generally, all the advantages that youth and old age possess separately, those in the prime of life possess combined; and all cases of excess or defect in the other two are replaced by due moderation and fitness. (*Rhetoric* 2.14)

At first glance, these two statements—separated in time by some four hundred years—may seem to be quite different in intent. The former, coming from the period at the height of physiognomic speculation proper, the second century of the Common Era, clearly delineates the character of a person based, in this case, on the appearance of the eyes and the expression of the face. Here the outward facial features function as a gateway to the inner character of the person in question. Moreover, in this particular case, facial features allow the one discerning to be on their guard against the evil-doings of the characterized personality type. In Aristotle's example, by contrast, the outward body plays less of an explicit role. Rather, someone at a particular point in their life is anticipated to display a specific inner disposition in outward behavior. In other ways, though, the two examples provide a complement to each other, as one demonstrates the focus on the outward manifestation of character in bodily features and the other illustrates a similar display in action. In both cases, a correlation exists between outward manifestation and inner virtue or vice. Further, the two foci could also be combined. For example, in his characterization of the Persians, Ammianus Marcellinus (fourth-century C.E. Roman historian) notes that

on the one hand, they are so free and easy, and stroll about with such a loose and unsteady gait, that one might think them effeminate; but in fact they are most gallant warriors . . . They are given to empty words, and talk madly and extravagantly. They are boastful, hard and offensive, threatening in adversity and prosperity alike, crafty, haughty, cruel, claiming the power of life and death over slaves and commons. (23.80)

Here both outward behavior, in particular the gait of walk, is combined with attitudes that also signal the "character" of the Persians (as constructed, of course, from the standpoint of the imperial center).

Whether or not the specific correlations and constructions of inner and outer character are consistent is beside the point. Important, rather, is to note the interest in placement, stability, prediction, and correlation of inner and outer character. Moreover, the lines drawn between outward appearance and inner character demonstrate the important role given to assessing and classifying bodies and their performances. That is, outward appearances are a critical signifier of one's place in the ancient world and, as such, they have a primary meaning in the context of *social relationships*, most often hierarchical ones. Indeed, it is precisely in this mapping of the social sphere onto the body that the hierarchies of power can be constituted and maintained within a system of meaning and representation. Further, the "able" and "normal" body serves as the primary figure of reference, as deformity and disability, in physical form or, for that matter, in outward action and moral character, were considered deviant and disruptive of the social hierarchies.[13] Thus, it was not just any body that counted, but primarily the body as ideally constructed by dominant discourse.[14] Granted, as noted at the outset of this chapter, even ugliness could be considered a valued trait in certain contexts (such as the philosopher whose true value lies in his inner moral beauty). Still, we should not lose sight of the fact that these reconfigurations—or even disfigurations—of the normative body were ultimately permutations that allowed the hegemonic body (of the penetrating, elite male citizen) to inscribe itself in diverse forms, thereby often masking its basis of authority and power.

In this light, one might well conceptualize the ancient world as a whole in physiognomic terms—that is, outward appearances mattered quite a bit. It is easy to understand how, then, that "being, for the ancient Roman, was being seen" (Barton, "Being in the Eyes," 221). Body markers not only denote existence, they in some respects call someone into existence in the ancient world. In other words, this focus on the external markers and manifestation of identity assume a context of spectatorship, a surveillance of the subject in question—it is a spectacle of the gaze (wherein the fixation on "looking" evokes a pleasure [potentially perverse] in the viewer). Thus, visibility takes on a major role in the regulation of ancient identity, and is one of the fundamental building blocks of the larger societal structure.[15] In this framework, regulation, being so closely wedded to the policing of society, evokes Foucault's use of the concept of the Panopticon (originally a design by Jeremy Bentham for the construction of a fully surveillant prison) in his *Discipline and Punish* (1995), where the possibility of always being seen in the prison by an "unseen guard" "induce[s] in the inmate a state of conscious and permanent visibility that assures the automatic functioning of power" (201). In this framework, even though the inmates might not always actually be seen, they would comport themselves as if they were always seen. While Foucault had in mind the emergence of modern institutions, these insights are helpful for imagining the ancient world as well, not in small part because of the way in which being seen and being visible—and being constructed within that frame of outward appearance—is fronted in the sources. True, unlike the system that Foucault had in mind, where the "perfection of power" in this high mode of visibility made the "actual" (overt) use of power unnecessary, in the ancient world there were very public displays of power, from huge spectacles of pageantry in the arena to crucifixions, where the body, either corporately or individually, was displayed for the public, thereby creating a context for control and the molding of non-elites, subordinates, enemies, the penetrable, and so on.[16] Nonetheless, in all of these modes, the body was regulated within a tightly controlled system of meaning and representation—disciplined, if you will—and it was precisely in this manner that social relations were established, reified, but also contested. It is in this broader context, then, that gender formation must be assessed and analyzed, especially with respect to the imperial and colonizing accent of both Greek and Roman social ordering, which had a distinctive masculine framework, focused on the authority of the "father," even as the precise patriarchal configurations were played out in a variety of ways across time and space in the ancient world.

Gendering bodies

Within this system of meaning, then, physiognomy should be viewed as more than just a framework for categorizing visual appearance, since it was not only used to determine a person's identity, but also served as a manual for the molding of male and female bodies and their behavior in the desired direction. Gender was not so much considered to be a given, but rather something that had to be acquired and proven, a process that began even before birth and that never ended (although it took on different shape and meaning as one aged). For instance, the way in which one moved their eyes, head, hands, and hips were all deciphered as signs of masculinity or femininity. The body-language of a person could give away their "true" nature and, as such, needed to be shaped and regulated in the process of maturation. Important to note here is that anatomical sex was not considered decisive for gender determination. As we pointed out in the previous section, both men and women could display masculine and feminine characteristics, and the balance between the two determined where one ended up on the male to female scale. In this way, discipline and self-control were of utmost importance, as one's identity was scrutinized and could always be questioned on the basis of one's appearance and behavior.

Of course, this framework was mostly the concern of those who had something to lose to begin with, and herein emerges a complex intersection of conceptions of gender, sex, and sexuality with other markers of identity, such as class, status, and race/ethnicity. The result is a hierarchy that reflects the norms and values of those in power. For instance, the idealized images of masculinity and femininity one finds in the literature of the time reflect and support the values of the upper class. Moreover, elite households had both the means and expertise at hand to shape the bodies of their members in the desired direction. Starting at birth, nurses molded and corrected the infant's body through swaddling. Instructions for that purpose appear in the work of physicians such as Soranus (late first century/early second century CE) and Galen. Education and physical exercise took the task further. In fact, given the framework outlined earlier, it is evident that ancient writers perceived a correlation between the mind and the body, and that the training of the physical body had to be correlated with rigorous conditioning of one's mental abilities.

For example, looking at the *progymnasmata*, the elementary rhetorical training manuals for ancient primary education for Greeks and Romans, one can immediately observe the importance placed on order and arrangement in composition. Theon's manual (ca. first century CE, written in Greek), one of the most extensive examples surviving from the ancient world, emphasizes throughout the critical role of imitation in the formation of one's pedagogy: "we imitate most beautifully when our mind has been stamped by beautiful examples."[17] Here we see the emphasis placed on imitation transmitted through pedagogy. In other words, the body and mind so molded are constantly reinscribing the normative (and ideal/ized) body and mind of the past. The normative body is thus constructed "naturally" and "universally" through this process, which continued through to adulthood, as advanced rhetorical training furthered the educational process, at least for elite male citizens. Using Quintilian's rhetorical handbook *Institutes of Oratory*, dated towards the end of the first century CE, Erik Gunderson (*Staging Masculinity*) has shown how the orator's body was to exhibit the *vir bonus* (literally "good man"), which denoted ideal masculine control in performance. Mastery over the body is thus instrumental in proving the virtue of its master and evidencing his authority and confidence. This endeavor requires both self-awareness and discipline from the student, as the body has to be harnessed and trained. Moreover, nothing can be taken for granted or escape reflection. The orator's attitude, expressions, and movement all contribute to the effect of his speech, and the most important tool in this public performance—his voice—should be strong and express manliness. Such a voice is associated with a solid body, obtained through regular exercise as well as sexual abstinence (or at least sexual control). The orator's voice is to reflect both his status as a member of the ruling class and his masculinity, while softness, associated with eunuchs and women, should be avoided. This focus is all the more important since oratorical techniques could easily be associated with deceptive forms of speech ascribed to both women and slaves. Given oratory's inherently performative character, it could also be closely associated with acting, an identification that equally had to be avoided, not in the least because actors were often slaves. It was crucial therefore to avoid such associations and to display behavior that expressed one's "natural" superiority over these other groups, which served as negative foils for elite male identity-formation. The practice of oratory thus demonstrates that self-mastery and mastery over others are two sides of the same coin. In order to control the other, one has to demonstrate control of those elements associated with the other in oneself. Norms and values therefore play a central role in oratorical practice and reflect the ideology of those in power, which, in turn, justifies the dominant social and moral order, thereby supporting its ideology.

A good illustration of this larger framework is provided in the oratorical discussions related to women and slaves, who, as members of the same household, were the proximate others of elite males in antiquity. At the same time, precisely given their proximity to these elite males, they also provided cause for anxiety. In the rhetorical practice of declamation, an exercise that was intended as a demonstration of one's eloquence, one sees this theme reoccurring throughout, especially in the popular form of the *controversia*, which was a speech in which a fictive case was argued. Several collections of such speeches dating from the first century CE have been preserved. In these speeches, both women and slaves often appear in stereotypically denigrating ways (Connolly, "Mastering Corruption"). Most of all, these representations seem to reflect the anxieties and fears of those in power, who are ultimately dependent on the labor of both groups for their existence, the manual labor of slaves on the one hand and the labor of reproduction by women on the other. These *controversia* thus reflect an intercalation between the structuring of individual bodily control and the configuration of broader social relations and practices in everyday life. The body as constructed and maintained does not exist in isolation, but always in relation, with an abject other further substantiating the power of the norm(ative). Thus, women and slaves represent socially what disfigurement does physically for ruling male elites.

As Holt N. Parker ("Loyal Slaves and Loyal Wives") argues, this picture is further complicated in that, from the Roman perspective, both groups—slaves and females—have in common that they consist of outsiders that are incorporated in(to) the *familia*. The wife is an outsider because she comes from a different family, the slaves even more so because they are often also foreigners. The liminal position of women and slaves inside the household as intimate outsiders therefore makes constant surveillance necessary, which is legitimated by the stereotypical portrayal of both women and slaves as gluttonous, and given to excessive alcohol consumption and sexual desire. Another characteristic that both groups share is their inferior status, even if for different reasons. Sandra R. Joshel and Sheila Murnaghan ("Introduction") use the expression "differential equations" to express how both categories—slave and female—are constantly compared without necessarily being identified. Women, on the one hand, are different but subordinate to men because of their gender, but a wife is free and thus superior to any slave. Moreover, she has this freedom in common with her husband. Although slaves lack this honorable status, male slaves on the other hand have their (ideal masculine) gender in common with their masters. The intersections of these categories become most ostensibly clear in the figure of the female slave, who is subordinate both because of her gender and status. Even here, however, there is a crossing over of sorts. The female slave can add to the master's property through the bearing of children, but she can also serve as nurse to his free children. That she has her gender in common with the free woman offers a potential for alliance but also for antagonism (as the female slave becomes a potential rival to the free woman). As such, the female slave embodies a disturbing mix of categories that in principle should be kept separate. Similarly, the problem with male slaves is that they have the same gender and sex as their master, which forms a potential threat. They are therefore often presented as effeminate and thereby denied a normative masculine identity. For instance, male slaves are often associated with the vices of women, which is part of a larger strategy to create distance between them and their masters.[18]

Furthermore, the difference between the master and those subordinate to him finds further sexual expression in the distinction, already mentioned earlier, between penetrator and penetrated, which reflects the social hierarchy in both the household and society at large. To be a penetrator is the prerogative of adult free males, while the status of the penetrated is shared by women, boys, and slaves, both male and female. This distinction is expressed, among other ways, in that according to the Latin language slaves are often called "boy" (*puer*), thus reducing them to a childlike status. As a result, there is a complex relationship in the hierarchy of bodies, with numerous differentiations existing between various social classes of people, while, at the same time, a clear line of authority, control, and domination is also present in the same structure.

The body politic

In the discussion of the last section, an important distinction was made between those who rule and those who are ruled. The idea that there are basically two groups of people, rulers and ruled, is much older than the Roman period. Plato already considered this distinction to be a basic characteristic of life, present on both the micro-level of the household and the macro-level of the city, a perception that reflects prevailing social and cultural values in antiquity. Women, children, and slaves belong to the category of the ruled in the context of the household, even if for different reasons. In fact, there are specific treatises that deal precisely with how to execute superior household management (literally: *oikonomia*). Together these texts offer access to a variety of *topoi* (commonplaces that assume a tradition of use and meaning) related to the running of the household. One such text is Xenophon's *On Household Management* — *Oeconomicus* (362–361 BCE), which is written in the form of a dialogue between Ischomachus and Socrates, and treats, among other things, the respective tasks assigned to the husband and wife. Xenophon presents their duties as complementary, grounded in their different "nature," and concludes:

> For the woman it is more honourable to remain indoors than to attend to business outside; for the man it is more disgraceful to remain indoors than to attend to business outside. If someone behaves in a way contrary to the nature that god has given him . . . he will pay a penalty for neglecting his proper business or for performing his wife's work. (7.30–31)[19]

The husband is further presented as the one who instructs his wife about her duties. She is compared to a queen bee who is in charge of the hive, managing the other bees under her command (7.32–38). Xenophon's discussion maps out well the different hierarchies in place in the household, between husband and wife, between parents and children, and between masters and servants.

While Xenophon's treatment of these household matters is helpful for fleshing out the larger social and economic context for elite males, Aristotle's discussion of these issues in his *Politics* (335 BCE) appears to have been even more influential over time. Aristotle is especially interesting here, since he warns that mismanagement of the household has far-reaching consequences on a larger scale, specifically the *polis* (the city-state):

> since every household is part of the state, and these relationships are part of the household, and the excellence of the part must have regard for that of the whole, it is necessary that the education both of the children and of the women should be carried on with regard to the form of the constitution, if it makes any difference as regards the goodness of the state for the children and the women to be good. And it must necessarily make a difference; for the women are half of the free population, and the children grow up to be the partners in the government of the state. (*Politics* 1 260b 12-21)

Aristotle's ideas were still alive in the first century CE, and are thus useful for elucidating the discourse more fully. For example, the Roman stoic Arius Didymus (ca. first century BCE–first century CE), who taught philosophy to the emperor Augustus, repeated positions from Aristotle's *Politics* when he argued that "The man has the rule of this household by nature. For the deliberative faculty in a woman is inferior, in children it does not yet exist, and it is completely foreign to slaves. Rational household management, which is the controlling of a house[hold] and of those things related to the house[hold], is fitting for a man."[20]

Although these texts span a considerable distance in both time and culture, a broad correlation can be identified here between the order of the household and the structure of the city-state, which are both aligned with the order of nature. Augustus would soon transfigure this metaphorical relation to that of empire, establishing the individual household as the basis for imperial rule (making him the ultimate *pater familias*). In all of these correlations, the relationship between the normative male body and his social others—particularly women and slaves, but also the males above and below him in status—becomes a crucial element in the ordering and control of the household. Thus, bodily comportment and appropriate gendered performance were more than just a private matter. They also sustained and nourished the colonial aspirations of both the Greeks and then the Romans, creating a social world of meaning wherein the individual's body became the site whereupon domination and control could be constructed and deployed. For instance, one of the features of a colonial context is a degree of instability in terms of social and political structures. On the one hand, there is an attempt to impose the hard and firm agenda of the dominant center on the margins, and there is much evidence of such an effort by the Romans in terms of their ruling of the provinces. On the other hand, this colonial structure is mapped over already existing frameworks of power, which both conform to and also strain against the colonial order. This milieu provides for a variety of gendered dynamics, interactions, and possibilities as a result.

Turning again to the paradigm of physiognomy, we note that someone's body not only revealed their character, but also potentially that of a whole people as well (as noted in the earlier quote by Ammianus Marcellinus related to the Persians). This idea presumed a form of environmental determinism, in that the place where one was born was believed to determine one's physical characteristics—and these characteristics were also presumed to be hereditary (largely class based). In his well-documented study of proto-racism in classical antiquity, Benjamin Isaac (*Invention of Racism*) demonstrates how these ideas were entrenched among both Greek and Roman authors, often involving the creation of a direct link between markers of physical appearance and the prescribed character qualities of a specific people. The characteristics thus attributed to a group are in turn believed to be present in all of its members. Bolstering this physical mapping of the imperial world were the sociocultural relations established therein, as both Greeks and Romans believed that they themselves inhabited the ideal center. Greek and Roman authors differed, however, in their assessment and positioning of the people around them. While the Greeks compared themselves mostly with the people situated to the East and West of them (in Asia and Europe), the Romans rather did so with those to the North and South. The axis of this map reflected where their most important enemies were situated, the Persians to the East for the Greeks, and the German and Gallic peoples to the North for the Romans. In this way, much as females and slaves were used to establish and maintain elite male identity, the "other" groups were utilized similarly to shape ethnic identity for the Greeks and Romans. This comparison with other groups of people thus often served to justify supremacy over the "marginalized," creating, again, a "natural" sense of authority and power, emanating from an imagined center. A good example of this perception is offered by Vitruvius (first century BCE), who writes:

> the truly perfect territory, situated under the middle of the heaven, and having on each side the entire extent of the world and its countries, is that which is occupied by the Roman people. In fact, the races of Italy are the most perfectly constituted in both respects—in bodily form and in mental activity to correspond to their valour . . . Hence it was the divine intelligence that set the city of the Roman people in a peerless and temperate country, in order that it might acquire the right

to command the whole world. (*On Architecture*, 6.1.10–11; trans. from Isaac, *Invention of Racism*, 84)

The idea of supremacy posited the belief that others were inferior, and led to the conviction that non-Greek or non-Roman peoples were natural slaves, which, in turn, justified conquering their territories and taking them into captivity. This theory of natural slavery was developed by Aristotle in his *Politics*, and is grounded both in his distinction between Greeks and non-Greeks on the one hand, and in the natural division between superior and inferior beings on the other. Just as the male is considered superior to the female and she is therefore subject to his rule, so, similarly, those who are free citizens rule over those who are slaves. As Aristotle argues, this natural difference is also expressed in "a physical difference between the body of the free-man and that of the slave, giving the latter strength for the menial duties of life, but making the former upright in carriage and (though useless for physical labour) useful for the various purposes of civic life" (*Politics*, 1 254b 25). But this difference is not restricted to the physical realm, it is reflected in their mental faculties as well, in that slaves were understood, for instance, not to possess the capacity for deliberation. This difference applies both to individuals as well as to groups of people.

Further, for Aristotle, this differentiation has a clear ethnic basis, in that the superior Greeks are to be identified with the rulers and inferior, non-Greek peoples with the ruled. The conquering and subsequent enslavement of non-Greeks therefore appears natural and justified. The Roman practice of differentiation varied to some degree. As Isaac notes, in contrast to the Greeks, Roman imperial strategies did not employ the ethnic distinction of "us" and "them." They did, however, believe that some peoples were more "slavish" than others and that these groups could become even more slave-like through their own cultural and social degeneration and corruption. Thus, Tacitus, in writing about the Gauls, states that they were "once renowned in war; but, after a while, sloth following on ease crept over them and they lost their courage along with their freedom" (*Agricola* 11.5; trans. from Isaac, *Invention of Racism*, 190). This image is also clearly gendered in that courage was considered to be a male quality present in rulers, the opposite of cowardice, which was associated with women. One strategy for denigrating other groups of people therefore was to effeminize them, by ascribing negative qualities associated with women to the men of the outsider group. In this way, gender played a critical role in both reflecting and substantiating the hierarchical division between those who dominated and those who were subject to domination.

Having established this larger framework, it is also important to note that power does not simply flow in one direction. Rather, colonial and imperial contexts create a milieu ripe for multiple social and cultural intersections and mappings. Indeed, we often understand the center best by reading it from the margins. While it is true that we have relatively less literature from the margins when compared to the center, there are still significant literary remains (e.g., from the Greeks, Jews, Egyptians) that attest, at the very least, to vibrant interaction with the Roman imperial center of empire (especially in the period 30 BCE–200 CE). Continuing the physiognomic emphasis delineated throughout this chapter, we might well articulate the disruption of the normative imperial body in terms of a *confrontation of body politics*, insofar as one way of looking at larger imperial interactions is precisely through the lens of diverse reconfigurations and redeployments of the individual body and the larger body politic within specific historical and sociocultural contexts. In other words, there was no stable, unitary body—individual or corporate—in the ancient world, for there were always shifts and movements in the interplay between individuals, cultures, and political entities. Yet it is precisely in the moment of contact and/or conflict that the body's meaning and significance comes into fuller light. Of course, in those same moments the body's meaning could also change. The divergence between the Greek East and the Roman West in the first and second centuries of the common era provides us with a unique window into this "clash" in the ancient world, and it is thus worth elaborating on this relationship more broadly, not in the least because it is precisely at this juncture and in this milieu that early Christian discourses emerged and took shape.

Bodies in empire

The Roman conquest of the Greek East was undertaken during the Republican era (ca. 200–30 CE), but the ongoing effects of colonial (re)settlement and imperial occupation were particularly acute in the period of the empire (especially 30 BCE–200 CE). The Roman conquest superimposed power and authority in the various Greek regions of the eastern Mediterranean area (e.g., Greece, Anatolia, Syria), while the preexisting cultures (e.g., Greek, Jewish, Egyptian, Celtic) continued to hold significant influence as well. The Romans thus provided an imperial overlay to an already existing Greek colonizing endeavor, and the milieus that were generated resulted from the bifurcated, hybrid, and complex interactions of various colonial powers, which did not necessarily all share the same operations and structures of rule and control.

The Roman Empire was an imperial force, focusing on creating stability and wealth for the "center" in Italy and Rome. The Romans established imperial rule in the provinces, and added a structural overlay (such as jurisdiction, administration, temples for the worship of the imperial family) to the existing social and cultural contexts of people in the provincial cities. The Greeks, however, had earlier created systemic cultural conduits in their colonized cities, including not only an overarching elite power structure, but also a full trickle down effect in terms of societal, political, and cultural ideologies and concomitant identities. In this way, the confrontation between the former and current colonizing powers may be perceived as creating a situation in which a wide variety of often ambivalent and even contradictory responses to power were possible. But the picture is much more complex than that. For instance, this conflict, as depicted in the literature of the first and second centuries CE, consists of minority Greek cultural elites seeking to reclaim past glory as a means of coming to terms with their identity under (recent) Roman rule. Multiple levels of colonial activity can be distinguished here—the Romans provided an overarching imperial authority, but the Greeks themselves had a longer history of colonialism in the East. Moreover, one has to consider the position of those outside the centers of power. The Celts of Galatia, for example, were not Greek, and yet they found themselves in situations of subordination to both ruling Greek elites and now also Roman imperial overlords. Moreover, within the existing social hierarchy, there were also the "others"— slaves, women, barbarians—who themselves were situated within the colonial order of things, but who were also seeking means to/of power. The result is a complex and often convoluted interaction between both elite cultural and political bodies, as well as between elites and their subordinates.

In terms of the interaction between Greeks and Romans, one of the fundamental sites for such engagements was in literary production, particularly in terms of the Greeks writing their own identity into and onto empire. The title of a recent book on postcolonial literature, *The Empire Writes Back* (2002), aptly captures how ancient Greeks sought to reconfigure their identity within a context of imperial Roman control and domination. Obviously, this move is complex, as the diverse regions of the eastern part of the Roman Empire were not identical in terms of how power was negotiated and distributed—Jerusalem, for instance, had different power and ruling structures in place than say Athens or Antioch (alongside other economic, social, and cultural divergences). Moreover, we should not forget that we are only referring here to a relatively small group of people, since the majority was not in a position to access education or even resources for writing.[21] In this larger configuration of power, then, gender, as it intersects with class and race, is an especially important facet of colonial engagement, being used both in the reinforcement of colonial agendas as well as in resistance of the colonized to the same.[22]

From the available literature, one can observe the cultural "gender clash" between Greeks and Romans in their respective characterization of each other. From the Roman "center," particularly in Roman Italy, adoption of Greek customs was frequently caricatured as effeminate, and was often used in association with general laments about the decline of Roman culture, society, and rhetoric.[23] Thus, from the "center," Greek language and dress came to represent a denigration of the hard masculine lines of Roman male identity (especially by the middle to later part of the first century CE). Yet, looking at it from the Greek perspective, there was rather a celebration and cultivation of the Greek heritage, with a relative sidelining of Roman imperial power. Indeed, this relative avoidance is an interesting facet of the Greek literary response to empire: whether one looks at the more philosophical literature such as one finds in Lucian of Samosata (ca. 125–180 BCE) or Dio Chrysostom (ca. 40–120 CE), or the novelistic tradition such as Heliodorus's *The Ephesian Tale* (mid-second century CE) or Achilles Tatius's *Leucippe and Clitophon* (ca. mid-second century CE), the Roman empire appears only at the periphery—on the outer edges of the world constructed in the text. This marginality should not be taken as a sign that Roman imperial force was not felt. Indeed, there were legions, proconsuls, temples, statues, and other visible reminders of the panoptic power of the emperor to be found throughout the Roman Empire. Rather, this marginality suggests something of the way in which the confrontation was negotiated: the Greek elites of the East constructed a landscape in which their days of glory continued uninterrupted.[24] The "imaginary" in this respect functioned as a means of resistance, even while many of the Greek elites themselves had to comply with imperial authority figures in their daily lives.

Further, Greeks such as Dio Chrysostom modeled themselves on philosophical and cultural heroes/exemplars from the past such as Socrates, a model of manly comportment that was evidently different in their view from Roman exemplars. This strategy served a variety of purposes, not least the need to construct alternative forms of identity in resistance to dominant forms of power and also, often in the same moment, reliance on that same power as the staged identity also mimics aspects of control, dominance, and authority present in the very structure that is resisted. Moreover, the colonizers themselves were also caught in this intricate web of identity formation. That is to say, not only are dominant norms reinforced in the process of colonization, but there is also an *anxiety* that takes hold in the process: every act of domination posits its opposite—humiliation and defeat. Thus, the normative identities of the colonizer are not just reinforced, but, in some respects, they are also destabilized as disruptive spaces for alternative (alongside mimicking) identities are opened up even from within hegemonic discourses.

Although there are many ways through which to explore the implications of Roman imperialism for the formation of gender in the ancient world, we focus on a couple of key features that are important for our assessment of early Christianity within this Eastern context of the Roman Empire. Following on the physiognomic theme that has run throughout this chapter, we note in particular the diverse ways in which the body is manipulated. One place to begin is with the ancient literature itself, which reflects something of the operative gender dynamics we have been describing. With respect to the genre of Roman epic literature, for instance, Llewelyn Morgan ("Child's Play") observes how a patriarchal emphasis on authority is fronted throughout the material. That is, epic literature had a strong pedagogical function in terms of communicating the social and cultural values of the Roman social hierarchy. Thus, both the act of writing and reading this literature was intimately connected to the reproduction and transmission of the culture embedded in these texts. One might also think of the public display of rhetorical skills in Rome, which favored a masculine comportment, that of the *vir bonus* (as we noted earlier). What do we make, then, of the Greek novels in such a context? That is, to what degree can we think of the literature of the Greek East as a counter-production of culture and also, therefore, offering a different kind of authority? At one level, this literature reproduces some of the dominant themes of male authority that we see operative in Roman epic literature. At the same time, there are divergences as well, particularly in the more malleable nature of masculinity as embodied in the hero. Scholars such as Eric Thurman ("Novel Men") have pointed out, for example, that one can perceive a colonial ambivalence and hybridity in the construction of the dominant male subject in certain novels: there is both a firm line of masculine identity, but that line is also subverted in places, with the main character manifesting more effeminate facets of behavior in the process (which creates a hybrid characterization that avoids strict binary classification). Is this a subversion of dominant Roman identities or simply an effect of Roman colonial dominance on the Eastern male subject?

These are important questions for any examination of the gendered and sexed nature of identity in this ancient imperial context. Experience is multifac-

eted and varied, and what we see in this counter-literature is a complex identity that may well reflect actual experiences of Greek elite males in empire.
Further, the subject of these novels also suggests something of a rather differently inhabited world than that of Roman epic—the themes are more mun-
dane and pastoral, rather than grand and sweeping. The characters are not
warriors and gods or political heroes, but men and women of relative unimportance. As a result, modern scholars have tended to devalue the novels as
largely insignificant in comparison with Roman epic, in the process thereby
mimicking the authoritative standing of the latter. For that matter, even with
respect to oratory, Roman rhetoric in Cicero and Quintilian receives greater
emphasis than say the corpus of Dio Chrysostom, and even someone like
Plutarch has often been viewed as a "collector" of ideas rather than as a genuinely innovative thinker. Thus, the gendered lines established by Roman discourse are followed, even if unconsciously, by modern scholars in their
evaluation of these ancient works. Viewed in this light, then, we note the
physiognomic character of literature itself in the ancient world—bodies of
literature carry particular markings that either make them more like the
"normative" (hard/masculine) center or less.

This aspect of "center" and "periphery" also points to important differences in
specific aspects of gender performance. The fluctuating lines of power in a colonial context opened up opportunities that otherwise might have been more difficult to achieve. For instance, it is noteworthy that many of the inscriptions that
scholars such as Bernadette Brooten (*Women Leaders*) have pointed to as attest-
ing to female patronage of Jewish synagogues come from the eastern part of the
empire. While there are a variety of explanations for this phenomenon, one can
query to what extent the shifting lines of power in the East made it possible for
elite females to (re)define their own gendered identities. Also, more opportunities for patronizing new religious movements may have sprung up precisely in a
context where male identities were being contested by other "upstarts" vying for
power. Free and wealthy women thus may have found doors opened that were
previously closed. While such opportunities may also have been available in
Rome, it does seem that the colonial situation (and its concomitant instability) in
the Greek East created a social and cultural context that was especially fertile for
ruptures in traditional modes of individual practice and corporate life.

In this same vein, one might also examine the role of religion in this
larger context. Although often read from a modern standpoint in which religion has a fairly definable essence, in the ancient world religion was a complex
category infused with strands of politics, culture, and social life. Technically

speaking, "religio" proper referred to officially sanctioned religions, yet, broadly conceived, a vast array of different contexts for religious practices existed, from the worship of ancestors in the household through to the honoring/worshiping of the Roman emperor in the official cult sanctuaries. Between the micro-level of the household and the macro-level of empire there were numerous other deities to be found along the way, the worship of which did not generally exclude worship of others (one could worship ancestral deities in the household, honor the emperor in the public temple alongside the goddess Artemis, and attend a festive meal and ceremony for the god Mithras after that, or, for that matter, worship none). The cultivation of indigenous religious traditions and their dissemination throughout the empire could also function as a means to inhabit the space of empire on the highest level possible—the sphere of the sacred. And here, again, the gendered nature of the formation and reception of religious practice was diverse. There was a tendency from the center to effeminize the "exotic" other of the Greek East. Yet, at the same time, while the priests of Isis or the followers of Cybele may not have been considered *viri boni* from the vantage point of the elite Roman male, the exotic other was also a spectacle to behold, one that could evoke the same kind of response (and victory) that Favorinus's effeminate performance did in trumping Polemo's masculine display in public oratorical competition.

Furthermore, soon after Alexander the Great spread Greek culture throughout the same regions, syncretism (the mixing of different traditions and cultures) became a common facet of cultural interaction. The Roman period attests to an increase in the reconfiguration of local religious and cultural practices. Thus, new religious formations and the cultivation of older religious practices were both a response to and a result of the power fluctuations that followed in the wake of Greek colonial and then Roman imperial conquests. The confrontation between cultures and religious expressions, moreover, largely followed the gendered and sexed lines of society. Thus, while females might be more involved in some groups (depending on the specific configurations of authority), given the significant amount of slander (particularly sexual and gendered denigrations) against both new religious movements and other culturally "deviant" groups there was also an evident attempt to bring these collective entities in line with perceived "normative" and "dominant" expectations for gender, sex, and sexual performances. This assessment of course presumes that the rhetoric reflects reality. But it may not. At the very least, the degree to which someone like Lucian of Samosata attacks Alexander of Abonoteichus (whom he calls the "False Prophet"), using a host of tropes related to his lack of proper masculine comportment (e.g., Alexander cheats, steals, tricks women into bed, uses spectacle rather than sound reasoning to promote his cult), would suggest that religion, along with other facets of social and cultural identity, was both contested and in flux, while also being constantly reconstituted by and reproduced from a dominant center (even if that dominant center happened to be Greek culture and civilization rather than Roman).[25]

At the same time, Lucian could also make fun of Rome and its "extravagances," particularly its character as a city of spectacles (itself a kind of effeminization of the center).[26] Whether locally or on a larger scale of empire, then, a philosopher such as Lucian was identifying himself over against an array of "contenders," even as he had more power over some than others. Thus, as we noted at the outset of this discussion, the body takes on its most essential meaning in its social relationship to other bodies, and much of that meaning depended on the way that one's gendered performance was "made" and "unmade" in local contexts and in contests for identity.[27] We can refer to the normative, dominant male body and, at the same time, point to numerous instances where that body was subverted by the very structures that it reified and supported. We highlight these facets of the ancient world because they are crucial for interpreting the place of the early Christian body within the larger sociocultural world of antiquity. From the individual body of early Christians to the collective bodies of diverse Christian communities, from the body of Christ to the body of early Christian literature, all of these aspects of the early Christian world took shape within this complex landscape, where competing clashes of body politics, on the micro- and macro-levels, created fertile ground for new religious groups to reconfigure both ancient traditions and contemporary social and cultural values to new ends. As a sociocultural and religious phenomenon, Christianity, in all of its diversity, is rooted in this complex ancient world of ideology and identity formation that we have briefly sketched in this chapter.

With respect to gender, sex, and sexuality, moreover, we must bear in mind that early Christians not only used conceptions from their diverse spheres of interaction, but they also redeployed various related tropes (often against imperial agendas) and in the process created distinctive discourses and identities. The genealogy of early Christian discourses on gender, sex, and sexuality is complex and varied (there are many genealogies in some respects), but understanding the early Christian movement in context entails analyzing this phenomenon as a "player" in the ancient world. There is much more that is needed for a fuller contextualization of early Christian discourses, and in the next chapter we explore further what other (especially internal) factors are necessary for thinking about early Christian discourses related to the body. The ancient world is, as we noted at the outset of this chapter, significantly different from our own, and, with respect to conceptions of gender, sex, and sexuality, there are fundamental divergences as well. If we are to understand Christianity as part of its world, then, we will also have to appreciate the categorical differences that separate early Christians from us. The first step is to grasp fully the distance between our world and the ancient one, and to situate early Christian social and cultural phenomena in *that* world, rather than our own. Finally, in line with the physiognomic paradigm we have developed in this chapter, we first and foremost want to examine how discourses related to the Christian body, both individual and corporate, not only fit into the broader milieu outlined in this chapter, but, even more so, how these created their own distinctive disciplining of the corporeal realities of early adherents. To that we turn in the next chapter.

Notes

1   The most famous example is the handbook compiled by Polemo (ca. 90–144 CE). For a translation, see Simon Swain et al., eds, *Seeing the Face, Seeing the Soul: Polemon's Physiognomy from Classical Antiquity to Medieval Islam* (New York: Oxford University Press, 2007). Mikeal Parsons's recent treatment of physiognomy in the Greco-Roman world (*Body and Character in Luke and Acts*) details much of the known evidence. He accentuates the Christian subversion of this ancient category (especially for those with flawed and disabled bodies).

2   These modern *male* interpretations represent well the way in which gender easily inscribes itself into constructions of the ancient world. As we explore further in the fourth chapter (and as already noted in the first), it is not by accident that male scholars have been significantly invested in cultivating and reclaiming an ideally masculine Paul from the ancient world.

3   The argument here relies on the analysis by Paul Zanker, *The Mask of Socrates: The Image of the Intellectual in Antiquity* (trans. A. Shapiro; Berkeley: University of California Press, 1995), 34–39.

4   That Thecla is introduced as an object of desire is a feature that lines up with the portrayal of other female figures in the apocryphal Acts (such as Drusiana in the *Acts of John* or Maximilla in the *Acts of Andrew*). Moreover, sexual desire (and danger) is a trope that further aligns a figure like Thecla with female characters in the Greco-Roman novels. For an analysis of gender patterns in the Greek novel, see Katherine Haynes, *Fashioning the Feminine in the Greek Novel* (London: Routledge, 2003). See also Kate Cooper, *The Virgin and the Bride: Idealized Womanhood in Late Antiquity* (Cambridge, MA: Harvard University Press, 1999), who explores the increasing tension between virginity and marriage as an ideal for women.

5   For a divergent perspective on the development, see Jonathan Ned Katz, *The Invention of Heterosexuality* (new edn; Chicago: University of Chicago Press, 2007), who focuses on the discursive

evolution of "heterosexuality" as it comes to denote those men and women who have sex for plea-sure. In this framework, "heterosexuality" becomes (at least initially) the discursive deviation rather than "homosexuality." Also see the helpful treatment by Holt N. Parker, "The Myth of the Hetero-sexual: Anthropology and Sexuality for Classicists," *Arethusa* 34 (2001): 313–62.

6 In terms of engagement and criticism of Foucault's work on the ancient world, see David H. J. Larmour, Paul Allen Miller, and Charles Platter, eds, *Rethinking Sexuality: Foucault and Classical Antiquity* (Princeton: Princeton University Press, 1998). In this volume, numerous classicists contend with Foucault's generalizations and male-centered constructions.

7 Amy Richlin offers a similar critique of Foucault's approach ("Foucault's *History of Sexuality*: A Useful Theory for Women?" in *Rethinking Sexuality: Foucault and Classical Antiquity* [ed. D. H. J. Larmour, P. A. Miller, and C. Platter; Princeton: Princeton University Press, 1998], 138–70), noting that he systematically avoids critical questions with respect to women's subjectivities related to sex and gender identity in the ancient world (146). She argues that Foucault had no interest in the "female desiring subject" (156), as evidenced, for example, by his lack of attention given to women who are described in medical texts while examining the males in the same (161). Richlin concludes her assessment with the following judgment: "Can a historical model that incorporates the absence of women and others be turned around and applied to the study of the very groups it omits? I don't see how that can be done without drastic alterations to the model" (169). In our approach in this book, and in contrast to these critics, we believe that Fou-cault is much more helpful and interesting for his analytic model than for the accuracy of his spe-cific historical and sociocultural observations and conclusions.

8 In his more recent book, *How to Do the History of Homosexuality* (Chicago: University of Chicago Press, 2004), Halperin develops his argument further, not only historically contextualizing the way in which sexuality is classified, but also arguing that subjectivity itself as related to sexuality and desire is historically and socioculturally contingent. Also see the excellent treatment of similar themes in Arnold I. Davidson, *The Emergence of Sexuality: Historical Epistemology and the Forma-tion of Concepts* (Cambridge, MA: Harvard University Press, 2004). For a contrary reading of the evidence, see Giulia Sissa, *Sex and Sensuality in the Ancient world* (trans. G. Staunton; New Haven: Yale University Press, 2008).

9 Even with respect to feelings, desires, and emotions, the way one experiences these sensations is dramatically shaped by historical and sociocultural contexts as well. There is no essential, universal "feeling" as such. We would argue that such a contextual perspective on "feelings" and "desires" also has to be employed with respect to the analysis of the ancient world. For an assessment of modern feelings related to "love" and "romance" as situated within a consumerist (and exchange) model of human relationships, see Eva Illouz, *Consuming the Romantic Utopia: Love and the Cultural Contradictions of Capitalism* (Berkeley: University of California Press, 1997).

10 The work of Niklas Luhmann is particularly insightful in terms of conceptualizing the relative (and limited) nature of models, especially his major study of social system analysis: *Social Systems* (trans. J. Bednarz and D. Baecker; Stanford: Stanford University Press, 1996). Luhmann emphasizes that all systems of social meaning and interaction are self-referential. Although Luhmann is focusing on modern societal interpretation and cultural meaning, we believe his larger theory can be useful for

analyzing ancient texts. Especially helpful is Luhmann's contention that complexity in viewing interpretive models arises from the acknowledgment that we are "forced to select" from a larger pool of data, which then creates "contingency" (25). In other words, classification and categorization of data could proceed in differing ways, depending on the interpreter and theoretical framework being employed.

11 For a discussion of the options available to women in the patristic period against the background of late Roman society, see Gillian Cloke, *This Female Man of God: Women and Spiritual Power in the Patristic Age, AD 350–450* (London: Routledge, 1995).

12 The classic study in this respect is Peter Brown's *The Body and Society: Men, Women, and Sexual Renunciation in Early Christianity* (second edn; New York: Columbia University Press, 2008 [originally published 1988]).

13 On deformity in the ancient world, see Robert Garland, *The Eye of the Beholder: Deformity and Disability in the Graeco-Roman World* (Ithaca, NY: Cornell University Press, 1995). In terms of the broader picture, one has to keep in mind the diversity of conceptions related to the "normative" body. Depending on age, class, or social standing, expectations of how one would look varied and changed. For instance, the body of a young boy was to look different than that of an older male citizen.

14 Illuminating from a theoretical perspective is Rosemarie Garland Thomson's work on disability, in which she postulates a primary relationship between the abject disabled body and the claims of the normative hegemonic one (*Extraordinary Bodies* [New York: Columbia University Press, 1996]). As she suggests, "the disabled figure operates as a code for insufficiency, contingency, and abjection—for deviant particularity—thus establishing the contours of a canonical body that garners the prerogatives and privileges of a supposedly stable, universalized normalcy" (136).

15 See further Eric Gunderson, "The Flavian Amphitheatre: All the World as Stage," in *Flavian Rome: Culture, Image, Text* (ed. A. J. Boyle and W. J. Dominik; Leiden: Brill, 2003), 637,–58; and idem, "The Ideology of the Arena," *Classical Antiquity* 15 (1996): 113–51.

16 For further discussion of the spectacles of empire in early Christian discourse, see Todd Penner and Caroline Vander Stichele, "Bodies and the Technology of Power: Reading *The Gospel of Peter* under Empire," in *Das Evangelium nach Petrus: Text, Kontexte, Intertexte* (ed. T. J. Kraus and T. Nicklas; Texte und Untersuchungen zur Geschichte der altchristlichen Literatur 158; Berlin: de Gruyter, 2007), 349–68. Also see Chris Frilingos, *Spectacles of Empire: Monsters, Martyrs, and the Book of Revelation* (Divinations; Philadelphia: University of Pennsylvania Press, 2004); and David Reis, "Surveillant Discipline: Panoptic Vision in Early Christian Self-Definition," *The Bible and Critical Theory* 4 (2008): 23.1–23.21. On the brutality of these spectacles, see especially Carlin A. Barton, *The Sorrows of the Ancient Romans: The Gladiator and the Monster* (Princeton: Princeton University Press, 1993).

17 This translation is taken from George A. Kennedy, trans. and ed., *Progymnasmata: Greek Textbooks of Prose Composition and Rhetoric* (Writings from the Greco-Roman World 10; Atlanta: Society of Biblical Literature, 2003).

18 This process of emasculation is most acutely present in the figure of the eunuch, who represents a disturbing conflation of slavery and femininity (which accounts for the popular portrayal of the

eunuch as a highly sexualized individual, a kind of monstrous hybrid of sexual desire). See J. David Hester, "Eunuchs and the Postgender Jesus: Matthew 19.12 and Transgressive Sexualities," *Journal for the Study of the New Testament* 28 (2005): 13–40.

19 This translation is taken from Sarah B. Pomeroy, trans. and ed., *Oeconomicus: A Social and Historical Commentary* (New York: Oxford University Press, 1994).

20 This translation is taken from David L. Balch, "Household Codes," in *Greco-Roman Literature and the New Testament. Selected Forms and Genres* (ed. D. E. Aune; Sources for Biblical Study 21; Atlanta: Scholars Press, 1988, 25–50 [42]).

21 In recent times, scholars have tried to rectify this neglect of non-elites in the study of early Christian history. Joseph A. Marchal, *Politics of Heaven: Women, Gender, and Empire in the Study of Paul* (Paul in Critical Contexts; Minneapolis: Fortress Press, 2008), 15–36, discusses the problems and prospects with trying to engage "people's history." Also see Richard A. Horsley's edited collection, *Christian Origins; Volume 1 of a People's History of Christianity* (Minneapolis: Fortress Press, 2006), where a concerted effort has been made to undertake such a historical project of recovery.

22 The colonial construction of gender, sex, and sexuality at the intersection of race and class has been aptly articulated by Ann Laura Stoler, *Carnal Knowledge and Imperial Power: Race and the Intimate in Colonial Rule* (Berkeley: University of California Press, 2002). Also see İrvin C. Schick, *The Erotic Margin: Sexuality and Spatiality in Alterist Discourse* (New York: Verso, 1999).

23 On this general theme, see the helpful study by Catharine Edwards, *The Politics of Immorality in Ancient Rome* (Cambridge: Cambridge University Press, 1993).

24 See further Todd Penner and Caroline Vander Stichele, "Script(ur)ing Gender in Acts: The Past and Present Power of *Imperium*," in *Mapping Gender in Ancient Religious Discourses* (ed. T. Penner and C. Vander Stichele; Biblical Interpretation Series 84; Leiden: Brill, 2007), 231–66.

25 See further, Erik Gunderson, "Men of Learning: The Cult of *Paideia* in Lucian's *Alexander*," in Penner and Vander Stichele, *Mapping Gender in Ancient Religious Discourses*, 479–510.

26 See the nuanced study by Tim Whitmarsh, *Greek Literature and the Roman Empire: The Politics of Imitation* (New York: Oxford University Press, 2002), 247–94.

27 We make allusion here to Elaine Scarry's classic study, *The Body in Pain: The Making and Unmaking of the World* (New York: Oxford University Press, 1985), as she has forcefully demonstrated the ways in which coercive acts against the body can destroy worlds, while, at the same time, providing a context in which creativity can also reclaim them.

Bibliography

Ammianus Marcellinus. *Roman History*. Translated by J. C. Rolfe. 3 Vols. Loeb Classical Library. Cambridge, MA: Harvard University Press, 1935–39.

Aristotle. *On Rhetoric : A Theory of Civic Discourse*. Translated by G. A. Kennedy. New York: Oxford University Press, 1991.

Aristotle. *Politics*. Translated by H. Rackham. Vol. 21. Loeb Classical Library. Cambridge, MA.: Harvard University Press, 1932.

Artemidorus. *The Interpretation of Dreams (The Oneirocritica of Artemidorus)*. Translated by R. J. White. Park Ridge, NJ: Noyes Press, 1975.

Ashcroft, Bill, Gareth Griffiths, and Helen Tiffin. *The Empire Writes Back: Theory and Practice in Postcolonial Literatures*. Second edn. New York: Routledge, 2002.

Bartky, Sandra Lee. "Foucault, Femininity, and the Modernization of Patriarchal Power." Pp. 61–86 in *Feminism and Foucault: Reflections on Resistance*. Edited by I. Diamond and L. Quinby. Boston: Northeastern University Press, 1988.

Barton, Carlin. "Being in the Eyes: Shame and Sight in Ancient Rome." Pp. 216–35 in *The Roman Gaze: Vision, Power, and the Body*. Edited by D. Fredrick. Arethusa Books. Baltimore: Johns Hopkins University Press, 2002.

Bollók, János. "The Description of Paul in the *Acta Pauli*." Pp. 1–15 in *The Apocryphal* Acts of Paul and Thecla. Edited by J. N. Bremmer. Studies on the Apocryphal Acts of the Apostles 2. Kampen: Kok Pharos, 1996.

Braun, Willi. "Physiotherapy of Femininity in the *Acts of Thecla*." Pp. 209–30 in *Text and Artifact in the Religions of Mediterranean Antiquity*. Edited by S. G. Wilson and M. Desjardins. Studies in Christianity and Judaism 9. Waterloo, ON, Canada: Wilfrid Laurier University Press, 2000.

Bremmer, Jan N. "Magic, Martyrdom and Women's Liberation in the Acts of Paul and Thecla." Pp. 36–59 in *The Apocryphal* Acts of Paul and Thecla. Edited by J. N. Bremmer. Studies on the Apocryphal Acts of the Apostles 2. Kampen: Kok Pharos, 1996.

Brooten, Bernadette. *Women Leaders in the Ancient Synagogue*. Brown Judaic Studies 36. Atlanta: Scholars Press, 1982.

Cantarella, Eva. *Bisexuality in the Ancient World*. New Haven: Yale University Press, 1992 (Italian edn, 1988; second edn, 2002).

Connolly, Joy. "Mastering Corruption: Constructions of Identity in Roman Oratory." Pp. 130–51 in *Women and Slaves in Greco-Roman Culture*. Edited by Joshel and Murnaghan.

—*The State of Speech: Rhetoric and Political Thought in Ancient Rome*. Princeton: Princeton University Press, 2007.

Dover, Kenneth J. *Greek Homosexuality*. New York: Vintage Books, 1978.

Dreger, Alice Domurat. *Hermaphrodites and the Medical Invention of Sex*. Cambridge, MA: Harvard University Press, 2000.

Foucault, Michel. *The History of Sexuality III: The Care of the Self*. New York: Vintage Books, 1988.

—*Discipline and Punish: The Birth of the Prison*. New York: Vintage Books, 1995.

Foxhall, Lin. "Pandora Unbound: A Feminist Critique of Foucault's *History of Sexuality*." Pp. 122–37 in *Rethinking Sexuality: Foucault and Classical Antiquity*. Edited by D. H. J. Larmour, P. A. Miller, and C. Platter. Princeton: Princeton University Press, 1998.

Gleason, Maud. *Making Men: Sophists and Self-Presentation in Ancient Rome*. Princeton: Princeton University Press, 1994.

Grant, Robert, M. "The Description of Paul in the Acts of Paul and Thecla." *Vigiliae Christianae* 36 (1982): 1–4.

Gunderson, Erik. *Staging Masculinity: The Rhetoric of Performance in the Roman World.* Ann Arbor: University of Michigan Press, 2000.

Halperin, David M. *One Hundred Years of Homosexuality and Other Essays on Greek Love.* London: Routledge, 1990.

Isaac, Benjamin. *The Invention of Racism in Classical Antiquity.* Princeton: Princeton University Press, 2004.

Joshel, Sandra R., and Sheila Murnaghan, eds. *Women and Slaves in Greco-Roman Culture.* London: Routledge, 1998.

Joshel, Sandra R., and Sheila Murnaghan. "Introduction: Differential Equations." Pp. 1–21 in *Women and Slaves in Greco-Roman Culture.* Edited by Joshel and Murnaghan.

Laqueur, Thomas. *Making Sex: Body and Gender from the Greeks to Freud.* Cambridge, MA: Harvard University Press, 1990.

Malherbe, Abraham. *Paul and the Popular Philosophers.* Minneapolis: Fortress Press, 1989.

Malina, Bruce J., and Jerome H. Neyrey. *Portraits of Paul: An Archeology of Ancient Personality.* Louisville: Westminster John Knox, 1996.

Morgan, Llewelyn. "Child's Play: Ovid and His Critics." *The Journal of Roman Studies* 93 (2003): 66–91.

Parker, Holt N. "The Teratogenic Grid." Pp. 47–65 in *Roman Sexualities.* Edited by J. P. Hallett and M. B. Skinner. Princeton: Princeton University Press, 1997.

—"Loyal Slaves and Loyal Wives: The Crisis of the Outsider-within and Roman *Exemplum* Literature." Pp. 152–73 in *Women and Slaves in Greco-Roman Culture.* Edited by Joshel and Murnaghan.

Parsons, Mikeal C. *Body and Character in Luke and Acts: The Subversion of Physiognomy in Early Christianity.* Grand Rapids: Baker Academic, 2006.

Reardon, Bryan P., ed. *Collected Ancient Greek Novels.* Berkeley: University of California Press, 1989.

Sissa, Giulia. "The Sexual Philosophies of Plato and Aristotle." Pp. 46–81 in *A History of Women: From Ancient Goddesses to Christian Saints.* Edited by P. Schmitt Pantel. Translated by A. Goldhammer. Cambridge, MA: Harvard University Press, 1992.

Skinner, Marilyn B. *Sexuality in Greek and Roman Culture.* Oxford: Blackwell, 2005.

Thurman, Eric. "Novel Men: Masculinity and Empire in Mark's Gospel and Xenophon's *An Ephesian Tale.*" Pp. 185–229 in *Mapping Gender in Ancient Religious Discourses.* Edited by T. Penner and C. Vander Stichele. Biblical Interpretation Series 84. Leiden: Brill, 2007.

Walters, Jonathan. "Invading the Roman Body: Manliness and Impenetrability in Roman Thought." Pp. 29–43 in *Roman Sexualities.* Edited by J. P. Hallett and M. B. Skinner. Princeton: Princeton University Press, 1997.

Williams, Craig A. *Roman Homosexuality: Ideologies of Masculinity in Classical Antiquity.* New York: Oxford University Press, 1999.

3 Boundaries and Bodies in Early Christian Discourse

And [the governor] ordered that Paul be brought before the judgment seat. Thecla, however, rolled herself on the place where Paul had been teaching while he sat in jail. But the governor ordered that she too would be brought before the judgment seat, and she went, exulting with joy. And when Paul was again brought forward, the crowd yelled even louder: "He is a magician! Away with him!" But the governor listened with pleasure to Paul about his holy works and, after taking counsel, he called Thecla and said: "Why don't you marry Thamyris according to the law of the Iconians?" She however stood there gazing at Paul. And when she didn't answer, Theocleia her mother shouted: "Burn the lawless one! Burn the unmarried one in the middle of the theater, so that all women who have been taught by him will have fear!"

—Acts of Paul and Thecla 3.20

The lines quoted above, taken from Thecla's first trial, are of particular interest to us in light of the issues we broach in this chapter. In the context preceding this scene in the *Acts of Paul and Thecla*, Paul himself stands on trial before the governor Castellius, on the charge that he "does not allow virgins to marry" (16). Next, Paul is sent to prison, where he is visited in secret by Thecla, who decides to stay with him. When her family and fiancé find out, they report the situation to the governor and, as a result, both Paul and Thecla are brought before the tribunal to be judged. While Paul is scourged and thrown out of the city, Thecla is condemned to be burned.

What makes this scene important for our purposes here is the change of location, from the more secluded sphere of the house and prison to the public realm of the tribunal and theater, for, as we will argue later in this chapter, there is a decidedly gendered and sexed nature to space and place in antiquity (in some sense, gender performance itself is on trial in this narrative). Spaces become places to think from, and they are evocative of specific discourses as a result—that is, space and language are interconnected, and discourse alters when spatial spheres shift. Overall, spatial dimensions perform a critical role in situating both Paul and Thecla within the larger framework of the *Acts of Paul and Thecla*. Although we meet him on the road to Iconium at the beginning of the story, Paul's initial location is in the house of Onesiphorus, where others come to see and hear him. After his trial before the local magistrate and his stay in prison, Paul is thrown out of the city and is next found inside an "open tomb." Time and again, we discover Paul thus contained within an enclosed type of space—from house, to prison, to tomb. It is striking that Thecla's spatial placement is significantly different. She moves from her house to the prison where she visits Paul and from the "judgment seat" to the theater, where she undergoes her first public trial. After meeting Paul in the tomb, they both enter Antioch, where Paul denies that he knows Thecla and rapidly vanishes from the scene when the suitor Alexander seeks to possess her. Meanwhile, Thecla repeats her Iconium experience in a similar trial scene at Antioch, but this time with even more intensity. In search of Paul, she next moves on to Myra, where she finds him, but then she returns to Iconium, the place where her journey all started, and she continues from there to Seleucia to teach the word of God.

With these changes in location, a crossing of boundaries also takes place, marked by shifting roles, spaces, loyalties, and identities. Thus, the bride-to-be readily becomes the follower of a preacher (or "magician" in the view of the outside community), and the devoted virgin and chaste ascetic seeks her beloved (Paul). This picture is further enhanced by Thecla's portrayal as a virgin, a woman in a liminal state (i.e., she is not yet incorporated into the marriage bond). Here also lies the danger perceived in Paul's preaching: he "does not allow virgins to marry" (16). As such, he threatens the status quo—a charge that, as the narrative unfolds, actually turns out to be true! Indeed, Thecla offers a case in point, as her own mother states: "Burn the unmarried one in the middle of the theater, so that all women who have been taught by him will have fear!" (20).

Boundaries thus play a formative role in the unfolding narrative. As we will argue in the following pages, it is often through an examination of these boundaries, as well as their crossings, that one can obtain a better sense of the broader normative structures of a given society and text, because such structures play a critical role in the formation and maintenance of the identity of a particular group.[1] In the ensuing discussion, we suggest that early Christian literature as a whole participates in the creation of both discrete and interrelated identities in the ancient world. Most often such identity formation takes shape over against other existing and competing identities. Thus, both mapping the boundaries established in the process and delineating the crossings of these boundaries can prove to be immensely helpful in detecting broader social and cultural borders that early Christians were both erecting but also transgressing. It is precisely here that a gender-critical analysis, in combination with postcolonial reading strategies, with their respective overarching attention to and challenge of structures of normativity, can help elucidate dynamics in the landscape of early Christian literature that might escape a more conventional mode of analysis. One critical task at hand in such inquiry is the deconstruction of the oppositional elements in discourses, illuminating the contextual, communal, and individual hybridity that underlies the construction of bodies in early Christian texts. Boundaries create difference and distinction. Hence, boundary-crossing, broadly conceived, is a particularly useful place to undertake more complex readings of ancient texts and discourses. When early Christians cross boundaries, we find a potential opening for learning about their rhetorical practices and the way in which their discourses were taking shape vis-à-vis competing conceptions of cultural and social formation.

Further, if we take seriously the structural dynamic of Thecla's multiple crossings, we also need to acknowledge that this dynamic is made possible by the fact that there are boundaries to transgress in the first place. If boundaries invite transgression, transgression in turn calls for boundaries. In this way, various boundaries point to broader facets of social and political power in the ancient world and in early Christianity specifically. Boundaries thus serve as symbolic codes that represent patterns of authority and control. Everything from location and space of characters to the representation of the body moves one beyond mere reference to the narrative plot towards larger power dynamics in both early Christian communities and in the larger sociopolitical context in which the narrative and its correlative symbolic (and real) world are situated. In other words, texts map out the sociocultural assumptions and values of both the community and the world of which the community is a part. In this respect, a gender-critical analysis seeks to expose the ways in which discourses in general and texts in particular embody (as well as reinscribe and contest) authority structures, which themselves persistently seek to discipline and regulate the body, both individual and collective. These avenues of inquiry, in the end, lead us to a better appreciation of the role of the body in early Christianity, elucidating more fully the complexity of the gender, sex, and sexual categories and conceptions that emerge therein.

One must think here about the body in a larger sense too, pushing beyond our literal notions of what constitutes a body to the larger corporeal structures that define and regulate societies and cultures. In ancient Greece, for instance, the city (or *polis*) was understood as the "body-politic" that governed and regulated the individual bodies of which the former was composed. The "body-politic" is a collective/communal body, and it takes on an identity formation not that dissimilar from individual subjectivity. One can push this conception even further. So far we have been discussing bodies mostly in terms of individuals or communities, but texts themselves also function as corporeal entities—bodies of literature. Herein we observe some intriguing facets of the *Acts of Paul and Thecla* as this narrative intersects with other early Christian texts, particularly those included in the "New Testament," a body of literature deemed authoritative for the life and practice of early Christians by the time of the third century CE. Examining the boundaries between these texts may help us understand more fully how it is that one text was incorporated in the New Testament canon while another one was not, or, more precisely, it may help us rethink the act of canonization itself as a social and political operation. In other words, when reflecting upon the canonical process, we may gain some appreciation for why, despite their similarities at some levels, the Acts of the Apostles became part of the New Testament while the *Acts of Paul and Thecla* did not.

Alongside the issue of canonization, it is likewise important to pay attention to the character of texts themselves. As we noted in the previous chapter, in the ancient world epic was considered to be a kind of "masculine" literature, one that contributed to the formation of males within the parameters of life in the city. That body of ancient epic literature tended to coalesce around particular themes and disciplined the reader in a specific socialized and gendered behavior. Odysseus and Aeneas, for example, were more than mere characters in a story; they provided exemplars of ideal virtue and practice that structured the life and duty (values) of the civilized male in Greece and Rome. In a similar sense, early Christian texts tended to cohere together and thereby provided a context for imitation. Moreover, we need to conceptualize this gendered dynamic on at least two levels—on the one hand, texts can be understood as gendered *bodies* themselves, in that there exists between them (individually and collectively) a broad thematic but also structural (grammar, style) cohesion, while, on the other hand, the bodies of both individuals and communities are shaped in the reading and hearing of these very same texts. Thus, the text has both a "life" and an "effect," and both of these can be examined from a gender-critical perspective.

life I

effect II

If in the first chapter we have focused on methodological issues, in the second we sketched the sociocultural background against which early Christianity needs to be situated. In the current chapter we are especially interested in examining the multiple ways in which a gender-critical perspective can help us reconceive the literary and social landscape of early Christianity itself. To that end, we will first discuss canonical and related conceptual boundaries. Our guiding question here is how to understand early Christian discourse from a gender-critical perspective. Second, we will turn our attention to the boundaries between early Christianity and the larger cultural contexts that shaped it. Third, we examine the political boundaries of empire, focusing on the way in which early Christian identity developed under imperial rule. Finally, in the last part, we center more squarely on how gender interacts with social spaces and places within early Christianity. Overall, we will argue that canonical, cultural, political, and social boundaries are interconnected as well as mutually reinforcing of each other, and thus are fundamental for understanding the development of early Christian identity insofar as it connects with gender, sex, and sexuality.

Canonical and conceptual boundaries

In terms of the formation of canonical boundaries, a natural place to begin is with the so-called "Church Fathers", who are considered to be authoritative teachers of the burgeoning early Christian churches. Among the more notable was Tertullian, who, born in Carthage (North Africa) around 160 CE., became one of the major pioneers of Latin Christian literature. In a treatise devoted to the practice of baptism, which he wrote in the beginning of the third century, Tertullian refers to Thecla as being claimed in defense of women's ability to teach and to baptize. Tertullian, who himself espoused a conservative stance on gender roles, discredits this claim, arguing that the *Acts of Paul* is a fraud, a document made out of devotion to Paul by a presbyter in Asia (*De Baptismo* 17). This statement makes clear just how much was at stake in determining which texts would have authority and which would not. Tertullian, moreover, backs up his argument with a reference to Paul's first letter to the Corinthians, in which Paul states that women should keep silent in the gathering of the community (1 Cor 14.35), a statement that bolsters Tertullian's attempt to control potentially unruly women. Elsewhere in his writings, Tertullian similarly appeals to Paul in an attempt to control the female body and to place it under severe strictures (see his *On the Veiling of Virgins* and *On the Apparel of Women*). It is not surprising, then, that he should be so adamant in his disdain for the Thecla traditions, as they offered a potential paradigm for female authority and public empowerment, to which he was stridently opposed. Herein, a gender-critical perspective helps us to appreciate better how the shaping of a body of literature has a correlating effect on the formation of early Christian identity. This literature plays a role in the articulation and construction of a normative early Christian male and female identity and performance (and, in the process, it also posits an "opposite," which provides a foil of nonnormativity that reaffirms the overall structure of the normative). It is therefore not surprising that the structure of ecclesial authority that Tertullian represents supported and promoted a reading list that would reinscribe that authority, while dismissing or denigrating (or even excluding) presumed alternative literary products that challenged such authority. The comment by Tertullian thus provides a helpful avenue into the larger debate about bodies of literature in early Christianity. It also demonstrates the critical role that discussions over legitimate and illegitimate bodies of literature played in shaping and disciplining the early Christian body, both individual and collective.

In this first part, our interest lies explicitly in the *canonization* process, by which particular texts became authoritative, possessing a disciplining function for a specific form of so-called "Christian orthodox" identity. It took a couple of centuries before this process came to relative completion. In his 39th *Festal Letter* (dated to 367 CE), Athanasius of Alexandria was the first to mention the 27 books that would later become known as the "New Testament."

By that time, Athanasius had become bishop of Alexandria and thus speaks from a position of ecclesial power. As a defender of "orthodoxy," he was, moreover, involved in a battle with a group of "heretics" (the Arians) regarding the identity of Christ. Athanasius himself did not create the list of books that were deemed "canonical" and authoritative for Christian use and practice. Rather, his declaration reflects a later stage in a long debate, one that took place in the context of a diversity and pluriformity of texts and traditions related to early Christian teachings and narratives. Some of these texts, such as the *Didache* (*Teaching of the Twelve Apostles*) and the *Shepherd of Hermas*, were held in high esteem, even though they did not make it into the corpus of New Testament literature. Others, such as the *Gospel of Peter* or the *Acts of Paul* (which includes the *Acts of Paul and Thecla*), received a mixed response, given their perceived divergences from "orthodox" practice and faith. Rather than just the process of canonization itself, however, we are interested in the implications of this process for the gendering and sexing of early Christian identity. In particular, at this junction we turn to the critical question of normativity in early Christian discourse, with a focus on the implications that the formation of an *authoritative* body of literature had for the establishment of a—predominantly *male*—authority structure among early Christian communities.

Eusebius of Caesarea (ca. 263–339 CE), a bishop and historian, plays an important role in this process, since he links a normative body of literature for Christian identity to an authoritative story of Christian origins and development, thereby setting out what would become the dominant paradigm. In his ambitious *Ecclesiastical History*, he constructs a narrative in which the first century represents the ideal of uniformity in Christian practice and belief. This uniformity then became distorted and corrupted over time as Christians deviated from the original and pure tradition. In "normative" terms, this deviation is known as "heresy," that which represents deviance from (and deformity of) orthodox or normative structures.[2] In fact, deviant belief and practice is often considered most dangerous by writers such as Eusebius precisely when this belief and practice seems to be most similar to that which is deemed normative. It appears, then, as a "proximate other," and its "passing" among some Christians as potential "truth" provides a specific danger, since boundaries potentially become blurred in the process. Thus, it is the resemblance to the pure tradition, but also the deviant character of heresy, that Eusebius sets out to account for. He accomplishes this goal by relating a story that constructs a lineage of the pure tradition down to his own present day, while also delineating the various points at which heresy diverges from the pure tradition.

The story is critical since it provides the "historical" or temporal grounding that stabilizes the body of tradition and teaching that supports the authoritative ecclesiastical structure that Eusebius endorses. In other words, his narrative serves to bolster a particular set of values and beliefs that are intricately tied to gendered and sexed—predominantly male—structures in early Christianity. Gender itself, of course, is only one aspect of a larger authoritative whole, but it is of crucial importance nonetheless. Indeed, as the earlier quote by Tertullian already made clear, male authority was premised in part on excluding alternative Christian traditions that might bolster female authority and power. It is thus not surprising that early Christian heresy-critics (heresiologists) would also gender and sex their assessments of the deviation from the norm. That is, there was a tendency to effeminize deviations from the pure, original lineage, affirming thereby the masculine nature of the normativity so constructed. This point cannot be overstated, since the constructed story of Christian origins and development did much to universalize male ecclesial power.

Through a variety of measures (e.g., slander, constructing narratives of female control and authority [as deviant]), stories like Eusebius's functioned to shore up male authority while also demonstrating the weak/ened and docile body of the heretic, thereby creating an "other" over against which the normative is formed and takes shape. Indeed, all of this comes as no surprise if we take seriously the point mentioned earlier in this chapter and in the previous one: the literature one wrote and consumed reflected one's own character. Roman epic literature, as already noted, sought to mold readers in their manly duties towards the state and family. In this same way, early Christian literature was understood to both reflect but also mold proper Christian character, which represents at least one edge of the imitative function that literature possessed in the ancient world. Thus, using a gendered frame of reference from the first century, there is a "hard" and "soft" nature to "orthodoxy" and "heresy." The normative tradition becomes a hard, manly line of imitation, which bolsters authoritative male control of church offices, while the heretical or nonnormative tradition forms a type of soft practice and tradition. Likewise, the normative hard body posits a soft, docile, and easily malleable body of literature with a concomitant deviant identity that has been molded in light of this body. In this construction, then, there is not only an emergent and distinct male authority structure that posits a less masculine (even effeminate/female) counterpart, but a temporal distinction is made as well. In particular, the first century becomes the pure, originary moment for this hard authority, while the second century is perceived as the context for deviancy and corruption of that prior authoritative body. As a result, the body of literature that coalesces most closely with the male founding figures of the Christian movement and that posits itself or can be situated closest in time to the "originary moment" bears more authority and power. The consumption of this literature, in principle at least, produces in turn a disciplining of the early Christian subject. Bodies of texts thus both reflect and influence bodies of readers and writers, and the larger community body is shaped in the process as well.

While the actual situation of early Christianity looks much more complex, convoluted, and "messy" than we have presented it here, we are especially interested in examining those discourses of normativity that seek to project a linear and simplistic picture of the nature of early Christian history and identity, leaving to one side literature that complicates that picture, thus becoming "non-canonical" as a result. Indeed, the historical impact of this gendered and sexed model of origins cannot be overstated. It is hardly accidental that the 27 books that finally became the "normative" New Testament canon for third-century orthodox Christianity cohere so surprisingly well with the Eusebian outline of Christian origins and development. The Acts of the Apostles, for instance, clearly provides the general structure for Eusebius's history, and the two mutually reinforce each other, therein providing a "true" image and paradigm of Christian beginnings. Moreover, because Acts forms a narrative bridge between the (Lukan) Gospel and the stories of the early church, but also provides a "historical" skeleton on which to situate the Pauline letters, a major portion of the "unity" of the New Testament rests on Acts.[3] It is therefore no coincidence that this text becomes so critical in Eusebius's construction, as it provides an initial impetus and rationale for the collection of New Testament texts, which is the central literary corpus around which Eusebius molds his story of the development of the "body" of early Christian faith and practice.

It is this New Testament "canon" or "rule" that, finally, becomes a true "body" that comports itself as a holistic entity. Moreover, this evolving body also received a "skin" in which to be contained, since so long as the various books were only promulgated in isolation but not themselves shaped as a whole, there was always room for "selection" (and possible "addition"). Not by accident, the rise of the early Christian normative body of literature closely parallels the introduction of the codex, the first "book" format in the ancient world, that could house the collection as a whole. This full embodiment was not possible on a single scroll, which, in the incipient period of Christianity, was still the dominant format used for literature.[4] Thus, material, physical conditions supported the ideologies that shaped the body of literature and, in turn, disciplined early Christian identity.

One should note here as well the way in which there exists a correlation between the rise of an authoritative body of literature and the development of authoritative institutions, which mutually reinforce each other. Institutional power can be seen to go hand in hand with the authorization of a particular retelling of the Christian past (temporally and spatially) and the bolstering of a hard body of canonical literature. That the authority figures were males should not be surprising, as the discourse that was generated largely sought to support masculine authority structures, closely mimicking the public power structures evident throughout the Roman Empire at that time. Indeed, in the development of early Christian ecclesiastical formation we can see a broad imitation of Roman imperial structures.[5] One might well suggest in this light that, at heart, early Christian authority had already been disciplined by larger cultural and social influences (delineated in the previous chapter), which were replicated in the formation of early Christian community structures. Thus, the body of early Christian authority is intricately connected to the institutions being established and to the canonical collection of early Christian traditions/texts. It is no wonder, then, that a text like the *Acts of Paul and Thecla* could be perceived as so problematic to early Christian authorities such as Tertullian. The multiple crossings of and in the text, especially by a female, presented a real danger to the disciplining of subjectivities that the normative body was inscribing and enacting on early Christian circles in diverse parts of the Roman Empire. That Tertullian, living in North Africa, knows and refutes the *Acts of Paul*, a text that, in his opinion at least, originated in Asia, aptly illustrates this point. Of course, the mobility of the text itself (that it reaches North Africa, for instance) also attests to the broad appeal of such crossings, with the crossing of empire geographically reflecting the crossing of empire textually.

This understanding of the disciplining function of the New Testament canon in gendered and sexed terms is a major feature of the gender-critical approach we are developing. Indeed, it becomes a key point of contention whether or not later readers of early Christian literature would choose to follow the normative paradigm as outlined by ancient male authorities or whether they would postulate alternative histories that illuminated voices, traditions, and bodies that were missing from the dominant discourses and story-lines. Of course, one must bear in mind that such alternative histories are not necessarily less authoritative, less patriarchal, or less masculine/hard in their orientation.[6] They may, however, offer differing lines of authority, and, as such, provide a glimpse of the outlines of the normative itself (in one of its manifestations). That is, as we noted in the last chapter, one often best perceives the normative from the vantage point of the margins, even as these margins themselves bear witness to something of the same power dynamics evident in the center.

In this same vein, one also has to take into consideration the effect this normative body of literature had on the modern reading and construction of early Christian history. The Eusebian paradigm and its concomitant story continue to hold powerful sway on modern scholarly perception. This influence should not come as a surprise. The body of New Testament literature has disciplined several centuries of modern readers to conceptualize Christian history and literature precisely from within that normative framework. Modern readers thus tend to replicate and reproduce the hard-lines of early Christian literature, including a penchant for considering the first century as the authoritative context for Christian origins. The same paradigms are even used by scholars dedicated to overturning the traditional, normative image of Christian origins and development. In these instances, the lines of development are simply reversed in establishing a "deviant" or "nonnormative" tradition as the primary, original, and pure one, which was then later usurped by traditions that became normative in their place.[7] It is noteworthy that the normative function of traditions thus continues to play a critical role in these modern alternative accounts of Christian origins. That is, what is normative may shift, but the decisive function of normativity itself remains firmly in place. This centrality of normativity in almost all constructions of early Christianity is vital to note in this context, as it may attest to a foundational impulse in the body of early Christian literature itself, which continually shapes modern paradigms in this dominant mode. Thus, the body as normative signifier is an inherent component of the early Christian tradition, and the disciplining function of this corpus continues well beyond the ancient world as a result.

Origins are always constructed in retrospect, and what is considered to be the beginning point is thus taken as normative, in that the foundational account explains and defines what comes after. Thus, every reconstruction is always already made from an "after the fact" perspective, which necessarily informs the selection and reading of the data. As a result, there is a tendency to "explain" how and why phenomena developed in the way that they did from the vantagepoint of what happened afterwards, which is then read back into and shapes our understanding of the earlier constructed history. Such an approach is inevitable, insofar as one cannot step outside of history or pretend one does not know what came after an earlier event, which, in turn, limits one's perspective on the past, because one is always already part of that history to begin with. Ultimately, our understanding of the past is informed by the present, but the reverse is equally the case in that our understanding of the present, wherein we situate ourselves, is informed by our interpretation of the past. All of this suggests, then, that, just as in the ancient world so also in the modern, readers and communities are being disciplined through the ordering and control of knowledge.

Moreover, modern scholars are equally engaged in the creation of different "beginning" stories. Even when these critics no longer canonize New Testament texts, they still tend to canonize particular versions of the formation and development of the New Testament and early Christianity. It is thus critical to examine not just the rise of the canon and early Christian story-telling (and myth-making) in relationship to the rise of male institutions in the ancient world, but also to investigate modern history-making practices and the effect such have on our reconstruction and interpretation of the former. As in the past, there are normative and nonnormative stories of Christian origins, and the "value" and "voice" given to different perspectives depends much on the relationship of any given "story" to hegemonic systems of knowledge production and control. While we will explore this issue in more detail in the next chapter, we raise it now to signal that there is a corollary between ancient and modern practices of establishing universal, normative stories, which discipline individual readers as well as communities.[8] As we have noted in the first chapter, ultimately there is no escape from ideology. That said, the approaches that conceal their own ideological perspectives are much more problematic than the ones that are overt about them (as Foucault notes, "Power is tolerable only on condition that it masks a substantial part of itself. Its success is proportional to its ability to hide its own mechanisms" [*History of Sexuality I*, 86]).

From the foregoing discussion, then, it should be clear that emergent Christian discourses are to be situated in the gendered and political contexts of both the past and present worlds. In particular, a close connection can be observed between the rise of early Christian institutions, the canonization of the New Testament, and the disciplining of early Christian subjectivities. Moreover, these various components all bear a gendered, sexed, and imperial edge, with male authority forming a critical element that constitutes the hard, "normative" and "universal" body of Christian power and control. However, as we have suggested throughout this discussion, the idea of a uniform and pure (in its origin) Christian movement is a fiction. Our argument is that from the beginning there was multiplicity rather than a monolithic Christian discourse, and that normativity, such as it ever existed, was gradually consolidated over time. Moreover, we also see a permeability of boundaries, from texts, to traditions, to individuals to communities, rather than a uniform essence or quintessentially distinct "Christian" identity. As early Christian communities were made up of people with multiple backgrounds and loyalties and drawn from different social strata, we need to think complexly about these communities and their contingent discourses. We can, for instance, use Paul's letters as sources of information for how certain communities were constituted, thereby constructing broad outlines of *some* early Christian communities, but even here we see pluriformity (and the limitations offered by a unifying, normative version of events and people). Paul's correspondence with the Corinthian community, for instance, attests to a variety of tensions, and, as a comparison between the first and second letter to the Corinthians makes clear, under the pressure of such tensions boundaries were redrawn and renegotiated. Thus, over time communities shift, morph, and mutate, often crossing their own previously established boundaries.

Our modern historical models often do not account for this more convoluted conception of community formation and evolution. In our estimation, however, this is one place where a gender-critical engagement of historical texts can be useful, as it aids in breaking down the binary logic embedded in normative and hegemonic discourses. When used more specifically to analyze early Christian texts, a gender-critical approach challenges both the normative structures and interpretations that play out across ancient writings. While there is always a temptation to replace one normative structure with another, a gender-critical perspective helps us to appreciate better the complexity of identity in early Christian communities and to pay more attention to the diversity of the material outside of the canon. In thus broadening the scope of inquiry, we also gain more insight into the ways that other stories and traditions/texts shape an image of Christian origins. That said, alternative traditions do not necessarily provide us with a non-patriarchal or even a non-colonizing form of Christianity. Rather, complexity emerges as we begin to recalibrate the very notion of a core or center by examining the literature often left at the "margins," treating these as equal partners in shaping our impressions of emergent Christianity.[9] Normativity is destabilized when one understands that the margins themselves have always been part of the broader phenomenon of early Christianity and that the discourses related to an existent center create the illusion of an "other" as inherently different and deviant.

Thus, in many respects, a gender-critical approach looks at early Christianity as a diverse and varied phenomenon, resisting the idea of a stable, unified, pure, universal center from which all else either flows or deviates. Such an approach instead seeks to reframe the literary and social landscape of early Christianity itself through an analysis of the boundaries (and barriers) and transgressions thereof as they have been socially constructed in dominant discourse. In so doing, a gender-critical perspective serves to illuminate the more complex character of early Christianity in the ancient world.

The ultimate result, in our view, is that biblical scholarship itself will transform in the process of asking a different set of questions about the past. That is, the object of study is not simply to investigate the past as a separate, discrete phenomenon, but also to inform the present through such study. There is thus much more at stake in our analysis than just an attempt to provide a new rendering of past objects of inquiry, as if all we need is yet another "new" interpretation and approach. Rather, such study of the past as we are advocating pushes us to see the ways in which these often presumed "universal" norms, including our notions of gender, sex, and sexuality, are, in the end, critically intertwined with a host of other sociocultural facets, thereby relativizing our own sense of identity and place. Herein the politics of our gender-critical methodology (see chapter one) are fronted in an open way, even as we fully realize there are also hidden ideological elements to which we ourselves are oblivious.

Cultural boundaries

When thinking about issues of gender, sex, and sexuality in early Christianity, one of the first questions that we want to discuss relates to the sources that groups such as the early Christians used to construct and develop their ideas. More precisely, what are the cultural influences upon which they would draw or that shaped (even if unconsciously) their perspectives related to gender, sex, and sexuality? As we will see in this section, when examining this phenomenon a complex interaction can be noted between ancient and modern worlds. Once again, these conceptions prove to be an intriguing lens through which to view ancient cultural dynamics (and our interpretation of them). It is not just that they are part of culture in a multifaceted and complex manner, but gender analysis also helps illuminate how bodies are constructed, both individual bodies but also, in this case, bodies of cultures themselves. Just as the canonical literature of the New Testament can be understood to form a body that disciplines readers and communities, so also cultures can be seen to perform a similar function. However, unlike the focus of the previous section, where the body of literature was selected, arranged, ordered, and promulgated by increasingly institutionalized forms of Christianity, in the case of early Christian discourses on gender, sex, and sexuality ancient cultures were foundational for how one came to perceive (and articulate) the substance of these conceptions. It was within the broader cultural sphere that early Christian discourses took shape and it was from there that categories and language were drawn to formulate argumentative strategies and bodily identities. That said, these cultural contexts are not easy to define and delimit. While modern scholars have tended to draw particular cultural boundaries in the ancient world, which then provide the sole or primary lens through which gender, sex, and sexuality are approached theologically, ideologically, and culturally, a gender-critical analysis aims at appreciating more fully the ways in which cultures form hybrid and porous entities rather than uniform and non-permeable ones. Thus, in line with the gender-critical approach being developed here, we question the ways in which ancient cultures have often been constructed by modern interpreters as static, uniform, and normative. Our gender-critical approach instead affirms that identities are shifting and morphing, always in the process of becoming rather than having an essentialist core. Culture—especially as it relates to individual and collective identity formation—therefore needs to be examined from a wider perspective than simply looking at discrete bits of historical and sociocultural contextual data (for comparative purposes). More attention needs to be given both to how cultures themselves are formed (there are diverse forces that act on cultures and variant threads that are woven together into larger assemblages) as well as to how individuals and communities are in turn shaped by these emerging cultural configurations.

This type of cultural analysis is especially important since discourses are related to the establishment of identities and cultures also function as a context out of which these discourses themselves arise. In ancient literature, for instance, a great deal of space is given to the production of a distinct Jewish cultural and religious identity in the ancient world. From Philo to the Maccabaean texts to the book of Jubilees to the later Rabbis, at various times and places individuals and groups developed ideas of what it meant to be "Jewish," and frequently the lines of that identity, as constructed in the discourses, were projected as being clear-cut. Yet the reality of the ancient cultural picture proves to be much more complex, as there were competing notions of what constituted Jewish identity, changing conceptions over time in particular communities, and, even more importantly, different views even within specific communities in any given moment of time. Further, rhetoric also has the effect of simplifying identity, because writers in their own interest or in the service to that of a particular group select certain tropes and characteristics to the exclusion of other possible identity markers. One can also see how the appropriation and adaptation of culture could be enacted differently by variant communities and, perhaps even more critically, how diverse threads or even distinct cultures (sometimes synthesized together) were drawn on to shape differing Jewish identities. For example, if one uses Greek philosophical traditions (such as Philo does), the Jewish identity that is constructed will look quite different than say if one draws on a version of Judaism such as one finds at Qumran. In both cases, gender and sex conceptions are constructed differently (although there may be significant overlap as well) precisely because of these cultural divergences. Discourses on gender, sex, and sexuality thus arise out of (while also forming a part of) this larger cultural assemblage. As a result (and rhetorical issues aside), there is a diffuse nature to the cultural grounding of the discourses themselves. It is precisely the modern obsession with precision and categorization that frequently leads one to narrow cultural and social contexts of meaning, when, rather, one should be seeking more nuanced understandings for many of the categories that are being reconstructed.

Still, it would be misleading to suggest that the projection of stability onto the past is simply a modern phenomenon. Early Christian writers, like their Jewish counterparts (such as Philo or the scribes of the Qumran community), similarly carved out distinct identities in their ancient world context. In the process, the discourse on "separation" and identity-formation produced a sense of a unity within early Christianity and, by contrast, also without.[10] That is, as communities defined themselves through language and social images they created a sense of self-identity that appeared to be stable and boundaried and in many respects also distinct from the surrounding cultural sphere. In the process, the surrounding culture is also reified and stabilized in contrast to this new Christian configuration—it is the "other" that is constructed (and indeed grounded) through clear and often stereotypical categories, against which Christians (in their discourses) appear comparatively different. Early Christians, like everyone else in the ancient world, thus created a sense of cultural stability in and through their language. It is this early Christian discourse that, in turn, informs the way that modern scholars themselves then think about and reconstruct ancient culture.

This broader understanding of culture is critical for assessing a wide variety of elements in early Christian discourses, not least the ones that we are dealing with in this book. We must therefore contend with both the apparent permeable nature of culture and the way it simultaneously presents itself as impermeable. With respect to the latter, identity tends to be produced within a set cultural framework and structure, with little room seemingly available for porous boundaries. Even in texts that seem to advocate boundary crossing as in the *Acts of Paul and Thecla*, the message that constitutes Christian identity (in that text)—the maintenance of sexual purity and renunciation—is never overturned or challenged despite the fact that Thecla is transformed throughout, shifting gendered roles. This phenomenon would suggest that even in a text in which the boundaries seem to be in flux, there is, nevertheless, a stability at the core with respect to the kind of identity that the text both assumes and reproduces. In fact, the various crossings we see operative in that text may ultimately affirm the fundamental normative identity that it would seem, at first glance, to deconstruct. In this light, it is critical to point out that every normativity that is produced in a text also postulates its aberrant and deviant other. In the *Acts of Paul and Thecla*, we catch numerous glimpses of the deviancy of the Roman upper classes in the various cities of the Greek East, particularly the inability of male elite citizens to control their own sexual desire and to mete out justice (the two being interconnected in many ways).

Similar rhetorical strategies are operative in Paul's letters. Thus, in the letter to the Romans, for instance, Paul opens with a demonstration of the depravity of the Greeks and Romans who have refused to acknowledge God, a deviancy that exhibits itself in overt sexual desire, which then ends in an insatiable sexual drive that leads men and women to have intercourse with members of their own sex (Rom. 1.26–27).[11] It is helpful to underscore this (in)famous Pauline text at this point because it so clearly demonstrates how discourse (here, a trope of sexual denigration—the inability to control one's desire/body) functions to both produce negative and positive aspects for identity formation. The main function of this argument is clearly to form, shape, and sustain particular patterns of Christian identity and practice (as indicated by the list of ethical exhortations at the end of the letter). In Romans, Paul nowhere else explicates what could be considered proper Christian sexual behavior, and yet the treatise opens with a statement regarding the sexual depravity of the Gentiles: the monstrous "others," who fall outside of the parameters of proper Christian comportment, and are constructed as a hideously, deviant—and sexually aberrant, in this case—counterpart. Christians, of course, are not like these "others," in Paul's reasoning, because "right knowledge of God" (which Paul delineates throughout his letter) leads to a very different, pure form of life. Thus, a distinctive Christian identity and sociocultural understanding is structured and stabilized by producing an image of the Gentiles as sexually "out of control," which is an indication, within the larger argumentative framework of the letter, of a systemic problem of social chaos and cultural degeneracy among non-Christians.

Several points follow from this discussion. First, when we engage and examine discourses related to gender, sex, and sexuality in early Christian materials, we need to keep in view that they are connected to broader discursive delineations of identity in the ancient world (as we noted in chapter two). Likewise, in early Christianity we see these categories intertwining with a broader articulation of identity. Gender, sex, and sexuality cannot be isolated from the construction of early Christian identity as a whole, both individual and corporate. Moreover, whatever else we may wish to draw out from references to gender, sex, and sexuality in early Christian texts, we have to give ample attention to the ways in which they function within a broader discourse on Christian identity and are situated within the context of particular early Christian writings or tradents of literary texts. In other words, it is tempting to simply examine early Christian attitudes toward gender, sex, and sexuality as if such an attitude or view can somehow be disentangled from a broader discursive framework—we believe it cannot. Rather, these attitudes need to be analyzed primarily as components in the construction and maintenance of Christian identities in texts. They are, in this respect, part of how (some) Christians defined what it meant to be a "Christ-follower" in the first centuries of the common era. Further, discussions in the primary sources related to gender, sex, and sexuality may not always have been primarily about "sex," "gender," and "sexuality" per se. When Paul chastises the Corinthians for sexual deviancy (1 Cor. 5), he not only postulates a "pure" opposite or "ideal," but in the process he also constructs weak opponents, thus undermining an opposition from within the community as well as promoting his own authority and his good character. In other words, modern readers often assume that texts that refer explicitly to "sexuality," for instance, must be about "sexuality"—but, as we noted in the first chapter, the rhetorical nature of discourse makes the end of argumentation the primary prism through which the various components of the discourse should be understood and assessed. Thus, Paul's argument about appropriate gender behavior of both men and women in 1 Corinthians 11 may, in the end, demonstrate not only his investment in the rationales offered for why a different comportment of the sexes is critical, but also his concern for the reputation of his community, which ultimately reflects back on Paul himself. There is thus a correlation between the various bodies present in this argument—the bodies of the individuals (Paul, the Corinthian men and women) and the body of the community itself. There is also, in Paul's argument, an intersection between the performance of the individual and the collective body, with Paul's own (gendered, sexed, and sexualized) body, seemingly absent from the text, being mediated through his language. Obviously, then, there is complexity in the way that various bodies overtly and implicitly intersect and interrelate in the text.

Second, discussions of gender, sex, and sexuality in early Christian literature form critical components in the construction of a distinctive Christian culture. It should be noted that this "culture" is essentially a hybrid construction, which owes its roots to a variety of strands from Jewish, Greek, Roman and other ancient cultures such as Egyptian, Anatolian, or Celtic (and none of these are themselves stable or uniform). It is impossible in fact to conceptualize a unique Christian culture, particularly in the first two hundred years of formation. The spaces and places that foster Christian community identity intersect in multiple ways with the larger world of which early Christians were a part. That said, an important accent should be placed on the way in which Christian discourse seeks to produce a *different* understanding of Christian identity and community formation than that represented by the "surrounding" culture. In other words, Christians frequently utilized a language of difference, and often articulated themselves as representing a superior form of social and cultural conduct. We see this move in Paul's writings as well as in the *Acts of Paul and Thecla*. Whatever differences may lie between these texts, what they have in common is that they produce a specific Christian identity over and against a Gentile "other." In the second century, a Church Father such as Justin Martyr, in his *Dialogue with Trypho the Jew*, would do something similar with respect to Jews.[12] Thus, Christian identity is marked off by divergence from others, be it Gentiles or Jews, particularly towards the end of the second century. In other words, as noted earlier, on the inside of the movement there exists the deviance of those who distort the "pure" original message and practice of Christianity, and on the outside there are the neighboring social and cultural contexts over against which Christians also articulated their difference. In many respects, these two moments of differentiation are part of the same process, and should be viewed in tandem. Further, if we take this point seriously, then the question can also be asked to what degree the two elements actually correlate in some respects: that is, to what extent do "heretical" perspectives and practices reflect cultural differences and not just theological ones? In other words, "inside" differences may also reflect "outside" ones (with correlative ideological bases) from the perspective of "orthodox" Christian communities.

Given these broader insights, early Christianity not only has to be thought of as having multiple origins (polygenetic) as we noted in the previous section, but the very categories of "beginning," "original," "pure," "pristine" are problematic entry points for analysis. Early Christians came from a vast array of places and spaces in empire, and they also emerged from diverse social levels in society. As a result, we cannot postulate a particular "ideal" early Christian reader or character—there is no such thing. The argument we are developing here pushes us in quite the opposite direction: there is already a rich diversity of both early Christian individuals and also communities, and one cannot assume a uniformity and normativity across the spectrum, although there is a disciplining function to the discourse that nonetheless creates an impression of cohesion. This view does not contradict our earlier assessment related to the emergence of early Christian rhetoric and its creation of identity, where there is a coalescence of themes, concepts, and language. The letters of Paul, for instance, consistently produce a vision of a *unified* Christian identity, even as there are undertones that strain against this notion. But that is precisely how discourse functions, and the creation of a sense of unity was all the more necessary in a context where there was substantive diversity and fluidity of identity, given that early Christianity was a *pan-regional* phenomenon, spread across the Roman Empire. The fictional quality of this discourse does not thereby mean that it did not produce real world realities in its wake—no doubt we need to be thinking in terms of the *production of Christian culture* in and through the rhetoric of early Christian texts.[13] However, it does not imply that this vision, even if shared, actually reflected reality. Discursive boundaries are often rigid and firm, but boundaries of daily lived life are frequently quite the opposite. It is thus critical to make a sharp break with an uncritical reconstruction of historical and cultural realities based on the discourses reflected in early Christian texts.

Third, we need to read these texts as if writers were negotiating with a plethora of cultural phenomena (which themselves are in flux and hybrid) out of which they emerged and from which they often sought to differentiate themselves. In other words, in our estimation, the production of unity through difference in early Christian texts needs to be deconstructed through a reading of what we know about these broader cultures. We understand this observation to mean that Christian discourse not only has to be understood in and through its cultural contexts, but it also has to be read against them. If on issues of gender, sex, and sexuality, for instance, early Christian discourse produces a normative understanding of individual and collective moral comportment, we cannot thereby assume that early Christian realities have thus been presented. The rigidity of the boundaries set by the discourse may well have been contested by the assumptions and values held by others (including Christians) in the ancient world. We therefore need to pay attention to those places in the texts that attest to a porous and less stable nature that often lies behind the discourse. In other words, inflexibility on the boundaries and borders is part of the discourse but not necessarily part of the culture. Thus, as we turn our attention to the formation of Christian culture, we should be thinking of this phenomenon as existing at the crossroads of discourse and lived-experience, and, while there is a definite interrelation between the two (they are dialogically shaping each other), there are still numerous gaps and fissures in lived-experience that attest to more complex realities in early Christian communities, despite what the discourse itself may suggest.

Fourth, following upon the observation presented earlier, and related to the production and projection of an idealized form of Christian cultural formation, we also need to take seriously the opposite effect of this discourse: the production and projection of an abject other, be it Greek, Roman, Jewish, or some alternate ancient people/group. Of course, as we have already implied earlier, being Christian in the first and second centuries CE was to be "Greek," "Roman," and/or "Jewish" (or "Celt," "Egyptian," etc.). The production of a distinctive Christian culture—and separation from the "other"—was not in small part a function of the discourses early Christians generated. That said, in the process of creating a distinct discursive identity, the opposite effect was to denigrate and abjectify the cultural contexts out of which early Christians emerged. The result is that early Christians also produced a discursive "other culture" of the Greeks and Romans that likewise did not necessarily exist in reality. Take for example Paul's claims about the Gentiles in Romans 1 that we discussed earlier, where he refers to their being out of control, seeking to satisfy every sexual urge and impulse. In the cultural context created for this discourse in chapter two of this book, it is clear that the lack of self-mastery displayed by these degenerate others is in effect a major characteristic of their weakness and even a sign of their effeminacy. Thus, we see an "out of control" non-Christian counterpart to the early Christian identity that Paul constructs in his text, a phenomenon we see paralleled in the *Acts of Paul and Thecla*, where Alexander definitely does not possess self-mastery. The operations of this discourse are fairly easy to perceive, but the lasting impact might be less clear to the modern reader. In effect, Christians not only produced a normative, stable identity for themselves through their texts, they also, in the process, proceeded to manufacture an alternative fiction (and necessary distortion) of the culture of the other. It is thus imperative, when thinking about gender, sex, and sexuality in early Christianity, to engage the ways in which both the identities of Christians and the identities of non-Christians were produced and projected through the discourse of early Christian texts. Clearly it is not so much a matter of whether or not non-Christians read this material and were affected by it. Rather, it is a matter of how our perception of the other continues to be shaped from the perspective of the early Christian literature.[14]

It is no wonder, as Jennifer Knust has recently shown in her book *Abandoned to Lust* (2005), that in the second century Justin Martyr could so readily imitate the tropes of sexual slander already evidenced in Pauline argumentation. Early Christians borrowed and developed patterns of thinking that were indebted to a rhetorical tradition, which focused on nurturing self-identity in positive terms and in denigrating the outsider or one's opponent. These early patterns were systemically linked to the process of community formation that Christians enacted, and thus had an enduring presence in and through the symbols, myths, images, narratives, and instructions that were passed on to and through the communities. Such a discursive interaction proved to be formative for creating a distinct impression of Christian difference and otherness, one that constructed a "purity" that matched, in many ways, the "purity" of origins in the normative Christian story of formation and development. In other words, the lasting image that is hereby sustained and nurtured is one of distinction, even as the tropes of argumentation by which this image is established are borrowed from the larger cultural sphere. This argument does not imply, however, that Christians did not create anything new as a result. To the contrary, early Christian discourse throughout evidences an ability to adapt and reconfigure language, images, tropes, preexisting sacred texts, cultural norms, and so on to the distinctive advantage of its survival and flourishing in an often inimical environment.

Finally, as we did in the first section, it is important to draw attention again to the way in which modern scholarship on early Christianity tends to reproduce the discourses reflected in the ancient texts. That is, just as scholars reconstructing Christian origins have tended to trace out an "originary impulse" or pure point of origin with later deviations and aberrations from that norm, so scholars examining gender, sex, and sexuality in early Christianity have tended to reproduce a Christian rhetoric of sexual difference. Following the discourse of the texts under study, historical critics have repeatedly postulated a strong moral focus in early Christianity out of which it developed a significantly different sexual ethic in comparison with contemporary Greek and Roman moral perspectives. Kathy Gaca (*Making of Fornication*), for instance, argues that Paul (following Philo) articulates an early Christian sexual ethic that is understood as an expression of devotion to God. The basis for this notion comes from the Septuagint (the Greek translation of the Hebrew Bible), and is thus biblically (and Jewish) based, rather than being grounded in Greek culture. The early Christians are thus constructed as wholly "other" just as their discourse would suggest.[15] Moreover, there has not only been a marked tendency to take the textual discourse as a stable indicator of Christian identity beyond the text, but there has, even more so, been a strong propensity towards reifying the cultural understanding reflected in the texts themselves. As we mentioned at the outset of this section, modern scholarship is inclined to construct culture as a boundaried phenomenon, which is fixed and stable in its meaning. That is, if a particular concept has a "Jewish" background, then it is Judaism that must be used to understand the meaning of that concept. One could enumerate study after study that focuses on a particular early Christian theme and traces it out with respect to its Jewish (or other) background (and within that larger category further narrows it down to more specific designations of "Jewish" such as Alexandrian, Hellenistic, Pharisaic, Rabbinic, Sectarian, etc.). This approach assumes a linear and fairly simplistic notion of cultural and ideological transmission, wherein ideas and influences maintain stability in the process.[16] But almost every received idea or influence is refracted through a blending with other ideas that an author or community possesses as a result of their own particular cultural and social *habitus*. It is thus just as problematic/misleading to talk about a "Jewish concept" in the ancient world as it is to talk about a "Christian" one. Cultural configurations are not only constantly in flux (differing as well as depending on regional location and social stratification), but they also intersect in various ways with other coterminous cultural contexts (one might think here of the Isis cult from Egypt being brought to Rome, where it becomes an exotic attraction and spectacle in this new context). Moreover, people are not always consistent in their appropriations and reconfigurations. Jewish culture in the ancient world interacts with Greek and Roman cultural features, and is shaped and changed in the process, and it is difficult to draw firm lines on where one ends and another begins, let alone delineating what "new" cultural product is birthed in and through this interaction.

Moreover, sexual discourse is also bound up with the rhetoric of a specific text, so the position that a particular writer holds may in fact shift from text to text and from audience to audience. For instance, rhetorical end will also have a substantive influence on the presentation of sexual perspectives in Paul. One should therefore ask what Paul is trying to accomplish in his argument, and how gender, sex, and sexuality are being used in that larger goal/*telos* of argumentation. At the same time, Paul's goal in argumentation may not be entirely consistent. Further, there is no guarantee that the reception of that argument will coalesce with the original purpose or intention of the argument. It is equally important to note that this reception will also shift depending on who is reading and from what vantage point that reading is undertaken. In other words, the stabilities that are frequently denoted in modern scholarship do not take into account that there is no "ideal" or "uniform" reader of these texts and images in both the ancient and modern worlds. The reading subject is constantly in flux on both a personal and collective level.

Political boundaries

In terms of thinking about gender in early Christian discourse, it is also important to situate tropes of gender, sex, and sexuality within a broader geographic and sociopolitical horizon. Early Christianity arrived on the scene during the emergence of the Second Sophistic, which was a literary, cultural, and intellectual movement of the first and second centuries in the Greek East that cultivated a revival of and celebrated traditional Greek cultural values and education at the height of Roman imperial power. As we noted in the previous chapter, when the Romans expanded their empire eastward, they essentially took over Greek colonies, providing a Roman imperial overlay to the latter but there still remained a strong Greek presence in the East. In this context, local elites found themselves in various unstable and precarious positions with respect to the changing social structures, and vast imperial influence of the Roman Empire. It was also a time of significant possibility for the creation of innovative identities and communities. Boundaries (social, cultural, political, economic, literary) were constantly in flux, and a budding new class of elites could begin to reposition themselves in local regional contexts as well as with respect to the imperial center of Rome.[17] In the process, the glories of ancient Greece were remapped onto the present through imaginative geographies that vividly redescribed the past so as to bring it to life for the present. Amidst the sometimes brutal violence of Roman domination, then, there also existed, in striking juxtaposition, openings for the creation of new identities as well as the recreation of past identities, out of which arose an arsenal of techniques to subvert imperial hegemony through rhetorical means. The shift to empire at this juncture is especially helpful for understanding the larger context in which early Christian discourses developed and deployed the tropes of gender, sex, and sexuality, as the imperial context allows us to engage the political backdrop (at least on the macro-level) that shaped early Christian perceptions. Even if the political sphere was often not explicitly engaged, the power relations of empire continually haunted the landscape in which early Christianity arose.

It is precisely this political aspect that provides a context for understanding the movement of religious traditions and practices through the empire. Already in the Hellenistic period, there was a strong impetus towards syncretism, the integrating and melding of diverse religious and cultural traditions into a new hybrid religious/cultural entity. Sometimes such syncretism was deliberately encouraged by foreign colonizing powers, as the effect was to assimilate more easily native indigenous cultures and divergent practices. During the Roman period, syncretistic practices were further fueled by the increase in mobility and travel, as ideas, texts, and new (and exotic) religious practices moved with seeming ease to remote places in the empire (and vice versa, from remote areas the same came to the regional centers). "Barbarians" took on a new role as well, as labor redistribution in the imperial period gave more control to local elites and offered traditional power positions to non-Romans. Ethnic identities were also redefined and set off against each other. Barbarianism was an identity that could be recultivated and salvaged, as the wide-open playing field created new spaces for intellectuals excluded from the traditional locations of power in the past.[18] All of these shifts brought more (and new) players into conflict with the "old men" of empire.[19]

This quick sketch of the environment in which Christian discourse developed helps us to appreciate more fully how boundaries and spaces in early Christian literature were being renegotiated. On the one hand, there was a vast Roman imperial presence that provided a colonial overlay to the regions of the predominantly Greek East where Christianity first took hold and spread. One cannot ignore this imperial context, as it drastically affected (albeit often implicitly) the way in which people articulated, cultivated, and contextualized their identities with respect to past and present cultures, traditions, stories, and social patterns. Rome was ever present in the East, not least through the use of imperial images in temples and city centers, in which local elites were erecting images of Roman emperors and their families as a way of paying tribute to their overlords. Wherever one walked in the ancient city, there were both overt and subtle reminders of the imperial panopticon (the ever present Roman gaze).[20] Naturally, not everyone was happy with this situation. The Jewish people in Judea, at the very least, resisted the erection of idols and similar kinds of dedications. Josephus (ca. 37–100 CE) records such incidents of resistance in his *Jewish Antiquities*, and, as would be expected, the Romans (as the Greeks before them) did not respond sensitively to such opposition. At the same time, there were also local Jewish elites who supported the Greek and Roman rulers. Thus, such dissemination of power through images and sanctuaries met with a variety of responses—from support to resistance to ambivalence.

At the same time, literary fiction and public rhetorical display opened up spaces wherein Rome appeared absent. Thus, the imaginative boundaries of empire could be redrawn, even as daily life itself may have looked very different. One might think here, for instance, of the Rabbis of the second and third centuries CE, who imagined the temple of Jerusalem in full daily operation even while it was long destroyed by the Romans in the first century (e.g., see tractate *Sukka* of the Mishna). Such imaginative journeys are by no means mere fictions, however, as they shape real attitudes towards the lived-reality of the world that the writers and readers inhabited. Narratives, therefore, were often empowering and transforming for individuals and communities, as literature imagined new ways of being in the world.

In line with the argument made earlier in this chapter, we want to stress the importance of assessing gender, sex, and sexuality in early Christianity within this complex landscape of meaning. Here again the body takes central stage, but now within the panorama of empire, as well as within the historical recreation and remembrance of the past and its infusion into a lived present. With respect to the vast geography of empire, the comportment and performance of the body in discourse provided an opportunity for a remapping of imperial space, for a counter-cartography of meaning, wherein individuals and communities, disciplined by empire, could reconceptualize meaning by creating their own spaces and places, with new boundaries for identity formation and the possibility for the emergence of new desiring subjects. The body of the characters in various early Christian narratives and the corporeality of the Christian community in general function within this broader sphere, and they do so on multiple levels and in complex ways. The body on display in the text maps out the personal and communal identity of early Christians. In some ways, one might construe this facet as the concomitant effect of the canonization process. As we delineated earlier, that process progressively disciplined early Christian communities into specific ways of thinking and acting. At the same time, alongside choice there was also coercion and it is often difficult to distinguish between them in the context of oppressive regimes of control, even as we find clear acts of resistance to that control. One thinks here of the stories of Thecla, which attest to the realities of life lived in fear (of persecution, of political tyranny), while also witnessing to the social and cultural power of emboldened perseverance in the face of death.

An entry point into this discussion of gendered and sexed boundaries is the Acts of the Apostles with its focus on travel through empire. A major feature of this canonical text is the emphasis on the gospel message moving outwards from Jerusalem towards Rome. The opening of the narrative has Jesus predicting this expansion to his followers. In Acts 1.8, Jesus explicitly states that the gospel message will spread, indicating both a geographic movement, as well as an ethnic reorientation as the message moves to the Gentiles alongside the Jews. In the history of interpretation, this focus of Acts has frequently been interpreted in theological terms. That is, the geographic movement has been read as a symbolic marker for Christian missionary expansion and vitality in the spreading of the "word." The focus has thus been squarely on "the Way" (Acts 9.2), from its origins in Judea to its arrival in Rome. Largely based on the letters of Paul read through the prism of Acts, the major scholarly concern has been to highlight the theological content or core of the gospel message, which forms the critical element for the expansion of the incipient faith. More recent interpretations, however, have shifted the focus towards viewing Acts as subverting Roman imperial domination. Just as Rome expands its territory through military force, so the gospel message in Acts spreads outwards through forceful words and deeds, but now in resistance to Roman imperial claims. Thus, scholars have argued that early Christian rhetoric, here on display in the book of Acts, depicts Christians subverting hegemonic categories of oppression, bringing the peace and mercy of Christ to the imperial outposts (and then to the center of empire itself).[21]

Part of the problem with such approaches to Acts, which we also see replicated in similar assessments of Paul's letters, is that so much of how the body functions more broadly in society and how it maps out community identity is overlooked in these analyses. The vast majority of scholarship continues to promote a view of Christian discourse that finds in it a transcendent, other-worldly dynamic, which is decidedly not invested in the negotiation of power.

Some scholars understand early Christians to be resistant to empire and Roman imperial aspirations, and thus they are seen to have developed an alternative system of meaning that undermined the dominant, patriarchal authoritative structures of the Romans.[22] Others stress that there are subversive elements in early Christianity (that draw on common cultural modes of resistance),[23] but sometimes then fail to appreciate the early Christian imitation of and desire for power. Yet there is much more going on with respect to the negotiation of power in these texts than simply "subversion," not least the consideration that every act of subversion easily becomes a reification of the very power being subverted in the first place. As Foucault notes, power always reconstitutes itself, even as it is constantly fluid and in flux (there is no outside of power).

Readings of gender, sex, and sexuality within an ancient context will therefore have to grapple seriously with early Christian investments in the performance of bodies. On the one hand, "manliness" and ideal gender performances were adopted from society and reinscribed on early Christian bodies. On the other hand, there is a critical edge to this rhetorical move, insofar as early Christians often reinterpreted manliness in the process. Thus, the main characters in Acts display ideal masculine behavior in the public forum. This situation is particularly the case with the apostles, who exhibit ideal comportment in word and action. The way that power is played out is intricately related to the construction of the normative male body set over against others in the text, who often act in ways contrary to the cultural ideals of masculine performance. One is reminded here of the showdown between Paul and Elymas, the advisor/magician who has the ear of the proconsul in Acts 13, or the Sons of Sceva, the Jewish exorcists casting out demons in Acts 19. In both cases, Greeks and Jews are shown to be inferior to the apostles (especially Paul), and their bodies are afflicted so as to accentuate the point (the sons of Sceva are beaten, while Elymas is made blind). It is the power of the apostles that exemplifies their character in the narrative, over against weak rivals. They also confront rulers/tyrants, such as king Agrippa in Acts 26, with bold speech. In this respect, Acts, alongside much of early Christian literature, maps out normative bodies and situates those over against bodies of non-Christians (Greeks, Romans, Jews, and others), who enact the opposite of expected normative behavior. An act of subversion it is, but one that also reinscribes in the process the basic power dynamics of empire—it is just that now the victims have changed, and the moral justification for this action comes from the deity constructed in the narrative. The boundaries of empire are crucial in this process, as it is the boundaries that dictate who is in power and who is not, and at the same time there arises an invitation for transgression and crossings of those same borders.

However, the identity formation that is enacted takes place on multiple levels. Thus, the Christian community imaginatively envisions itself expanding across the empire, hearing stories of its heroes in action, seeing how new territory is claimed for Christ, and experiencing the reworked tales of Hebrew prophecy now seen unfolding in their midst. Past and present blend in this enterprise, and Christians are portrayed as taking central stage in this cosmic imperial drama. They are herded into arenas, put to the test for their faith, shown to be strong in their resistance to tyrants, and at times narrowly escaping with their lives. The unfolding narrative spectacles dramatically enact the positioning of Christianity as a central trope in the reimagination of imperial geography (in the book of Revelation, for instance, Christianity takes its vital imperial place through a literal cosmic battle). The body of the community thus becomes a locus for the power of Christ, and the outward comportment of that community is critical in terms of negotiating the identity of its members. In Paul's letters we observe just this sort of enactment, even if on a local level. In the instructional material we observe how local communities were disciplined so as to imagine themselves as corporeal channels for the divine. It is no accident, for instance, that Paul uses an argument from creation in 1 Corinthians 11 to solidify the hierarchy of men and women in the community. Paul's mandates on sexual control earlier in 1 Corinthians 6.15–20 make a similar point: the individual body is a temple and its purity is critical for its ability to channel divine power.

In thinking about gendered and sexed boundaries in this context, then, it becomes clear that early Christians were both crossing and reconfiguring dominant boundaries (real and imagined) in order to create and sustain discourses that would prove effective in imperial realms, both local and global. One tactic was to play to the normative, masculine bodily representation, another was to utilize gender conceptions that pervasively reversed and transgressed cultural norms. One prominent example of the latter phenomenon is the manner in which early Christians, drawing on an already entrenched (particularly Jewish) tradition of martyrdom discourse, were able to recover the shameful and degenerate image of the martyr for argumentative ends. This move offers one example of how humiliating cultural images could be inverted and redeployed.[24] Obviously, the Christian embracing of these tropes of identity have close correlations with the crucifixion and death of Jesus, now reconstituted as ultimate signs of power. The modeling of this paradigmatic theme resonates throughout early Christian literature and, even though it takes on a variety of forms, it bears a remarkable coherence in terms of turning the abject other into a potent model for community formation. The versatility of concepts and images related to gender, sex, and sexuality were especially helpful in this process, as they were highly malleable when the rhetorical and ideological situation demanded such.

Other themes were also successful in the rhetorical engagement of empire. One such theme, which reoccurs throughout the apocryphal Acts, was the challenge to normative Roman family structures by wealthy women who adopted the lifestyle promoted by the itinerant apostles. This journey from one, often married, state to another independent one, free of family or societal obligations, includes a shift from the power of the culturally dominant elite male to the power of a more potent Christian apostle. In this way, early Christians were telling stories that subverted the local elite hierarchical structures, thereby reconfiguring lines of power by promoting a potentially culturally shameful message that turned the value system of Greco-Roman society on its head. This reversal, here of class and gender expectations, was also dangerous, as such reversals subverted traditional gender roles and threatened the institution of marriage, which was fundamental to the Roman moral code and the growth of empire. Further, out of control women (sexually, socially, in the public sphere) was a major fear of the upper classes, as the reaction of Thecla's mother makes evident. In this context we are reminded of the staunch patriarchal stance of the early Christian leaders as well (mentioned above), which Christian texts helped to bolster and to secure.

However, early Christians were not only creating and shoring up the boundaries of their own "household"/community, they were, simultaneously, telling stories about incursions into the upper strata of Roman society, upstaging elite male citizens in the process. Such a dual-edged focus might seem like a contradiction, but in some sense these were two complementary movements. Through narrative early Christians were imaginatively inhabiting various spaces and places of empire. At the same time, new channels were opened for a host of individuals who were excluded from previous configurations of power relations. As Matthew Keufler has shown (*Manly Eunuch*), Christians gradually created a sexual revolution in the ancient world. By the time the later monastic communities arrive on the scene, the larger implications of earlier Christian counter-discourses on gender, sex, and sexuality were settling in. The dominant image of the Roman male was disappearing from the scene and being replaced by that of the ascetic, who controlled desire and eschewed sexual pleasure. The "true" male was one who was willing to die for God, or at the very least he was ready to reconceptualize social and sexual relations within a framework of physical control (for the love of God). The outward display of masculinity that was so common in the Roman imperial period (taking on dramatic proportions in the militaristic imagery) thus became internalized. The control of desire and the passions, and the winning of that battle, came to symbolize a new masculine ideal, one that women (and slaves) could also participate in, albeit in disguise, as "female men of God."[25]

Early Christian discourse on gender, sex, and sexuality thus served to develop a strong counter-cultural identity, which eventually became dominant in the Roman Empire by the time of Constantine (272–337 CE). These discursive moves also influenced the themes and images that early Christians employed. On the one hand, images of kingship appealing to the royal Psalms (Acts 2) are invoked to depict Jesus' regal manliness. He is a powerful Messianic figure, who both vanquishes death and reigns at God's right hand, not unlike the deified Augustus. On the other hand, Paul could use a female metaphor depicting himself as a mother to his community.[26] However, such gendered imagery could also be used negatively. Thus, manly (authoritative) women in "heretical" circles, such as Prisca and Maximilla, who were prominent Montanists, were often viewed (by "orthodox" writers) as a sign of larger moral decay in such groups. And yet, in the popular imagination, Thecla or Perpetua (the heroine of the *Martyrdom of Perpetua and Felicitas*) could in fact embody masculine aspects in positive ways—in a manner that reflected well on the "new birth" that Christians were enacting through baptism and that directly challenged Roman imperial claims on the body of its citizens. Here we may catch glimpses of the reuse of marginalized images as a means to offset typically dominant paradigms of masculinity. At the same time, one should also bear in mind that under colonial subjugation identities are fractured and contested, and the permeability we find in the tropes related to gender, sex, and sexuality may also, at least in part, be related to this phenomenon. Thus, some of the images related to the portrayal of Jesus in Gospels may well represent such fracturing of masculine identity, which cannot maintain a stable structure under the pressures of colonialism. Some of the instability and fluidity with respect to cultural representation may therefore reflect the crushing power of imperial control and authority. Herein, there is a complex level of interaction between Christians claiming and propagating powerful images of themselves in their texts and the unconscious effects of living under imperial domination. We thus observe the dual side of bodies in empire, where discipline and punishment of the body mapped and remapped social and political space. Bodies give meaning to space, but they are also in turn determined by spatial and temporal conceptions, categories, and acts. There is thus a multifaceted interrelationship between corporeal transgression of the boundaries of empire (real and imagined) and the punishing effect of empire on the body.

Social boundaries

As we noted earlier in this chapter, location plays a crucial role in the *Acts of Paul and Thecla*. At the beginning of the story, we find Paul addressing the people gathered in the house of Onesiphorus. A less sympathetic group of people is present when Thecla and Paul are brought before the tribunal. The theater where Thecla is to be killed forms an even more hostile environment, with a multitude coming out to watch the spectacle of her impending death. Space thus sets up the scene for social interaction, bringing with it certain expectations of roles to be played by the various characters in the narrative. Onesiphorus serves as host to Paul and the people in his house. The governor performs his role as judge at the tribunal and presides at the execution in the theater. Further, far from being neutral, space also evokes diverse cultural and social associations. For instance, after escaping her trial, Thecla goes searching for Paul and finds him praying and fasting in "a new tomb" (3.23). While, on the one hand, the tomb itself suggests death, its being "new" on the other implies that it has not yet been defiled by a dead body. With the sharing of a meal, life is resumed, and Paul and Thecla leave for Antioch together. In some respects, this scene parallels the meeting of Paul and Thecla in the prison cell earlier in the story. Thus, places of "death" turn into places of renewal and even (in the case of the jail scene) erotic interaction between Paul and Thecla.

We learn from these observations that space can function in at least two different ways: 1) particular spaces and locations evoke specific language, discourses, and images, related to that space/location[27]; and 2) they also provide opportunities for the reconfiguration of conventional discourses (related to those places), thereby infusing narratives with new meaning and function. When conceptualizing gender, sex, and sexuality in early Christianity, then, one must pay attention to how discourse relates to specific places (e.g., public versus private social spaces, city versus countryside, Eastern empire versus Western, Christian versus "pagan"), but also to how discourse may be (potentially at least) reconfigured in the process. The complexity lies precisely in the interrelationship between language and (narrative) social context, as well as in the possibility that early Christian writers transformed (the meaning of) spaces through discourse. An examination of gender, sex, and sexuality in early Christian discourses should therefore accent the social boundaries present in the ancient world. In the following section, we explore several facets that are important to bear in mind as one conceptualizes social boundaries in early Christian rhetoric.

As far as the role of space and location in early Christian discourses is concerned, it is noteworthy that none of the places mentioned in the *Acts of Paul and Thecla* have an explicitly religious meaning or function. Religion, in fact, plays a minimal role with respect to the spaces and locations that the main characters in the narrative inhabit. The picture that emerges from the canonical Acts of the Apostles is strikingly different. Here, too, Paul travels to Iconium, in this case together with Barnabas, but when they arrive they enter "into the Jewish synagogue and [speak] in such a way that a great number of both Jews and Greeks became believers" (Acts 14.1). As a result, tensions arise in the city and the apostles have to leave in order to save their lives. This depiction of Paul preaching the gospel in local synagogues reoccurs throughout Acts. The result is that he appears firmly rooted in Jewish worship and tradition. In marked contrast, there is no fixed Christian place of worship in Acts. Only a few times is a place where Christians meet mentioned at all. In Acts 12, for instance, Peter, who is miraculously released from prison, goes to the house of Mary "where many had gathered and were praying" (12.12), and, in 20.7–12, Paul joins a meeting to break bread, which takes place in an undefined upstairs room. Paul's letters are hardly more specific. On two occasions Paul greets a Jewish couple, Aquila and Prisca, whose house appears to be a meeting place for Christians (1 Cor. 16.19; Rom. 16.5); the same goes for Philemon, Apphia, Archippus (Phlm. 1), and Nympha (Col. 4.15), who likewise host such meetings. The picture that emerges from these few texts is that the space where early Christians met with each other was in the (upper class) house (which we find paralleled in the opening of the *Acts of Paul and Thecla*, where Paul is hosted in the house of Onesiphorus). This representation, however, relates to only a few places in Jerusalem, Asia Minor, Greece, and Rome. All too often here as well the canonical writings have dominated the imagination and led to a generalized perception of early Christian communities as basically house churches (a social space that conceptually stabilizes early Christian identity by spatially containing it), blending out in the process all the differences that may have existed between those communities. There probably was a greater variety of communities than are depicted in our sources, especially if one keeps in mind that people with different and multiple identities joined these communities, bringing with them a variety of religious and cultural backgrounds, as well as diverse conceptions of nationality, class, gender, and social space.

Alternative models of community formation may have existed in different places of empire, depending on the models available in a particular region or among a specific group of Christians. Traces of such diversity can already be glimpsed from our sources. Early Christians did not invent these models, but took them over from the social world in which they lived in order to organize their own communities. Some functions, such as "elder," may have been adapted from Jewish culture, others, such as "overseer," from Greco-Roman culture, still others, such as "teacher" or "leader" could be found in both. The primary function of these designations will also have depended on the location and composition of the Christian community in question. A Jewish Christian community in Judea likely would have been organized differently than a largely Gentile one in Asia Minor, because the people who joined the group brought their prior cultural knowledge and social practices, to that community which would have shaped the structure of the space in which it gathered. Thus, when people met in a synagogue, a house, or a "school," as for instance is the case in Ephesus (cf. Acts 19.9), this social organization brought with it a different set of expectations regarding the roles people could or should perform in that particular social setting.[28] Still, the boundaries between these diverse settings may have been less clear-cut than may seem at first glance. When one thinks about the relation of gender and sex with respect to social spaces, then, one has to bear in mind that there is no uniform social setting for early Christian communities, and that even within a particular space (such as the house) there are different expectations for the various "players" in that space (as a slave has a different role than, say, the master).

The domestic context provides a good point of departure for exploring further the various social complexities we are outlining in this section. Spatial organization creates boundaries for gender, sex, and sexual performances, but at the same time it also provides a context in which boundaries can be crossed or at least permeated in certain respects. The social lines will likely be blurred when a mixed group of people (in terms of gender, class, and ethnicity) meet in a house, and this may have resulted in the permeability of the dividing lines between them. Also, small meetings with a more private character may have grown over time and become more public as a result. Some texts in the Pauline letter corpus seem to reflect tensions that arose from such situations, followed by the concomitant concern to keep certain groups of people, notably women and slaves, in check. Precisely the domestic character of the house may have offered women and slaves possibilities that were not present in the public forum, which tended to be dominated by elite male citizens. Christian meetings, with both their (often combined) public and private character, may therefore have turned the house into an ambiguous space when it comes to the behavior expected of those involved and the role they could play within that context. The potential blending of Christian ideology (e.g., "in Christ there is no male and female") with cultural ideologies related to social space may therefore have led to boundaries being crossed or at the very least contested.[29]

A text such as 1 Corinthians 14.33b–35, is revealing in this respect, as it limits the speech of women present at the meeting of the community. 1 Timothy 2.8–15 goes even further in imposing not only a particular dress code aimed at more wealthy women who can afford to wear gold, pearls, and expensive clothing, but also in excluding women from positions in which they appear superior to men. Instead, the women are told to be submissive and referred back to their domestic role as child bearer, which is understood to be their road to salvation. A similar interest in keeping women, as well as children and slaves, in their designated subordinate place can be found in Colossians 3.18–4.1 and Ephesians 5.22–6.9. While these texts are clearly prescriptive, they may also reveal underlying tensions operative in the early Christian communities for which they were presumably intended. Scholars have expended significant energy attempting to reconcile a Pauline egalitarian community ethic with some of the more hierarchical statements found both in Paul and in the post-Pauline literature (e.g., the Pastoral Epistles). These tensions probably cannot be reconciled, however, and we require more nuanced models to appreciate the seeming contradictions we find in some of the early Christian texts. In the communities reflected in the Pauline letters, ideology frequently conflicts with the realities of the social and cultural contexts in which Christians in empire found themselves. People may have lived with these contradictions, possibly giving them less thought than modern scholars are inclined to do, as the latter are seeking to create consistency and coherence in early Christian thought when there may have been much less than we anticipate. These tensions become even more complicated when we add class differences to the mix. In 1 Corinthians 11.17–22, for instance, Paul refers to a scenario in which, when the community meets for the common meal, some go hungry and others partake excessively. This inequity might suggest that those members from the higher classes were indulging while slaves (and other lower class people) were in need or treated as "second" class members of the community.[30]

As the last example makes clear, social class was also intricately linked to shifts in gender expectations and performance. Perhaps this facet is most evident in the interrelation of class and gender performance with respect to higher class women, who could play a more public role than other women precisely because of their social status. In both the apocryphal and the canonical Acts, we find references to such women. In the *Acts of Paul and Thecla*, for example, Thecla is taken under the protection of a rich woman called queen Tryphena (3.27). In the canonical Acts, references are made to both wealthy women and female leaders of a household. In Acts 16.14–15, 40, a certain Lydia is mentioned, who is described as a dealer in purple cloth at Philippi and a leader of her own household. In this text, she is the one who offers hospitality to Paul. Elsewhere in Acts, women of high social standing are mentioned as Paul's opponents (13.50), converts (17.4; 17.12), or simply his audience (Bernice in Acts 25.13; 25.23; 26.30, and Drusilla in Acts 24.24). Shelly Matthews has drawn attention to this phenomenon in her book *First Converts* (2001), suggesting that the fact that these women are explicitly mentioned in Acts may reflect an interest on the part of Luke, its presumed writer, in gaining social prestige for the Christian movement through its association with elite women. This move is predicated on the public role of benefactors that wealthier women would play in Greco-Roman society of this time period. In this case, class can be seen to overrule gender and, as a result, the boundaries between domestic and public sphere are blurred. Claiming the support of these female benefactors is more specifically expected to raise the social and cultural acceptability and prestige of the Christian communities themselves. If such women also became members of the community, they may well have been expected to play as prominent a role within this community as they did without. A woman like Phoebe, for instance, who is mentioned in Romans 16, may have been in just such a situation. She is explicitly acknowledged by Paul as a benefactor and also called "deacon of the church in Cenchreae" (16.1).[31] Women who were leading a household may have had similar expectations placed on them, especially if meetings took place in their own homes. However, it is made clear in letters such as 1 Timothy and Titus that at least certain leadership roles were to be reserved for men (in some communities).[32] Such is the case for the function of "overseer" or "bishop" in

1 Timothy 3 (where the command that the "overseer" be "man of one woman" makes clear it is a male leadership role; also for deacons in 3.12 and for "presbyter" or "elder" in Titus 1.6). Still, again, we note that these conceptions may not have been ubiquitous across all early Christian communities, but may rather reflect localized concerns (and even customs).

We are obviously not trying to provide a comprehensive picture here of early Christian meeting places. Rather, we are detailing a few of the threads that are present in our texts. Our point is that space plays a significant if not formative role in how gender is configured in early Christian discourse. Spaces evoke specific behaviors and expectations, and they also provide contexts in which conventional language and images can be reconfigured and redeployed. Early Christians were not only part of their local communities, they also partook of broader social and economic associations within their cities and larger regions. Since language—and the performance that is evoked therein—intersects with the lived-realities of the people who made up these communities, we should pay careful attention to the ways in which spaces and locations map out how people conceptualized their own gendered and sexed performances. In reading the Acts of the Apostles, it is not difficult to see how, when in the public forum, the apostles and Paul consistently perform as ideal male citizens: they are consistently debating, speaking with authority and boldness, and persuading others to join the "new way." One might also note that the apostles' opponents and various other figures of authority do not ideally comport themselves in public. For instance, the trial of Stephen (Acts 6–7) ends in a chaotic scene in which the spectators lose control and kill Stephen in an act of mob violence. Here, Stephen is portrayed as the ideal public figure, including the offering of final words of mercy (in imitation of Jesus; cf. Luke 23.34) for his perpetrators, whereas his adversaries are shown to be quite the opposite in character, being unrighteous, lacking control, and evidencing injustice. In this contrast with Stephen, the mob is shown to be unmanly as they fall victim to their passions in comparison to the superior performance of masculinity and control offered by Stephen. Early Christian writers could thus manipulate the images, with an eye to what was ideal or expected in a specific location and space.

The examples just mentioned are drawn from narratives and thus it is easier to map ideal performances. These would be more convoluted and less ideal were they intertwined with actual lived realities. Making the latter even more complex was the varied nature of social spaces throughout the Roman Empire. Rome, as an imperial power (moving goods and people from the extremities of the empire to the center—Italy), played a significant role in creating images (artistic, cultic, social, and militaristic) that impressed upon the people in the conquered territories that Rome was their master. However, while Romans exported a specific image, it was contextualized differently throughout the empire.[33] Moreover, the rise of industry, labor, and trade in the Roman imperial period focalizes the city as the central space in which identity was both connected to a larger entity of "Romanness" and also to a more localized configuration of that larger imperial image, all channeled through local elites. Similarly, gender and social categories would also have differed throughout the empire, and in many ways would have been reconfigured in local contexts depending on a variety of factors that intersect with the social spheres of everything from individual domestic space to the public meeting places (such as the civic forum or the local temples) to the loci of regional governance and imperial presence.

In this context it might prove illustrative to rethink Tertullian's perspective on gender, which we delineated earlier in this chapter. We began the discussion with mention of Tertullian's negative stance on female participation in ministry. We noted, moreover, that Tertullian emphatically sought to heighten the "veiling" of women, keeping them modest and situated within the home. Modern feminist analysis has highlighted the patriarchal nature of his stance, but one could also understand his position as reflecting a Christian, North African appropriation of Roman values, since, beginning with the Augustan reforms, Roman imperial discourse focused on (re)establishing the household as the microcosm of empire. Thus, we may read Tertullian's thought on the necessity of proper (and demure) female comportment as being an attempt to domesticate Christian females by adopting Roman moral codes that had as one focus the relegation of females to the household. Or, it could instead be understood as the recovery of a regional North African identity over against a perceived out-of-control and luxurious Roman world, consumed by spectacle and illusion (just across the Mediterranean Sea). We could thus read Tertullian as accommodating or being resistant to Roman domination in this act of female subjugation. Such a reevaluation also allows us to see how gender and sex conceptions are played out between elite males in order to create alternative community identities. Granted, when we examine Tertullian from the perspective of modern feminist concerns, he looks quite different than if we position him over against Roman imperial aspirations. Also, the geographic and social space that we identify him as inhabiting vis-à-vis Rome/Roman imperial power brings with it a different way of interpreting his discourse as well.

When read in this way, it is clear that the social space of the domestic sphere is framed differently depending on the various interpretive factors taken into account. Tertullian's attempt to control the domestic sphere, reigning in the female body and bringing sexuality under control, surfaces throughout his work. When read against the story of Thecla, Tertullian's approach appears to represent a male dominated configuration of the household and church. At the same time, when Tertullian's position is evaluated over against that of the Roman *imperium*, and particularly within a North-African context that is seeking to establish a specific regional identity over against Roman culture, one can also see in Tertullian's control of social space something of a nationalist agenda. Social space can thus be viewed as a place of resistance as well as a locus of authoritative control. Our point here is not to suggest that one reading is more correct than another, but rather to note that how we read and interpret the function of social space as well as its intersection with Christian discourses depends a great deal on how we understand the social space in question in the first place. In this framework, then, given the many ways in which they can be read in their local urban and larger regional contexts, the gendered and sexed discourses of early Christians appear multi-interpretable.

One further aspect that bears consideration in terms of the complexity of early Christian social space is the role that language plays in shaping these spaces. This emphasis moves beyond the notion of spatial reconfiguration (as in the domestic household becoming a public place for Christian worship) or of change in social meaning shaped by differing kinds of comparison (as in the case of Tertullian). Here we shift our focus to the function that language itself performs in reshaping social relations and boundaries. For instance, Christians early on invoked kinship language for delineating the contours of their relationships to one another. This move no doubt played a formative role in the reconfiguration of the relationships within the Christian community, as well as the restructuring of space itself. For instance, when a slave, who is a social inferior, suddenly becomes a "brother" in the discursive framework of the community (or at least in a letter written to that community by its founder), then the social structure of the community is partially reframed as a result. This kinship language features most prominently in Paul's letters, as the recipients of his missives are frequently addressed as "brothers," on the one hand evoking the closeness of family relations, but on the other doing so within the boundaries of a firmly established patriarchal order. In this communal ordering, Paul situates himself in the paternal, disciplining role ("I became your father through the gospel"; 1 Cor. 4.15). He emerges as a father figure most prominently in 1–2 Timothy and Titus, where he addresses both Timothy and Titus as his "child[ren] in the faith" (see also 1 Cor. 4.17), giving them instructions regarding the organization of the Christian communities.

Thus, on the one hand, we see how Paul uses family language to position himself as "head" of the new kinship group, which invests him with authority and power, playing out an ideal type of manly comportment in the ancient world. On the other hand, one cannot overlook the powerful effect such language must have had on community formation and identity. One should also note, moreover, that the kinship and friendship language that early Christians invoked played itself out in community rituals, such as the Lord's supper. As communities enacted these and other rituals (some of which may have been relegated to specific regions) space itself begins to take on new meaning, as the discourse (here both through language and ritual enactment) stresses the change in traditional patterns of kinship, thus offering a realignment of collective identity with and loyalty to Christ. Moreover, ritual embodiment of this collective identity would serve to further strengthen the boundaries. In short, the new language of kinship ("brother," "father") brings with it a reorganization of social space, and in the process old boundaries are crossed while new ones take shape. In this way, we have to conceptualize existing social boundaries as permeable and malleable, open to reconfiguration and change. In the discursive perspective we develop in our gender-critical approach, language itself (rather than mere human action) has the power to reshape perceptions and promote (or prevent) boundary-crossing. Gender, sex, and sexual performances in early Christianity, then, are intricately linked to the language that inhabits a specific social space in early Christianity. Just as social space evokes gendered and sexed performances, so language also re-genders and reorients social space, consolidating as well as altering perceptions of and expectations relative to social relations and locales in early Christianity.

Our discussion in this section has only been illustrative of the larger interrelationship of space and language, focusing on how the two mutually interact. On the one hand, gendered and sexed language and performances are related to location and place—specific discourse and actions are anticipated relative to particular spaces in the ancient world. On the other, space itself is reconceptualized through the use of discourse and ritualistic action. When, for instance, the household space becomes a place for the invocation of the kingdom of God, then the household has shifted in meaning from a merely domestic sphere to the primary (as is often the case in the Gospels) locus for the in-breaking of God's new world order or kingdom. This kingdom discourse is just one example, but it demonstrates the power that language has in reshaping the social landscape of early Christians. With this shift come challenges to and changes in the gendered and sexed expectations of new adherents. One of the central themes across the diversity of earliest Christian literature is in fact the ways in which roles can be contested and potentially reversed. This element in turn creates a variety of responses in various communities (or alternative responses even within a single community). As space changes, people find themselves out of place, and this shift has both a potentially liberating effect but also a more liminal side, as we see early Christian leaders constantly trying to discipline community members towards moderation and appropriate conduct. As Foucault notes, "It has often been said that Christianity brought into being a code of ethics fundamentally different from that of the ancient world. Less emphasis is usually placed on the fact that it proposed and spread new power relations throughout the ancient world" ("Subject and Power," 131). Foucault defines this particular Christian manifestation as "pastoral power" (131–32). While "pastoral power" may only be one facet of early Christian power dynamics, it nonetheless aptly captures a major feature of the material we have been looking at in this chapter.

Beyond the role of the "pastor" and in line with the broader emphasis of this chapter, we might also note that, while social boundaries discipline individuals and communities in specific discourses and performances, at the same time they are acted upon too, changing as a result. Power is thus enacted and embodied in multiple ways, and, insofar as power is played out with respect to performance, both are constantly in flux. Looking at the data in this way we gain a better appreciation for the dynamic nature of early Christian discourse. It is not simply a matter of the discourse bearing a disciplining function, since it is also transformative, creating fluidity and permeability with respect to cultural and social conceptions (and their inherent boundaries).

Conclusion

In this chapter we set out to demonstrate how a gender-critical approach might help us to better understand early Christian discursive dynamics. Overall, we have argued that boundaries are a critical element in the formation of early Christian concepts and language. Moreover, we have suggested that these boundaries can be perceived to function in multiple ways in early

Christian discourse. We have sought to employ the critical feature of a gender-critical approach, that of deconstructing the binaries (of all sorts), to help us more fully appreciate both the boundaries of and in early Christian discourse, but also the permeability of the same. We have also argued that the body plays a central role in boundary-making and crossing. We suggested, for instance, that the canon of the New Testament functions like a body, which serves to discipline early Christian readers and communities, as it sets up a seemingly natural demarcation of insider and outsider status with respect to meaning-making. We delineated how social and cultural boundaries further determine space and place for men and women in early Christianity and how spaces and places in empire provide the larger framework that helps situate and configure the gendered, sexed, and sexual conceptions and discourses of early Christianity.

As Jonathan Z. Smith notes, "It is the relationship to the human body, and our experience of it, that orients us in space, that confers meaning to place. Human beings are not placed, they bring place into being" (*To Take Place*, 28). As this quote makes clear, the body (in and through discourse) is what gives space meaning, providing social and political significance and fostering ideologies and practices of identity formation. Mapping the body in its political, social, cultural, and canonical contexts, then, amounts to deciphering the meaning of these very categories themselves, as well as understanding the connotation the body acquires in relation to these diverse (yet interconnected) spheres. From the microcosm of the household to the macrocosm of the vast imperial territory, in multiple ways the body gives meaning to the world and to the language used to interpret, contest, and reconfigure that world, even as the body itself is unstable in terms of its meaning and function in this ancient context (despite all of the ancient and modern attempts to provide stabilized versions of these early Christian bodies). Still, the language of gender, sex, and sexuality in early Christianity proves formative for plotting out the conditions by which the Christian rhetorical logic could succeed in creating the context in which such language would make sense (and have appeal). Thus, attention to boundaries, real and imagined, and to bodies (human, literary, cultural, social, political) in relation to these boundaries, is critical for assessing and appreciating how early Christian discourses on gender, sex, and sexuality both arose from within broader Greco-Roman cultural and social spheres and diverged with respect to its (at times) distinctive argumentative aims and concomitant applications. Boundaries and borderlines there were for sure, and Christian discourses functioned simultaneously and in varying ways to keep those in place, while at the same time also providing impetus for the shifting of those lines alongside the crossing of them, all as a means of asserting the social and cultural power that would shape early Christian identity and help calibrate its influence in the ancient world.

Notes

1 We use the term "identity" throughout this chapter, and do so somewhat loosely. We understand the problematic nature of attributing modern identity notions to the ancient world. Even the term "identity" itself is essentially a contemporary concept. As Charles Taylor has recently pointed out in *A Secular Age* (Cambridge, MA: Harvard University Press, 2007), ancient people were embedded in broader clan, tribal, societal, and sacred structures in a way that modern individuals are not. In terms of this chapter, we understand "identity" to represent the manner in which ancient people defined themselves within embedded social and cultural structures and outwardly comported themselves in line with these identities. We are not thinking, however, of the specific individual inward identifications that modern people are likely to make. Rather, we conceptualize through this terminology an outward, public enterprise.

2 In this respect, "normative" versions of Christianity constructed the heretical "other" as a monstrous entity, with its own hideously distorted "canon" of literature. The physiognomic connections we delineated earlier in chapter two help frame this monstrous "other" through constructions of the body, which are represented from the perspective of the "normative" masculine center. Rosemarie Garland Thomson (*Extraordinary Bodies* [New York: Columbia University Press, 1997]) aptly sums up the physical construction of this difference: "focusing on cultural representations of disability reveals a politics of appearance in which some traits, configurations, and functions become the stigmata of a vividly embodied inferiority or deviance, while others fade into a neutral, disembodied, universalized norm" (135). As we explore throughout this chapter, the normative constructions of early Christian identity provided such a model, wherein the normative seemingly emerged "naturally" through the conceptualization and abjectification of an opposite.

3 Christopher Mount, *Pauline Christianity: Luke-Acts and the Legacy of Paul* (Novum Testamentum, Supplements 104; Leiden: Brill, 2002).

4 See particularly the thorough treatment in Harry Y. Gamble, *Books and Readers in the Early Church: A History of Early Christian Texts* (New Haven: Yale University Press, 1995).

5 For this imitation as evidenced in Acts, see Gary Gilbert, "Roman Propaganda and Christian Identity in the Worldview of Luke-Acts," in *Contextualizing Acts: Lukan Narrative and Greco-Roman Discourse* (ed. T. Penner and C. Vander Stichele; Society of Biblical Literature Symposium Series 20; Atlanta: Society of Biblical Literature and Leiden: Brill, 2003), 233–56; as well as Brent Allen, *The Imperial Cult and the Development of Church Order: Concepts and Images of Authority in Paganism and Early Christianity before the Age of Cyprian* (Vigiliae Christianae, Supplements 45; Leiden: Brill, 1999).

6 In her groundbreaking study, Elaine Pagels, *The Gnostic Gospels* (New York: Random House, 1979), makes this critical error regarding the Gnostic writings, constructing them as proto-feminist texts.

The discourse of these texts is rather phallogocentric, however, even as women and the feminine are configured differently in the material when compared with "orthodox" writings.

7 The famous work of James M. Robinson and Helmut Koester, *Trajectories through Early Christianity* (Philadelphia: Fortress Press, 1971), offers a good example of this phenomenon in contemporary scholarship. See further Todd Penner, "'In the Beginning': Post-Critical Reflections on Early Christian Textual Transmission and Modern Textual Transgression," *Perspectives in Religious Studies* 33 (2006): 415–34.

8 For an example, see Jonathan Z. Smith, "On the Origin of Origins," in his *Drudgery Divine: On the Comparison of Early Christianities and the Religions of Antiquity* (Chicago: University of Chicago Press, 1994), 1–35.

9 Such efforts have, for instance, been made in feminist commentaries, such as Elisabeth Schüssler Fiorenza (ed.), *Searching the Scriptures: A Feminist Commentary* (New York: Crossroad, 1994); and Luise Schottroff and Marie-Theres Wacker, eds, *Kompendium Feministische Bibelauslegung* (third edn; Gütersloh: Chr. Kaiser/Gütersloher Verlagshaus, 2007); as well as the Feminist Companion Series (Cleveland: Pilgrim Press).

10 See especially, Daniel Boyarin, *Border Lines: The Partition of Judaeo-Christianity* (Divinations; Philadelphia: University of Pennsylvania Press, 2004); as well as the contemporary example of the same phenomenon in Jonathan Z. Smith, "Close Encounters of Diverse Kinds," in his *Relating Religion: Essays in the Study of Religion* (Chicago: University of Chicago Press, 2004), 303–22, where he convincingly demonstrates that "discourses of the other" are essentially "discourses of the self."

11 See the excellent treatment of this theme in Jennifer Wright Knust, *Abandoned to Lust*. Also helpful is the study by Diana M. Swancutt, "Sexy Stoics and the Rereading of Romans 1.18–2.16," in *A Feminist Companion to Paul* (ed. by A.-J. Levine with M. Blickenstaff; Feminist Companion to the New Testament and Early Christian Literature 6; London: T&T Clark International and Cleveland: Pilgrim, 2004), 42–73.

12 We are oversimplifying the complex rhetoric on identification here. Denise Kimber Buell, in her book *Why This New Race: Ethnic Reasoning in Early Christianity* (New York: Columbia University Press, 2005), demonstrates with more complexity how someone like Justin uses the category of "race"/*genos* to describe early Christians. She notes that the distinction from the Jews (and heretics) is both fixed and fluid, and that each element is critical in terms of creating a useful rhetorical strategy (and consequent social space) for inclusion and exclusion. Also see Boyarin's *Border Lines* (n. 10 above). See most recently, Laura Nasrallah and Elisabeth Schüssler Fiorenza, eds, *Prejudice and Christian Beginnings: Investigating Race, Gender, and Ethnicity in Early Christianity* (Minneapolis: Fortress Press, 2009).

13 See now the especially rich work of Vernon K. Robbins, *The Invention of Christian Discourse* (Rhetoric of Religious Antiquity; Blandford Forum, UK: DEO Publishing, 2009).

14 We thus see a coalescence of sorts between modern scholarship and the early Christian literature itself, in terms of mapping out normative bodies and situating those over against deformed, mutilated, and abnormal/nonnormative bodies. As Rosemarie Garland Thomson has noted, "gender, ethnicity, sexuality, and disability are related products of the same social processes that shape bodies according to ideological structures." In this framework, she argues, "the disabled figure operates as a code for insufficiency, contingency, and abjection—for deviant particularity—thus

establishing the contours of a canonical body that garners the prerogatives and privileges of a supposedly stable, universalized normalcy" (*Extraordinary Bodies*, 136). As we noted earlier in note 2, heresy functioned as just such a "disability" in early Christian discourse. Similarly, culture also functions to enable a Christian normative body that is then defined against the deviance of the abject culture out of which the normative body arises or against which it is defined. Thus, critical readings of early Christian discourses must interrogate and challenge the subjects of normativity and privilege that are continuously being constructed and reconstructed in discourse, both ancient and modern.

15 Thus, modern scholars frequently construct lineages for sexual and gender ideas in early Christianity that operate from within the viewpoint of the texts, rather than at the intersection between text and culture. For instance, the following recent studies are illustrative of how different cultural contexts have been proposed for understanding specific issues in early Christian conceptions of sexuality. In *The Making of Fornication* (2003), Kathy Gaca affirms the role of the Septuagint (the Greek translation of the Hebrew Bible) in shaping early Christian ethics on sexuality and argues for a thoroughly Jewish Hellenized influence on early Christian self-understanding. William Loader, in his *The Septuagint, Sexuality, and the New Testament* (Grand Rapids: Eerdmans, 2004), makes a similar case. By contrast, Will Deming's recent study of Paul, *Paul on Marriage and Celibacy* (Society for New Testament Studies, Monograph Series 83; Cambridge: Cambridge University Press, 1995), uses the Stoic-Cynic debate on marriage to elucidate Paul's stance in 1 Corinthians 7. Bruce Winter, in his study *Roman Wives, Roman Widows* (Grand Rapids: Eerdmans, 2003), reads Paul's take on women in his community against the alleged outrageous behavior of "new women" in the Roman cities of the Greek East. In each case, the selection of the appropriate cultural and social background reflects modern scholarly ideologies, which are negotiated through the proffering of specific cultural and social backgrounds deemed to be best suited for interpreting these early Christian texts. These approaches, moreover, require postulating fixed cultural contexts and stable individual and corporate identities.

16 In terms of the cultural contexts that are posited by modern scholars for understanding early Christian phenomena, it should also be noted that Judaism in particular offers a cultural context that provides a buffer zone (and "clearing house") for the transmission of various cultural and social facets to Christianity. Because of the stigma of "paganism" in especially Protestant biblical scholarship, earlier scholars used Judaism as a way of protecting Christianity from the surrounding "pagan" environment. Greek and Roman religious ideas were thus seen to be mediated through Judaism to early Christianity. Christianity thus receives the traditions through this filter, while at the same time transcending Judaism in the process. In this way, the choosing of the cultural context for best understanding early Christian ideas and practices is *not* ideologically neutral. See the study by Smith, *Drudgery Divine* (note 8).

17 Especially useful for elucidating these dynamics is Douglas R. Edwards's study, *Religion and Power: Pagans, Jews, and Christians in the Greek East* (New York: Oxford University Press, 1996).

18 In a recent article, Laura Nasrallah ("Mapping the World: Justin, Tatian, Lucian, and the Second Sophistic," *Harvard Theological Review* 98 [2005]: 283–314) outlines the importance of placing early Christian writers (here Tatian and Justin in the second century) within the context of the

Second Sophistic. Nasrallah argues that early Christian writers were mentally mapping and discursively situating themselves with respect to major centers of military and cultural power, such as Rome and Athens. She goes on to show, by drawing the famous second-century satirist Lucian of Samosata into the discussion, that ancient writers in the Eastern part of the empire were seeking to define their place within imperial historical time and culture, as well as to negotiate their imagined places vis-à-vis alternatives inhabited by elite rivals. Also see Todd Penner and Caroline Vander Stichele, "Script(ur)ing Gender in Acts," in *Mapping Gender in Ancient Religious Discourses* (ed. T. Penner and C. Vander Stichele; Biblical Interpretation Series 84; Leiden: Brill, 2007), 231–66.

19 In the second century, for instance, we find a brilliant intellectual like Lucian of Samosata battling it out with Alexander of Abonoteichus in his *Alexander the False Prophet*. Alexander was giving Lucian a run for his reputation and respect (if not finances) in the region. From Lucian's urgent tone, it may well be that Alexander had been winning the support of Lucian's patrons. For Lucian, it was the spectacle of the words and charades of Alexander that he set out to expose for his readers. We thus catch a glimpse here of a wider phenomenon, of old(er) men like Lucian battling for their reputation and for classical Hellenic values and education over against newly minted power-brokers, itinerant philosophical sophists, and magicians who had risen to prominence (and certainly as rivals) in this period. See further Erik Gunderson, "Men of Learning: The Cult of *Paideia* in Lucian's *Alexander*," in Penner and Vander Stichele, *Mapping Gender in Ancient Religious Discourses*, 479–510. At the same time, it is important to note that, while new avenues to power were open to some happy few, the vast majority, including slaves and women, were still largely relegated to the margins. Economic capital was the easiest way for people to make relative advancement in this system. But there was also alternative capital—cultural and social gain—to be found in new religious movements (either by becoming an adherent or by taking on the role of benefactor and patron). Christianity gained a foothold in this respect. It also provided another avenue for those who could not easily accrue economic gain: to shift power from external authority to internal control. Thus, in the early Christian emphasis on mastering the passions and controlling the body, we find a significant alternative to the values of the Roman elite class (and the *Acts of Paul and Thecla* makes clear just how threatening that could be).

20 See especially Davina C. Lopez, "Before Your Very Eyes: Roman Imperial Ideology, Gender Constructs and Paul's Inter-Nationalism," in Penner and Vander Stichele, *Mapping Gender in Ancient Religious Discourses*, 115–62; and her *Apostle to the Conquered: Reimagining Paul's Mission* (Paul in Critical Contexts; Minneapolis: Fortress Press, 2008).

21 See Yung Suk Kim, *Christ's Body in Corinth: The Politics of a Metaphor* (Paul in Critical Contexts; Minneapolis: Fortress Press, 2008). Kim argues that only undertaking social and political readings of Paul's use of the metaphor "body of Christ" fails to probe his deeper theological and ethical thought regarding community formation. Our argument, however, is that all theological mappings are intricately connected to politics and society. Seyoon Kim, in his recent book, *Christ and Caesar: The Gospel and the Roman Empire in the Writings of Paul and Luke* (Grand Rapids: Eerdmans, 2008), goes one step further, seeking to disentangle Paul and Luke from empire altogether. His focus is on explicit parallels, whereas ours is rather on the principle that imperial power structures

are impossible to evade. Consequentially, there is *no* pure realm of thought in any historical context.

22 Kathy Ehrensperger (*Paul and the Dynamics of Power: Communication and Interaction in the Early Christ-Movement* [New Testament Library; London: Continuum, 2007]), for instance, concludes that Paul is not invested in the dominating, hierarchical power as evidenced elsewhere in the Greco-Roman world. For a more nuanced and complex analysis, see Joseph A. Marchal, *The Politics of Heaven: Women, Gender, and Empire in the Study of Paul* (Paul in Critical Contexts; Minneapolis: Fortress Press, 2008).

23 Another version of this argument is found in scholarship on colonialism in the ancient world, which frequently tries to show that Paul and other Christians were resistant to empire, perhaps through the use of "transcripts of resistance," which were the small, everyday ways in which imperial power was undermined by the colonized. See especially the work of Richard Horsley (e.g., his most recent edited collection, *In the Shadow of Empire: Reclaiming the Bible as a History of Faithful Resistance* [Louisville: Westminster John Knox, 2008]). Also see Mikeal Parsons's book on physiognomy and Luke-Acts, where he argues that the writer of Luke-Acts rejects the hierarchical bodily classifications of empire (*Body and Character in Luke and Acts: The Subversion of Physiognomy in Early Christianity* [Grand Rapids: Baker Academic, 2006]).

24 As Judith Perkins has argued, early Christians constructed subversive identities that both empowered the community and offered a means for developing a resistant subjectivity in the face of imperial power (*The Suffering Self: Pain and Narrative Representation in the Early Christian Era* [London: Routledge, 1995]). Virginia Burrus has likewise argued that early Christians developed a language for embracing shame, employing culturally abject tropes of identity as a form of empowerment (*Saving Shame: Martyrs, Saints, and Other Abject Subjects* [Divinations; Philadelphia: University of Pennsylvania Press, 2007]). Also see Judith Perkins, *Roman Imperial Identities in the Early Christian Era* (Routledge Monographs in Classical Studies; London: Routledge, 2008), where she pursues more thoroughly the contribution of resurrection tropes to shaping early Christian perceptions under domination.

25 See Gillian Cloke, *This Female Man of God: Women and Spiritual Power in the Patristic Age, AD 350–450* (London: Routledge, 1995); as well as Chris Frilingos, "Wearing It Well: Gender at Work in the Shadow of Empire," in Penner and Vander Stichele, *Mapping Gender in Ancient Religious Discourses*, 333–50.

26 On the latter, see Beverly Roberts Gaventa's new book, *Our Mother Saint Paul* (Louisville: Westminster John Knox, 2007).

27 It is important to note in this context that ancient writers were trained in constructing *appropriate* narrative settings and also character representation, both of which were to (ideally) avoid excess and dramatic emphasis in representation. Thus, in line with the rhetorical training of ancient writers, stress was placed on the suitable language that should be employed relative to particular contexts. A judge in a courtroom comports himself in a particular way given the judicial context and the fact that he himself is (presumably) an elite male citizen. Conversely, non-Greeks and non-Romans were similarly depicted in stereotypical ways, but often times with negative overtones.

In this way, the ancient educational system reinforced the spatial dimensions of context and character deemed appropriate to specific discourses (see further, Todd Penner, *In Praise of Christian Origins: Stephen and the Hellenists in Lukan Apologetic Historiography* [Emory Studies in Early Christianity 10; New York: T & T Clark International, 2004], chapter 3; and idem, "Reconfiguring the Rhetorical Study of Acts: Reflections on the Method in and Learning of a Progymnastic Poetics," *Perspectives in Religious Studies* 30 [2003]: 425–39). For further discussion of this theme, see chapter five of this book.

28 The social space of the (predominantly) male (guild) associations will have differed significantly from the household. See especially Richard S. Ascough, *Paul's Macedonian Associations: The Social Context of Philippians and 1 Thessalonians* (Wissenschaftliche Untersuchungen zum Neuen Testament 2.161; Tübingen: Mohr Siebeck, 2003), who argues that Paul's language in Philippians and 1 Thessalonians closely parallels the public (inscriptional) terminology found in voluntary associations in the ancient world, and that these, rather than synagogues, provide a better analogue for early Christian community formation. For a thorough focus on the household as the context for thinking about gender and sex (especially as these concepts relate to women) in early Christianity, see the detailed study by Carolyn Osiek and Margaret Y. MacDonald, with Janet H. Tulloch, *A Woman's Place: House Churches in Earliest Christianity* (Minneapolis: Fortress Press, 2006).

29 At the same time that Christian space was reconfiguring the gendered and sexed expectations of the household, Augustan social reforms were changing the nature of domestic private life, giving it a more explicit role in the formation and maintenance of the empire. Political discourse began to take on tropes and themes from the domestic sphere as well. Thus, there was a larger intersection of private and public in the Roman imperial period of the early first century CE, and it is perhaps not surprising that early Christians readily situated their discourses and practices within this Augustan shift (see Kristina Milnor, *Gender, Domesticity, and the Age of Augustus: Inventing Private Life* [Oxford Studies in Classical Literature and Gender Theory; New York: Oxford University Press, 2005]). Also see Mary Rose D'Angelo, "Gender and Geopolitics in the Work of Philo of Alexandria: Jewish Piety and Imperial Family Values," in Penner and Vander Stichele, *Mapping Gender in Ancient Religious Discourses*, 63–88.

30 See the analysis by Gerd Theissen, *The Social Setting of Pauline Christianity: Essays on Corinth* (trans. J. H. Schütz; Philadelphia: Fortress Press, 1982).

31 On this emphasis at the end of Romans, also see Eldon J. Epp, *Junia: The First Woman Apostle* (Minneapolis: Fortress Press, 2005).

32 This hierarchy is not present in all communities, as the Montanist movement attests, where the two female prophets had significant authority. See the important analysis by Christine Trevette, *Montanism: Gender, Authority and the New Prophecy* (Cambridge: Cambridge University Press, 1996).

33 Recent analysis of the spread of Roman culture in the ancient world has moved towards a model of "globalization" rather than strict "imperialism" (as the latter was understood in the nineteenth and early twentieth centuries). See especially the detailed analysis by Richard Hingley, *Globalizing Roman Culture: Unity, Diversity and Empire* (London: Routledge, 2005).

Bibliography

Ehrman, Bart. D., ed. and trans. *Apostolic Fathers*. 2 Vols. Loeb Classical Library. Cambridge, MA: Harvard University Press, 2003.

Eusebius. *The History of the Church*. Translated by G. A. Williamson. Rev. edn. New York: Penguin Books, 2004.

Foucault, Michel. *The History of Sexuality I: An Introduction*. New York: Vintage Books, 1978.

—"The Subject and Power." Pp. 126–44 in *The Essential Foucault: Selections from Essential Works of Foucault 1954–1984*. Edited by P. Rabinow and N. Rose. New York: The New Press, 2003.

Gaca, Kathy L. *The Making of Fornication: Eros, Ethics, and Political Reform in Greek Philosophy and Early Christianity*. Hellenistic Culture and Society 40. Berkeley: University of California Press, 2003.

Josephus. *Jewish Antiquities*. Translated by H. St. J. Thackery et al. 9 Vols. Loeb Classical Library. Cambridge, MA: Harvard University Press, 1930–65.

Keufler, Matthew. *The Manly Eunuch: Masculinity, Gender Ambiguity, and Christian Ideology in Late Antiquity*. The Chicago Series on Sexuality, History, and Society. Chicago: University of Chicago Press, 2001.

Knust, Jennifer Wright. *Abandoned to Lust: Sexual Slander and Ancient Christianity*. Gender, Theory, and Religion. New York: Columbia University Press, 2005.

Justin Martyr. *Selections from Justin Martyr's Dialogue with Trypho, the Jew*. Translated by R. P. C. Hanson. London: Lutterworth Press, 1963.

Matthews, Shelly. *First Converts: Rich Pagan Women and the Rhetoric of Mission in Early Judaism and Christianity*. Contraversions. Stanford: Stanford University Press, 2001.

Shewring, W. H. *The Passion of SS. Perpetua and Felicity*. London: Sheed & Ward, 1931.

Smith, Jonathan Z. *To Take Place: Toward Theory in Ritual*. Chicago Studies in the History of Judaism. Chicago: University of Chicago Press, 1992.

Tertullian. *The Ante-Nicene Fathers*. Edited by A. Roberts and J. Donaldson. 24 Volumes. Edinburgh: T & T Clark, 1866–72.

—*Tertullian's Homily on Baptism*. Text Edited with an Introduction, Translation, and Commentary by E. Evans. London: SPCK, 1964.

Gender and the Modern Interpreter

4

Chapter Outline

And Thecla was taken away from Tryphaena. She was stripped, received a loincloth, and was thrown into the arena. Lions and bears were set loose on her. A wild lioness ran forward and lay down at her feet. A crowd of women cried out loud. Then a bear ran to her, but the lioness ran toward it and ripped it apart. Next, a lion from Alexander, trained to fight human beings, ran toward her, but the lioness wrestled with the lion and they perished together. Then the women lamented even louder, since the lioness that had come to her rescue had died. And when other wild animals were released, the women screamed with horror and some threw herbs, others nard, still others cinnamon or amomum, so that there was plenty of perfume. And, as if they were hypnotised, none of the released animals touched her.

—*Acts of Paul and Thecla* 3.33, 35

Having been miraculously saved from the fire the first time around, Thecla is again sentenced to death and sent into the arena to fight with the wild beasts, all of this for having made a laughing-stock of Alexander, one of her potential suitors. This fascinating scene links up with issues related to sex and gender that have been raised in previous chapters. First, there is the aspect of female bonding between Thecla and the lioness who comes to her defense and kills a lion that belongs to Alexander. Second, the female spectators sympathize with her and come to her defense. This alliance based on sex is further played out on the level of gender, as the women use perfumes to overpower the wild beasts. They thus move from passive support to action, resorting to (stereo-) typically feminine strategies to conquer the enemy.

In looking at this interpretation, we are immediately aware that a concept such as "gender," which we are using for our analysis of the interaction between the characters in this text, has only developed relatively recently. In other words, the way we read this text (and interpret it) is connected to our *modern ways of conceiving and seeing*. Earlier interpreters could not read the text in this manner, because the tools for doing so did not yet exist. Thus, we start this chapter with the observation that our ways of reading are shaped by our own cultural and historical contexts, and that any interpretation of ancient texts must always bear in mind the contextual nature of all interpretation. Further, as we will show, interpretations are also shaped by particular biases and assumptions. For instance, the scholars we mentioned in the first chapter (Stevan L. Davies, Dennis R. MacDonald, Virginia Burrus) all aligned the *Acts of Paul and Thecla* with female communities, in part because of the apparent female focus in the text (e.g., the female lioness rescues Thecla, then women in the audience take her side, Thecla is shown to evidence strong male characteristics such as courage in the face of imminent death), but they did so largely based on a series of assumptions that were still taken for granted in the 1980s, in particular, dualistic notions of gender, sex, and sexuality (men versus women; male versus female; homosexual versus heterosexual). However, these perceptions have changed in the ensuing years, and with that shift has come differing assessments of the gendered and sexed relations in the *Acts of Paul and Thecla*.

Understanding these shifts in interpretation, and their interaction with the cultural and historical context of a given time period, are critical for appreciating the ideological nature of all reading practices. In the past three chapters we focused on the way gender is constructed in ancient texts; in this chapter we shift our focus from the object of interpretation to the interpreter, in order to explore more fully how reading and understanding gender, sex, and sexuality in ancient texts correlate with constitutive features of the formation of modern identity, including the important role that academic learning and disciplinary training have in shaping the modern reader. In part, this emphasis goes back to our discussion in the first chapter, where we detailed Foucault's importance for understanding the emergence of specific discourses and their attendant disciplinary practices. As Michael Clifford (in a play on the famous line by Simone de Beauvoir that "one is not born, but, rather, *becomes* a woman") aptly states, "the political subject is made, not born" (*Political Genealogy after Foucault*, 106). While academics tend to place significant emphasis on the *freedom* of the *individual* to act (here "interpret"), Clifford pointedly remarks that individuality rather is a way of disciplining the subject in a particular direction. Clifford goes on to discuss the surveillance system that makes the individual subject (so produced) complicit in the very tactics that shape their identity to begin with (108). While Clifford is thinking specifically of the emergence of the *political* subject, his observations hold true for the *gendered, sexed,* and *sexual* subject as well. For our purposes in this chapter, this approach would suggest that our conceptions of what constitutes gender, sex, and sexuality are also a product of modern disciplinary processes. In the first two chapters, we already discussed different approaches as well as theoretical positions that lead to a more nuanced understanding of gender, sex, and sexuality in the ancient world. We now turn to the other side of the equation: assessing how modern scholarship is both gendered/sexed as well as informed by particular interpretations of gender/sex/sexuality.

By way of introduction to the various issues raised above, we analyze the transformation of the reading of one particular interpreter—Virginia Burrus—with respect to Thecla's role in the narrative of the *Acts of Paul and Thecla*. Observing both the continuity and discontinuity in Burrus's treatment of Thecla in her work set 20 years apart allows us to examine more closely how scholarly discourse shifts and changes, how discourses not only shape the way in which ancient material is read but also how the scholar herself or himself can choose to construct their own identity as an interpreter, how institutions are intricately wedded to the way in which scholarship is played out (and the hearing it receives), and how specific fields of study perform an ongoing disciplining effect in the formation of scholarly paradigms.

Since Virginia Burrus has written several important pieces on the apocryphal Acts more generally and on the *Acts of Paul and Thecla* in particular (among which are her book of 1987 and a more recent publication in 2005), she provides an excellent example through which to assess how modern scholarship connects with gendered and sexed identities. Burrus's first work on the apocryphal Acts became something of a landmark in feminist interpretation, and offers a markedly different framework of engagement than her later publications. This shift between her earlier and later work is worth highlighting in terms of the production of knowledge in, and the disciplinary effects of, academic institutions and the scholarship that specific guilds and disciplines employ. The earlier work, Burrus's master's thesis, was entitled *Chastity as Autonomy*. Here she focused squarely on providing a framework for assessing and recovering the historical and social conditions of the virginal-ascetic female stories in the apocryphal Acts. She lays out her methodology in her 1986 essay of the same name (which was a distillation of the argument in her published book). Drawing on methods used in the study of folklore, she argues that the focus on chastity in the apocryphal acts should not be linked with the Greek novels (where similar chastity features occur), but rather with independent oral traditions that circulated in diverse forms in early Christianity. The comparison with folklore assumes that such stories "focus on subjects of real conflict in the societies in which they are told" ("Chastity as Autonomy," 111). Functionally separating the chastity stories from the novels allows Burrus to better account for 1) why the Christian chastity stories do not embrace the social order of the late antique city with its focus on marriage (as the novels do), and 2) how the chastity stories as oral tales reflect a socio-historical reality (which, if they were related to the fictional novels, might well not be the case). To dislodge the oft-assumed connection between the apocryphal acts and the novels thus opens up the possibility that the chastity stories in the Apocryphal Acts provide a "woman's point of view" (107).

Burrus's conclusion with respect to Thecla is that "every time she leaves the house she is crossing boundaries, intruding into the male world, and provoking disapproval, hostility, and suspicion" (110). For Burrus, the story of Thecla represents the viewpoints of real women who experienced tension within the patriarchal system of marriage. Moreover, for Burrus the role of the apostles in the chastity stories is rather marginal. They are present for social legitimation and for psychological reasons (in that they replace the love of a husband), but they are of little consequence in terms of the female identity established in the text. Particularly relevant for the interaction of Paul and Thecla is Burrus's observation that "the apostles remain on the sidelines of the woman's struggle, and their stay with the woman is temporary" (116). The spirit of her earlier essay is clearly feminist in orientation, insofar as Burrus seeks to recover the voices and communities of women behind these chastity stories, those who were empowered in and through their telling of them.[1] Moreover, the use of folklore for the categorization of the chastity stories helps to isolate this material in order to recover the "real world" behind the stories.

Burrus's approach is further illuminated in conversation with the response of Jean-Daniel Kaestli to her essay, which was published in the same volume. In his response, Kaestli raises two objections to her argument: 1) there appears to be no trace of any original oral framework in the chastity stories, and 2) one cannot use folklore approaches to analyze these stories. First, he suggests that the separation of the chastity stories from the larger Hellenistic novel tradition is unfounded, and therefore the appeal (in this instance) to conventions of interpretation based on folklore are not appropriate. Rather, he argues that the stories were likely *written* (perhaps by women) rather than told as *oral* narratives in female communities. This shift from orality to textuality undermines a basic premise in Burrus's argument, as Kaestli turns her focus on the populism of the female movement (which allegedly transmited the chastity stories) to one of class orientation (i.e., consisting of those upper class people who could write). As a result, some of the features of the chastity story can no longer be attributed to "real history" but should rather be viewed as literary motifs (adopted in his view from the novels). Kaestli also challenges Burrus's marginalization of the role of the apostles in these stories. He thus seeks to recover the prominence of not only the apostles, but also some of the other males in the narrative, those who convert to Christianity as a result of their wives' chastity ("Response," 130). He concludes with the following observation on Burrus's approach: "The opposition of a feminine world to a masculine world postulated by Burrus can lead to a selective and sometimes erroneous reading of the texts" (131).

In her response to Kaestli, Burrus highlights their differences regarding the literary and oral character of the stories, and acknowledges that if the stories were not oral in nature they are less likely to reflect a genuinely "female perspective," since, as literary documents, they would rather represent male perspectives (as males were most likely, in ancient culture, to be the writers of such texts). Most illuminating for our purpose at present is Burrus's final comment. In distinguishing her approach from Kaestli's, she states that "our distinctive perspectives as male and female scholars also affect our responses: Kaestli emphasizes the positive and important roles played by males in the chastity stories, while I cast males as villains or mere 'helpers' and identify females as heroines. Given our biases, how is it possible to attain an acceptable degree of 'scholarly objectivity' in interpreting these stories?" ("Response," 135). This citation from Burrus is intriguing not simply for her acknowledgment of the gendered bias of the interpreter, but even more so for illuminating Burrus's resolute focus on female subjectivity and agency in this story about Thecla. One can easily understand the position taken by Burrus, especially when it is contextualized in the feminist movement of the time.

Some 20 years later, in her article "Mimicking Virgins: Colonial Ambivalence and the Ancient Romance," Burrus takes a significantly different view on these same matters. In the ensuing time period, she not only developed a substantively divergent discourse and method of analysis, but her position shifted in essential ways as well. It is worth highlighting that shift in order to appreciate more fully the disciplining function (i.e., how, in this case, the configuration of the discipline and its guild shape and order the ways in which we see data and enforce that ordering) of method, theory, and academic structures in our modern ways of knowing and reading. Twenty years later, Burrus no longer relies on methods from folklore study to isolate the chastity stories in the apocryphal Acts. She is also no longer interested in separating a text like the *Acts of Paul and Thecla* from the Greek novelistic tradition. Relying on the postcolonial theory of Homi Bhabha, Burrus instead understands the *Acts of Paul and Thecla* to be closely aligned with the Greek novels, since she recognizes the latter as a "hybrid genre" that is a "quintessentially colonial literary product … at once disputing and colluding with the universalizing aspirations of empire" (50). Whereas earlier, Burrus stressed more clearly a binary opposition of the virginity stories to the patriarchalism of Roman society with its focus on marriage, her more recent approach appreciates the fluidity and instability inherent in texts, societies, and ideologies. Moving from what seemed to be a more strictly conventional feminist approach, Burrus now situates herself in the sphere of postmodern engagement, where the stability of the individual subject is contested. That said, she is still invested in a liberationist reading of the Thecla story (66), and so she avoids any purely deconstructionist interpretive strategy. Rather, in continuity with her earlier agenda, she aims to disrupt the dominant paradigm against which the Thecla narrative can be read and positioned.

By appreciating the chastity stories as instances of "colonial mimicry" (54), Burrus has moved away from the sociohistorical context of the story (as oral traditions passed among women) and shifted her attention to the function of the narrative within its sociocultural world. She understands the narrative to be a hybrid narrative that borrows themes from the larger culture (while excluding others), and the process it becomes a challenge to the colonial, hegemonic order. It mirrors the dominant order back to itself, but in a way that challenges the dominant ideology of the Roman imperial structures of family and society. One observes the traces here of Burrus's earlier themes and approach, but the final assessment moves away from her previous feminist conclusions. In this postcolonial approach, Burrus argues that the chastity stories of the apocryphal Acts disrupt the novelistic conventions of marriage and social structure. Social identity shifts as the female figure desires the apostle over her husband/betrothed (55). In this reconfigured interpretation, the shifts from Burrus's earlier study are fairly evident. She presents the story of Thecla as a challenge to the dominant order (now understood as imperialist rather than solely patriarchal). Further, while she continues to understand the narrative as different with respect to the larger literary environment, she no longer interprets the chastity stories within the folklore paradigm. She argues now that the novelistic tradition as a whole is a hybrid genre developing under colonial auspices while also challenging that same imperial order. In her earlier work, to the contrary, the novels were understood to represent the dominant perspective of society, which were juxtaposed to the apocryphal Acts. She has thus reclaimed the novelistic tradition for her own ends, which would mean that, on the one hand, she has conceded to Kaestli's argument (regarding the unlikelihood of separating the chastity stories from the novelistic tradition), but at the same time she has moved her agenda forward in spite of that shift. Also, her movement from "real" historical women to an emphasis on the function of the narrative itself represents a further acquiescence to the ambiguity of constructing historical communities for which we have very little information. Moreover, the complex theoretical framework of Homi Bhabha's work has shifted her into territory in which characters are not "either/or" but "both/and" in terms of the cultural and social values they embody. Her interest, then, is in deconstructing the binary, which, one might add, she tended to affirm in her initial response to Kaestli, where she noted that their perspectives were in larger part determined by their being "male" and "female." Within this newer paradigm, however, this binary gendered framework—both ancient and modern—collapses.

This disruption of the binary is also evidenced in Burrus's new focus on eros in the story of Thecla, especially with respect to the narrative's violence and asymmetry (64). In her analysis of how dominance and submission play out in the act of eros, Burrus highlights that there is no simple binary or symmetry of the two, but they are both constantly in flux and as a result there are "no stable orders of 'equality'" in the narrative (64). Thecla is both passive and resistant, while Paul, a notable apostolic figure, has a contested masculinity in the text, which is "markedly ambivalent." Paul, the "hero," "has become a pseudo-man . . . [and] a mimic-woman." Oddly, in this new framework Thecla becomes a "man" by enacting "resistant submission," which results in her becoming "unnaturally virile." Conversely, for the male in the text to achieve the same, he is now forced to "act like a woman" (64). The logic of this argument rests on the way in which the hybridity of Thecla's chastity story disrupts dominant cultural paradigms, unmaking men and making men out of women. The structure of the story itself accomplishes this effect, and it is done at an unconscious level. Because of the contradiction that lies in the notion of submissive resistance, the two forces of domination and submission interact together, and therefore destabilize a binary notion in which one is *either* dominant *or* submissive. For Burrus, then, the desire of eros brings with it this potentially liberative function in the text. Eros itself represents an unstable and asymmetrical entity that not only poses "a threat to the political order but also [forms] the threat that lies at the heart of that very order" (68). Thus, like her earlier treatment, where she understood the oral stories as subversions of the social and political order, here the forces of eros to which the chastity stories bear primary witness can also be used to challenge the universal order of empire. At the same time, there is no absolute fixed standpoint for the resistant subject in the narrative of Paul and Thecla, since, in the very act of resistance to empire, we can see the instability of the subjectivities of both characters. The narrative mimics the instability that both reflects the dominant order and subverts that same hegemonic order. It is in this way that the "either/or" option—the binary system of cultural and political power—is subverted.

The specifics of Burrus's arguments aside for the moment, we note that, in studies 20 years apart, there can be both dramatic differences in method and analysis but significant similarities as well. However, beyond the particularities of this example, this development also illustrates the disciplining function of and the ideological context for scholarship on early Christianity more generally. It is intriguing, for instance, that in Burrus's later study of 2005, she makes no reference to her earlier work on this same subject. In fact, one almost gets the impression that there is a conscious omission of that earlier period, a gap to be filled by this more sophisticated rhetorical and theoretical piece. Burrus's work 20 years later is indeed invested in a theoretical discourse that owes as much to the shifting nature of institutional contexts and of the field of early Christian studies as it does to the increasing use of theory-laden language, wherein particular academic discourses often carry social weight, acadamic authority, and enhancement of cultural status for the individual scholar who deploys that language. It is noteworthy in this respect that scholars on the *Acts of Paul and Thecla* still frequently appeal to Burrus's earlier work not in small part because it is more accessible and readable. While there is little ambiguity or confusion in that earlier discourse, using Bhabha's postcolonial theory, which draws on the psychoanalytic work of Jacques Lacan (1901–1981), moves one, on the contrary, into much more convoluted and ambiguous linguistic territory.

Developing from a graduate student to one of the leading scholars of late antique Christianity no doubt also played a formative role in the way that Burrus reconfigured her earlier work and thinking. Burrus's increasing institutionalization may well leave a mark on the later sophistication of her work, in both its rhetorical flourish and its ambiguity. In that same shift comes a renegotiation of power relationships, since as one becomes further institutionalized this entrenchment brings with it more complex (and potent) power positions for particular academics. Moreover, using the theory of Bhabha has a particular cultural cache for a group of more liberal (politically, socially, and culturally) scholars in American academic discourse. Not only is this postcolonial discourse in vogue, but it also shifts the location of Burrus's own intellectual context/audience to a field in which some of the most socially and culturally formidable academic players of the moment are located. Many scholars shift and change their positions, approaches, and views over the years, so there is nothing new per se in Burrus's own change. Rather, our point is that forms of scholarship are interrelated with academic institutions and alliances, and that guilds discipline scholarship in specific ways. Moreover, the shift in how gender functions between Burrus's early work (where it clearly had a more explicit feminist slant) to the later binary-challenging approach demonstrates that methods are integrally linked to how gender, sex, and sexuality in the ancient world are conceptualized (and how conceptions can change within the time span of one's scholarly career). But these conceptions themselves are products of the modern political order, and they are constructed in relationship to class, social status, economics, and so on.

The gender, sex, and sexual identities of interpreters are also closely connected with the modern conceptions in and by which they are disciplined. While the majority of scholars are trained to mask (mostly unconsciously) these facets in their scholarship, these identities nonetheless often play themselves out in interpretation. And even as they are hidden, they are also made manifest. In this respect, Burrus is connected with her work in more open ways than most scholars usually are, which is a refreshing feature of her work. In conclusion, then, no truly critical study of gender, sex, and sexuality in the ancient world can take place without paying careful attention to the way in which these categories play out in our own world. If we take the disciplining function of institutions and academic fields seriously, then they necessarily impact the way we think and speak about gender, sex, and sexuality, *and* how we construct ourselves (or are constructed) as gendered, sexed, and sexual interpreters. It is precisely this ideological aspect of modern interpretation (and its consequences) that we explore in the following pages.

Race, gender, and the formation of modern biblical scholarship

In chapter two we already noted the importance of modernity as the context in which gender, sex, and sexuality were reconceptualized. In this chapter we focus more squarely on how these new understandings also informed modern biblical scholarship. Gender, for instance, intersects with a host of social and cultural structures, and one cannot analyze gender in isolation from these broader configurations. Our discussion of Burrus's interpretation of Thecla shows, more generally, how we have inherited a "genealogy of interpretation" that impacts in critical ways our reconstructions of the past. Our readings of ancient texts are intricately linked to modern formations of thinking and being. As Burrus's changing interpretation further demonstrates, new theoretical models are developed and employed, and this advance also changes the way we understand, in this case, gender. Moreover, these models do not develop in isolation from our social, political, and cultural worlds, as we formulate new ways of seeing as a result of the shifting contexts in which we "see."

In the following discussion, our aim is to delineate some of the facets of modernity that we believe are critical for appreciating the complex intersections of our own ideologies with those of the past. Our point of departure here is Shawn Kelley's analysis in *Racializing Jesus* (2002), where he deals with racial biases in the rise of biblical scholarship. Modern views on both race and gender were developed largely coterminous with biblical scholarship in the same European context and, as we will show, multiple intersections can also be observed between the two.

The racializing of modern biblical scholarship

Kelley follows David Theo Goldberg (*Racist Culture*) in using the concept of "racialized discourse" to illustrate how, on the one hand, modern discourse helped shape the concept of race and how, on the other, that concept in turn racialized modern discourse. As Goldberg notes, the term "race" as such already existed before the Enlightenment and was used to refer to groups of   "stuff" plants, animals, and people that had natural and/or social features in common (62–63). However, the development of a *system* of racial classification only arose in the post-Enlightenment period, when classification became a critical component of methodology in the natural sciences. Human beings were now divided into species and subspecies on the basis of differences that were understood to be "natural," arising either through inheritance or environmental influences. Anatomy in particular became the most important lens through which to study differences, employing, for instance, craniometry (the measuring of the skull) as a way to register race and to determine dissimilarity. Far from being irrational, racial differentiation was based on rational argumentation, thus expressing its firm belief in reason as a modern, universal value. Biology, however, was not the only means by which to determine race. Another way was to define race in cultural terms. Thus, linguistic classification was used to categorize languages among different family groups, distinguishing between the perceived superior European linguistic groups, which had their roots in ancient Greek and Latin, and languages derived from Semitic or Asian roots that were considered inferior.

Around this same time, the social sciences, particularly anthropology, arrived on the scene, primarily using linguistic classification systems as a means by which to categorize cultures and peoples. Based on the model of language expanded upon by the German philosopher Johann Gottfried Herder (1744–1803), the common assumption was that all languages bore the essential characteristics—social, cultural, aesthetic—that were uniquely indicative of a particular people group. Thus, the scientific study of language, following the classification systems of the natural sciences, could readily be associated with anthropological models of analysis. The development of the museum in Europe, for instance, was directly related to the burgeoning European interest in displaying the results of such classification and analysis for public dissemination and consumption.[2] Differences between races were thus "explained" with the aid and authority of science, legitimating in the process a racial hierarchy with Europeans at the top, while also justifying colonial imperialist politics and practices such as the enslavement of people considered to be racially inferior. All of these developments followed closely the rise of European colonialism and the burgeoning post-Enlightenment movement towards the formation of nation-states and the creation of nationalistic identities.[3] Here one can see how modern colonial formations offered a binary structure that closely regulated the ways in which inclusion and exclusion—and access to power and institutional support—took shape.

The broader understanding of race in cultural terms also made it possible to define Jews as a separate racial group, even when they were living in Europe. In her book *Regulating Aversion* (2006), Wendy Brown documents how throughout the nineteenth century the incorporation of the Jews into the modern European nation/state required Jewish people to assimilate.[4] This process of assimilation went hand in hand with the redefinition of Jewishness in racial terms, one of the results being, however, that their difference became an ontological phenomenon, inscribed on the body, thereby forming a permanent identity marker. As a result, Jews were no longer considered a separate nation within the larger nation; rather, "the racialized Jew became highly individuated as well as physiologically, intellectually, and emotionally saturated by Jewishness" (54). Marked as different from the surrounding dominant cultures in which Jews lived, tolerance was seen as the appropriate response to their presence, but, as the history of European anti-Semitism makes clear, such tolerance could never be taken for granted. In effect, tolerance, on the flip side, was a mechanism for regulation and control, as it was *difference* that was to be tolerated. This focus on difference (even when it is a tolerated difference) rests on the notion that one can identify that difference—that it has distinguishing characteristics, that it can be separated out and classified. In short, even in the midst of toleration, the system upon which toleration rests demands that there be a regulation and a surveillance of differentiation.[5]

The formation of the discipline of modern biblical study is to be situated in this broader framework. According to Kelley, this discipline, which developed largely in the nineteenth and twentieth centuries, became increasingly racialized as a result of its larger social and cultural context. This development occurred first and foremost through the influence of major philosophical thinkers of the time, especially Georg Wilhelm Friedrich Hegel (1770–1831) and Martin Heidegger (1889–1976). Kelley documents the influence of, more specifically, Hegel's view of history on the work of Ferdinand Christian Baur (1792–1860), one of the "founding fathers" of modern biblical scholarship, as well as the impact that Heidegger's earlier work had on the famed New Testament critic Rudolf Bultmann (1884–1976) in the earlier part of the twentieth century.

As far as the impact of Hegel and Heidegger on biblical scholarship is concerned, a key element to highlight is the racial dichotomy between the West and the Orient, which reflects both the Orientalism of the West (the exotic otherization and consequent differentiation and marginalization of the non-Western part of the world) and the emerging anti-Judaism of that same time period. Hegel combined this dichotomy with the idea of a progressively unfolding history in which an Oriental stage preceded a Greco-Roman one that then ultimately culminated in the Prussian/Germanic/European stage, in which true freedom was finally and fully realized. Hegel notes that "from Oriental culture we have fine pictures of patriarchal conditions, paternalistic government, and devotion on the part of the peoples; from the Greeks and Romans we have descriptions of popular freedom, where the constitution admitted all citizens to participation in the deliberations and decisions concerning general affairs and laws" (*Introduction to the Philosophy of History*, 50). The result of this interpretation is that modern European representational government appears as the synthesis of these two systems. Even more important is that the principle of reason and rationality emerge in Hegel's framework as a distinguishing characteristic of the modern period. Freedom, subjectivity, and individuality are consequently woven together through universal Reason, which resides most palpably in the modern nation-state. In this way, class (particularly the Prussian elite), intellectual culture (situated in the modern university), the state (especially the institutions of government, law, and military), and masculinity (identified with the rational principle and universal reason, and embodied in the males who run the state and educational institutions) become key strands in the formation of modern identity.

In Hegel's framework, it is in and through history that the divine spirit manifests itself. As a result, history "makes sense" and is accessible to reason. Important to highlight in this context is the role of modern historical study, since the focus on rationality (and its androcentric character) is tied closely to the development of modern methods to interpret history and to study the past. The historical methodologies that developed in this time period thus presuppose a real objectivity, which one can only comprehend with the use of philosophy, because "without philosophy history remains eternally dead and silent" (Baur, *Symbolism and Mythology*, 1824, xi). This view reveals the Enlightenment values underlying the historical projects of this period: a firm belief in the critical faculty of human reason, which should have the freedom to investigate all products of the mind, including the Bible, without dogmatic presuppositions; and an equally strong commitment to the possibility that through reason one can discover universal truth in history. These values are part and parcel of the historical-critical method for the study of early Christian texts that was developing in this same period. In this approach, early Christian texts were to be read as historical documents and analyzed with the use of one's rational faculties, paralleling in the field of history the objectivity that was to be found in the sciences. Since "reason" in Western tradition became increasingly male gendered when perceived through the modern lens of a male-female dichotomy, this focus on reason as the scientific means to access objective truth thoroughly gendered and sexed both the method and the results of the historical projects linked to these evolving methodologies and their inherent assumptions.[6]

The historical methods provided one context in which gender sex, and sexual categories, alongside broader class, cultural, and also racial classifications, were shaped and given meaning. The development of these methods for the study of ancient texts was, moreover, intricately linked to other developments of the time. As Dipesh Chakrabarty argues, "so long as one operates within the discourse of 'history' produced at the institutional site of the university, it is not possible simply to walk out of the deep collusion between 'history' and the modernizing narrative(s) of citizenship, bourgeois public and private, and the nation-state" (*Provincializing Europe*, 41) One can see how these elements were played out through interpretations of early Christian history, including the employment of the gendered and sexed principle of rationality, since those not included within the boundaries of modern European nation-states in many respects were associated with irrationality (itself a trope—even if implied—of female identification). This dichotomy was adopted by Ferdinand Christian Baur and his academic heirs, who applied it to their reconstruction of the history of early Christianity. This move resulted in the translation of the distinction, and in many ways also the opposition, between the Orient and the West into one between Judaism/Jewish Christianity and Hellenistic Christianity. According to Baur, Christianity inherited its belief in one God and the expectation of a messiah from Judaism, but in spiritualizing and universalizing those ideas it superseded and purged its Jewish form. Thus, in his major work on Paul (1866–1867), Baur states that "through his death, Jesus, as the Messiah, had died to Judaism, had been removed beyond his national connexion with it, and placed in a freer, more universal, and purely spiritual sphere, where the absolute importance which Judaism had claimed till then was at once obliterated" (quoted by Kelley, *Racializing Jesus*, 77). According to Baur, the initial opposition between the particularity of Jewish Christianity and the universalism of Hellenistic Christianity ultimately gave way to a reconciliation between the two in the form of early Catholicism, which inherited its moderated universalist spirit from Hellenistic Christianity and its hierarchical form from Jewish Christianity. Baur's ideas were taken up by the Tübingen school of which Baur was the founder, thereby informing and even facilitating the development of biblical scholarship in Germany through his students. It was this version of historical-critical scholarship that formed the foundation of modern biblical study as a whole, as the methods of interpretation that developed therein were exported throughout the West.[7]

Baur's emphasis on Christianity as embodying the principle of freedom in history went hand in hand with his focus on the "great men" and "traditions" of early Christianity.[8] This focus is hardly surprising, since the scholars studying early Christianity were themselves elite males, tied to cultural centers of learning. As such, they took an interest in Hegel's "world-historical individuals," those men who had accomplished great acts relative to the unfolding of the Spirit in history. As a result, the modern cultural structures ensured that the principles of the modern nation-state—including class, gender, and race—were reinscribed on the study of the past (not least in part because antiquity was understood to represent a critical stage in the development of the modern world). Baur also applied the idea of evolution through successive stages to the history of Christianity itself, where the particularity of Jewish Christianity was superceded by the universalism of Hellenistic Christianity. Both factions were represented by male protagonists, the apostles of Jerusalem and especially Peter in the first case, and Paul together with Apollos in the second. Thus, the history of Christianity was identified with struggles that were fought in the public forum. Taken together with the emergent gender, sex, and sexual binary, in which the public sphere is male gendered and sexed, this system of interpretation implied a further identification of Christianity with the actions of its male leaders as well as the rationalization of its patriarchal history.

As already noted, Kelley stresses that another major influence of philosophical thinking on biblical scholarship was mediated through the work of Martin Heidegger, who impacted biblical analysis mostly through his earlier work *Being and Time* (*Sein und Zeit*). Heidegger's aim was to analyze existence within the framework of authentic versus inauthentic ways of being. In his view, inauthentic existence is an alienated form of being, in which one is absorbed into the presence of other humans, the public, or "the They" (*das Man*). As such, this form of being represents a static, fallen condition. Authenticity, to the contrary, is a dynamic and future oriented way of being. It is a primordial, lived experience, the condition in which one is truly oneself, an existential condition that expresses one's true humanity. Heidegger maps out these two forms of being in time, insofar as a state of inauthenticity both precedes and follows authenticity, in the latter case as a moment of deterioration, a fall from authenticity.

The racialized nature of these categories becomes clear in Heidegger's appreciation of the Greeks as the forerunners and racial ancestors of the German people. In his view, the Greeks represented an authentic form of existence, while the Romans are understood as the beginning of decline, a falling back toward inauthenticity. This decline ultimately results in the crisis of modernity, but is followed by a Greek revival in modern Germany. The underlying model of Western history that thus comes to the fore is one of origin, fall, crisis, and revival. Precisely this reading is taken up by Rudolf Bultmann in his reconstruction of the origins of Christianity. He merges more specifically Heidegger's formulation with Baur's periodization of early Christian history into Jewish Christianity, Hellenistic Christianity, and early Catholicism. The resultant picture is one in which Jewish Christianity, with its presumed Jewish legalism, represents a state of inauthenticity over against Hellenistic Christianity, which appears as the authentic locus of true, Christian freedom. The Pauline letters, with their emphasis on individual freedom, are thus to be understood as expressions of authentic existence,[9] while the Gospel of Luke and the Acts of the Apostles represent, in Bultmann's assessment, the early Catholic spirit of accommodation, which mediated between Jewish and Hellenistic Christianities, thereby producing a synthesis of the two.

As Kelley further points out, Baur's and Bultmann's reconstruction of the history of early Christianity is Eurocentric as well as racialized and androcentric. In both cases, Judaism is equated with inauthentic legalism over against authentic Christian freedom, with the former representing the Orient and the latter the West. This view reflects the modern perception of "the Jew" as an altogether different race, rather than a religion or nation. Generally, we note that the origin of modern biblical scholarship was preoccupied with classification and categorization, seeking to interpret the past meaningfully through binary oppositions. However, in the process, prejudices of the present were projected onto the past, and, in turn, the past came to reflect palpably the biases of modernity. Thus, the past came to look surprisingly like the present. This accent was also the case in terms of the themes that were highlighted for study and reflection, as the elite male culture of Europe naturally focused on those subjects from the past that supported the principles of freedom and reason, projecting onto history a male principle of rationality, with an implied denigration of literature and traditions that seemed to work against this stream of thought. Finally, in line with the theme of this chapter, it is worth emphasizing here the critical function that context played in shaping interpretation in the origins of modern biblical scholarship. The study of early Christianity, especially the methods and the assumptions employed for analysis, bolstered the racialized and gendered/sexed discourses of the eighteenth and nineteenth centuries. It was these facets of historical study that generated many of the assured results that in turn shaped the way that gender, sex, and sexuality would play out in modern interpretation.

The gendering of modern biblical scholarship

As we show in what follows, structural parallels can be noted between the construction of race and gender in the modern period and the way these concepts intersect with each other. One parallel relates to the importance of the body, especially anatomy, for the classification of race and gender. This classification is further reflected in scientific language, producing a conceptual hierarchy between races and sexes. Another parallel relates to the role philosophy played in how these changes made their way into biblical scholarship in that time period and later. This intersection is particularly important for understanding the historical and cultural context of the discipline of biblical studies, including an appreciation for the ideological nature of its traditional historical methods.

We begin with an observation by Thomas Laqueur, who notes, in his book *Making Sex* (1990), that the same mechanisms at work in the construction of race during the modern period reemerge in the construction of two hierarchically ordered, oppositional sexes. This development took place, at least in part, in response to a shift in the perception of the body insofar as it functions as a source of knowledge. Instrumental for this change in perception was the philosophical work of René Descartes (1596–1650), who advocated the idea of a radical separation between the body and the mind. Since he understood the mind to be sexless, the only material basis left to explain, and also to justify, the differences between the sexes had to be located in the body, which thus came to provide the new biological basis for the social order, replacing the older conception that this order originated with God's will. As a result, nature replaced creation as an authoritative source for grounding gender, sex, and sexuality.

At the same time, a new set of technical terms was introduced in order to distinguish the female sexual organs from the male. This intervention provided a linguistic framework for delineating the difference between two, irreducible sexes. The word "vagina," for instance, only made its entry into the English language in the early part of the eighteenth century as a name for the female organ that parallels the male penis. Here language both reflects and causes shifts in perception, triggered by changes taking place in society at large. Moreover, medical experts also became interested in reexamining the "in-between" sexual category of the hermaphrodite, attempting to define this "fluid" state out of existence. In her study *Hermaphrodites and the Medical Invention of Sex* (2000), Alice Domurat Dreger uses diverse historical documents to illustrate the way in which the discovery of and scientific investigation into hermaphroditic individuals (particularly in France and England) gave rise to discourses related to sex differentiation. Dreger suggests that from the eighteenth through nineteenth centuries a shift occurred in the conception of what constituted a "true hermaphrodite." At first, there was scientific appreciation of and fascination with this "in-between" sex category, but, when matters of social control became more tightly wedded to definitions of sex differentiation, the difference between "male" and "female" became crucial, being based now on the presence of gonads, which was thought to offer a stabilized form of sex distinction. While this is just one instance, it is noteworthy that such conversations were taking place precisely at a time when society was changing rapidly in other spheres as well.

One of these changes, coming in the wake of the Enlightenment and the French Revolution, was related to the roles men and women were understood to play in the public sphere. In the development of the modern world, the *nuclear* family becomes a critical social unit for the maintenance of broader economic and social boundaries and hierarchies. In *The Origin of the Family, Private Property and the State* (1973), Friedrich Engels (1820–1895) understands the family to be the basic economic unit of capitalist societies, which rested on the "supremacy of man" (125). For both sexual reproduction and for the control of private property, marriage and family are quintessential. Using a Marxist economic classification, Engels argues that "within the family [the husband] is the bourgeois and the wife represents the proletariat ... The modern family is founded in the open and concealed domestic slavery of the wife" (137).[10] Gender and sex distinctions become all the more crucial, then, as the modern family structure was further wedded to the rise of industrial capitalism, with the family providing an essential role in the social and cultural configuration of the politics and economics of this new mode of existence. In other words, the ability to differentiate the sexes became pivotal in a new way, as the sphere of the home and domestic space was linked to industrial development. Moreover, the notion of two oppositional but complementary sexes also provided a firm basis for heterosexuality as an essential social norm.

These varied developments also gave rise to a coalescence of discourses related to distinctions between the sexes, which were then reified in the scientific lab. In other words, the evolution of the scientific method went hand in hand with the development of language related to sex differentiation, the former providing that language with an objective, universal, and normative standing.[11] As the preceding discussion regarding the racialized and gendered nature of modern discourse makes clear, both race and gender become increasingly inscribed on the body as a source of knowledge about the self in response to developments in society at large. Moreover, where racial and gender hierarchies intersect, they also appear to reinforce each other. Such is the case, for instance, in *The Descent of Man and Selection in Relation to Sex* (1871), where Charles Darwin (1809–1882) cites scientist Carl Vogt (1817–1895), the latter of whom pointedly states that "The difference between the sexes as regards the cranial cavity increases with the development of the race, so that the European male excels much more the female, than the negro the negress" (quote from Laqueur, *Making Sex*, 208). Not only is the hierarchy between men and women thus universalized, it is also racialized. The higher up the ladder the race, the greater the difference between men and women becomes. In both cases, a turn to biology can be seen to ground the differences in question, with the European male appearing as a point of reference for both.

These changes taking place in the perception of gender and sex also had an impact on biblical scholarship. As in the case of race, philosophical discourse played a role here too. In her book *The Man of Reason: "Male" and "Female" in Western Philosophy* (1984), Genevieve Lloyd shows that, before modernity, women were considered inferior or deficient compared to men, who set the standard for rationality. However, once men and women were understood to be complementary, rationality was increasingly identified as male gendered and sexed. She cites Jean–Jacques Rousseau (1712–1778) to illustrate this point: "The search for abstract and speculative truths, for principles and axioms in science, for all that tends to wide generalisation is beyond a woman's grasp" (quote from *Emile*, V, 349 in Lloyd, *Man of Reason*, 75). Again, it can be noted that modern discourse on gender, sex, and sexuality, notwithstanding its claims to universality, is thoroughly gendered and sexed.

We can bring in Hegel again to further elucidate this intellectual and cultural environment. Alongside the focus on reason highlighted earlier, another idea that Hegel developed in his *Phenomenology of Spirit* (1807) is relevant in this respect: the antithesis of the two sexes with a focus on the Family as constituting the realm of female consciousness. As Lloyd points out, Hegel identified the family as the "nether world," the inner realm of unconscious Spirit where women belong (*Man of Reason*, 83). However, it is in the man's realm, that of public life, that the unfolding of conscious Spirit takes place, and woman can only participate in that sphere through man. Her existence is determined by the Family, while his existence aims at the truly universal experience. Gender, sex, and sexuality are thus caught up in a web of correlative but still opposite realities, of public and private, universal and particular, reason and intuition, the outer and the inner world, culture and nature; the first of each pairing being associated with man, the second with woman. As males thus became identified with the universal principle, women were consequently wed to the particular in history (as Jews were in racial terms). One can easily observe herein how it was possible to extend these gendered and sexed associations to whole groups of people—those more closely tied to the particular were more female than those more thoroughly identified with the universal principle.

It is useful at this juncture to examine the feminist movement that developed alongside (and responded to) the androcentric system we have been outlining thus far. Two different positions were taken in the counter-discourse that emerged. One was to reverse the hierarchy in claiming that women are in fact superior to men, the other to advocate for the equality of the sexes. The contrary claim, that because of their biological predisposition women are in fact superior to men, was, Laqueur notes, the position taken by physician and women's rights activist Elizabeth Blackwell (1821–1910). In her view, women take the higher moral ground. She also believed that civilized people are more chaste than primitive or working class people, a statement that reflects both her cultural and class biases. That women's rights advocates did not escape reproducing other forms of prejudice is also illustrated by the fact that, at the end of the nineteenth century, the American women's rights movement advocated for the abolition of slavery, but did not support equal rights for black people. This apparent dichotomy was not just an issue of race, but even more so of class.

More widespread than the view that women are superior was the claim that they are equal. According to Wendy Brown (*Regulating Aversion*), the women's emancipation movement in the eighteenth and nineteenth centuries followed Descartes in making a distinction between body and mind, in order to argue that sexual difference related first and foremost to the body, not to the mind. As far as their mental capacities were concerned, women were considered to be equal to men—difference was grounded only in their bodily form. Thus, in *A Vindication of the Rights of Woman* (1792), Mary Wollstonecraft (1759–1797) offered a strong plea in favor of the education of women, repudiating the view of Rousseau, who argued in his work on education, *Emile* (1762), that the sexuality of women determined every aspect of their being and that their appropriate place was in the domestic sphere.[12] The gender, sex, and sexual binary could thus also be used for female advancement even in a largely androcentric environment. Although feminists such as Wollstonecraft appealed to the universality of the mind shared by men and women, "mind" and "rationality" were essentially male gendered phenomena, and thus, even as women could claim "mind," they did so largely on male terms.

As becomes clear from the preceding observations, the women's movement was confidently rooted in modernist thinking, in terms of sharing the latter's optimism, idealism, and universalism. Its optimism was reflected in the belief that social structures could be changed, its idealism in the affirmation that a better future for women was possible, and its universalism in its appeal to women's experience as a universal category. Moreover, woman's experience was used more specifically as a source of authority to challenge traditional (usually male) views and institutions. This movement was also ideology-critical in unmasking and rejecting social structures as patriarchal, androcentric, and sexist. Women were considered to be oppressed by these structures and therefore in need of liberation. This view, however, was heavily predicated on an essentialist understanding of womanhood and its collective situation of oppression, an understanding that has rightly been criticized by women of color as being ethnocentric and imperialist, universalizing the experience of white, Western, and often also wealthy women. Thus bell hooks notes in her book *Ain't I A Woman?* (1981), "The first white women's rights advocates were never seeking social equality for women; they were seeking social equality for white women" (124).[13]

This particular premise regarding the women's movement is aptly illustrated with Elisabeth Cady Stanton (1815–1902), who was one of the more reknowned early feminist interpreters of the Bible and the one who initiated *The Woman's Bible* project (1895–1898), a compilation of biblical texts and comments by women. As most of the commentators in this volume came from a socially privileged background, their observations, while focusing on gender issues and advocating equality for women, often ended up reproducing racist and classist discourses in the process. Moreover, *The Woman's Bible* also reflected the interests of especially Christian women, and, as such, also reproduced current anti-Jewish stereotypes in its evaluation of biblical statements regarding women. For instance, in her comments on the creation stories in Genesis 1.1–2.4a and 2.4b–3.24, Lillie Devereux Blake remarks that in her opinion "the second story was manipulated by some Jew, in an endeavor to give 'heavenly authority' for requiring a woman to obey the man she married" (*Woman's Bible*, 18). Thus, Christian feminists, in an effort to reclaim their own tradition and raise their status vis-à-vis males, tended to create an opposition, on the one hand, between the Hebrew Bible/Old Testament and Jewish traditions (such as rabbinic sources), and, on the other, between the Old Testament and the New.

As Judith Plaskow points out, compared with earlier forms of anti-Judaism, this proto-feminist standpoint resulted "in a new antithesis: Judaism equals sexism, while Christianity equals feminism" ("Anti-Judaism in Feminist Christian Interpretation," 119). This perspective is most apparent in the assessment of Jesus as a feminist, and also in the evaluation of Paul as being divided between his Jewish background and his new Christian identity. This distinction makes it possible to attribute negative statements about women in Paul's letters (cf. 1 Cor. 14.34) to Jewish influence, while more positive statements (cf. Gal. 3.28) are understood to reflect his new perspective in Christ. Thus, for instance, in her discussion of Paul's comments on women, Constance Parvey notes that "on the theological level, by envisioning the new interdependence of men and women in Christ, Paul makes a fundamental breakthrough in new images for women, but on the cultural, social level, he clearly identifies himself as a first-century Jewish teacher for whom arguments from custom have authority and validity of their own" (*Religion and Sexism*, 128).[14] In these instances, Judaism is used as a foil against which both Jesus and Paul appear as enlightened figures.[15] As a result, the dichotomy established between the particularity of Judaism and the universalism of Christianity, which we noted earlier with Baur, is reproduced here in a different form. Thus, female scholars, seeking to overturn the patriarchal perspective (and authority) of their male peers, were subject to and limited by their own ideological contexts. Some of these were held in common with the males of their time, others were uniquely related to the emergent feminist argument of the period, where class values were still held to be sacrosanct or at the very least they went unquestioned. In some respects, what we see emerging in the formative period of biblical scholarship, then, parallels the phenomena we outlined in chapter three, where we noted that men and women, slaves and freemen, were carving out their identity with respect to their proximate others, often creating an abjectified other by which they could differentiate their own higher status.

Of course, it is always much easier to identify the abjectified entity in another system's configuration than our own. Still, it is helpful to assess this phenomenon not least because it allows us to reflect more fully on our own interpretive situation. We do not want to suggest that somehow scholars in the twenty-first century are more enlightened and no longer dogged by such prejudices. In fact, we think quite the opposite is the case: our own era is every bit as biased in its operative historical methodological assumptions as this earlier period. The nature of the assumptions and values may have shifted or changed (or not), but the contextual character of our scholarship itself, relative to our own time and place, has definitely not. In the end, we cannot escape the cultural and social assemblages of meaning in which we are situated and that shape our values and viewpoints.[16] Even the recent advances with respect to re-envisioning gender, sex, and sexuality in antiquity, which we outlined in chapter two, are in large measure the reflection of changes in our current conceptions, now read—once again—onto the past. We are not promoting a nihilistic view of interpretation here, but one in which the interpreter is fully aware of the contextualized nature of knowledge, a situation that can never be fully perceived or grasped by the individual located within the larger system of meaning.

Finally, if we take our own context seriously as a source for the formation and development of the study of early Christianity, we can readily appreciate the ways in which the methods themselves, along with their embedded assumptions and values, produced a particular kind of knowledge, discipline, and guild related to the interpretation of early Christianity. In many respects, this legacy of biblical interpretation (institutionally, methodologically, and ideologically) is still a phenomenon with which modern scholars must contend. It is also the legacy that a gender-critical approach to early Christianity, such as the one we are developing in this book, seeks to engage, since the way we "see" the material of early Christianity in many respects continues to be enmeshed in the genealogy of the discipline. Thus, the older models of interpretation explored earlier continue to shape the ideologies of interpreters, even as we may not be aware of the presence and influence of past paradigms. Our analysis above, as it relates to both male and female interpreters, suggests that much of former scholarship was effectively reading modern identities (and concomitant agendas) into the past, all of which were connected with gender, sex, and sexual identities (at the intersection of class and race) in the present. So far we have focused on how these components of life in the eighteenth and nineteenth centuries influenced, often unconsciously, the kinds of prejudices and biases interpreters held, as well as the ways in which modern interpreters went about formulating methodologies for historical study that reflected the same perspectives. In the next section, we explore this facet further, moving from the formative period of biblical scholarship to our own, examining the way in which the power of the discipline of the earlier period is still very much alive in our current time, even if in a different guise.

Gender and power in the discipline of biblical studies

In what follows, we explore themes that arise from the various issues set forth in the previous section, only now, instead of looking at the formative period for Biblical Studies, we examine more closely the role that gender, sex, and sexuality play on the contemporary scene, related specifically to the guild, discipline, and institutional locations of scholars in the field. On the one hand, we want to elucidate from an ideology-critical perspective the social production of knowledge in the guild. On the other, we are also interested in the knowledge itself so produced, particularly the effect it has in shaping biblical scholarship. Here, gender criticism can explore how gender, sex, and sexuality inform not only the rhetoric and ethic of but also practices of self-legitimation within Biblical Studies, including elucidating the boundaries that are likely to be crossed and the ones that are not, as the guild plays an important self-regulating role in maintaining its power structures.

We begin this discussion by examining more closely an essay written by Averil Cameron, a well-known scholar of late antiquity. In her "Sacred and Profane Love: Thoughts on Byzantine Gender," Cameron assesses the "male" character of Byzantine discursive constructions of love and gender and what effect such discourses would have had on society, especially on the women in that context. In the midst of presenting this research agenda, Cameron poses a rather unexpected question: "In this connection, it is worth considering our own subjectivity as scholars and writers" (3). She continues by quoting from philosopher, linguist, and psychoanalyst Luce Irigaray (1932–): "there are centuries of sociocultural values to be rethought, to be transformed. And that includes within oneself" (3, quote from Irigaray, *Je, Tu, Nous*). Cameron then turns to an analysis of her relationship to the guild, particularly in terms of how her own subjectivity was shaped by the prevailing standards operative in her earlier years as an academic. She queries, for instance, why it took her so long to become aware of the "women's movement," which was quite active when she began her career as a scholar. Indeed, in a series of rather revealing claims, Cameron notes that the affirmation that "female scholars" are *just scholars*, devoid of gendered, sexed, and sexual identities, is precisely the "internalization of the surrounding (male) cultural values" (4). Drawing on a comment from Anaïs Nin (1903–1977), who was (in)famous for her erotic writings, Cameron underscores the often problematic nature of female embodiment in society when it does not meet the expectations of societal and cultural norms: "no one has ever loved an adventurous woman as they have loved adventurous men" (5). By using Nin in this way, both as a trope connecting Cameron (even if at a distance) to the embodied self and as a *prima facie* example of how gender and sex, understood from a "female" point of view, have a noted societal effect, Cameron underscores her larger point about gender in the Byzantine period: much of how we read and interpret this material will depend on our own sense of self in relation to modern societal norms and standards of gender, sex, and sexual performance.

Most interesting for our current analysis is Cameron's admission that she only became aware of this observation—on the contextualized nature of knowledge production and dissemination—as she progressed further in the guild. In other words, what became self-evident in the late 1990s was rather obscure to her (and other scholars) in earlier decades. There is no simple line of explanation for this shift—it is, rather, multifaceted. As the discourses of feminist, women's, and then gender criticisms developed, they also provided a structure and a context in which scholars came to think differently about themselves and their data. Moreover, as Cameron herself notes, as a more established scholar she also had the freedom to develop alternative and perhaps more traditionally marginalized perspectives. These observations fit well with the trajectory of Cameron's own career. Not only is she considered one of the premiere scholars in her field (the study of late antiquity), but, within the institutional structures of higher education in England, she also has one of the top posts—not only as professor at Oxford University, but also as the erstwhile university's pro-vice chancellor. In other words, one could argue that as she became more established within the guild, more opportunities arose for her to explore topics that were, earlier, considered more problematic. As a result, she was instrumental in opening up a discourse on gender, sex, and sexuality in late-antique studies, in some sense using her own status within the field to legitimate the discourse she was employing. One might also add that her use of Nin (in the essay cited earlier) for charting, even if implicitly (or unconsciously?), her own journey of self-discovery reveals the inherent connection between experience and the process of knowledge-making: how we view ourselves will affect how we construct the personal and sexual nature of our subjects of inquiry. As we already noted with Virginia Burrus at the outset of this chapter, the questions one asks of the material may in fact change over time, as one's own perspectives on the world and self change.

We use Cameron in this context because she poses not only interesting questions, but also particular dilemmas in the very same moment. She aptly attests to the power of the guild in shaping perceptions and in excluding particular options both in *what* is studied and *how*. Even more, Cameron points out the limitations we often place on ourselves, which in turn can prevent us from "seeing" anything other than traditional and culturally normative meanings. At the same time, as her references to both Irigaray and Nin make clear, Cameron promotes an essentialized notion of feminine subjectivity, without assessing the emergent complexities in modern sex and gender identity (something of which Burrus is more clearly aware). This facet of her thought provides some nuance for her broader observations. In the end, then, Cameron may have thought about and performed her personal identity in ways that the guild was willing to accept, even if not initially. Or, more likely, she herself still assumes many of the traditional views from that earlier scholarly world related to the gendered and sexed identity of the interpreter (limited by a narrow definition of what constitutes "male" and "female").

Cameron thus opens up a variety of avenues into the question of how, in this instance, concepts of gender, sex, and sexuality both limit and expand the fields of knowledge production. In other words, as much as one may see differently, and understand discourse another way as a result, there are also normativities that are constantly being reconfigured even in the moment of appearing to be challenged. Thus, although Cameron does something radical by bringing Nin into the discussion, it is also strategic that it is Nin in particular, because her feminine identity-markers are manifestly evident. The radical moment, then, both provides a disruptive in-breaking of sexuality and sexual expression into an academic piece, but at the same time it privatizes and relativizes the very same within the discourse. By making the chosen sexual identity clearly "feminine," to be identified as such by a predominantly "male" guild, the essentializing and normativizing function of the guilding process remains fundamentally unchallenged. As we have seen, in a field adamantly committed to objectivity as a masculine principle of scholarly operation, female subjectivity can be included as either a masked objectivity (passing as "male") or as a moment of fetishism, allowing the experience of female subjectivity to be both easily coded and then readily taken off the scene, creating the illusion of disruption that in turn allows the male-centered discourse to remain central and all the more powerful.

Worth mentioning at this point is Louis Althusser's (1918–1990) famous analysis of the educational system as an ideological state apparatus (i.e., the delivery mechanism for the propagation of ideology). In an essay entitled "Ideology and Ideological State Apparatuses," Althusser suggests that the School has replaced the Church in that the educational apparatus now plays a dominant role as it introduces people into the ruling ideology: "It takes children from every class at infant-school age, and then for years, the years in which the child is most 'vulnerable,' squeezed between the family State apparatus and the educational State apparatus, it drums into them, whether it uses new or old methods, a certain amount of 'know-how' wrapped in the ruling ideology or simply the ruling ideology in its pure state" (29). It thus turns individuals into "subjects," who freely accept their subjection, largely through the powerful hold that ideology has on the individual. Elsewhere Althusser claims, "ideology is the *lived* relation between [people] and their world. This relation, that only appears as '*conscious*' on condition that it is '*unconscious*,' in the same way only seems to be simple on condition that it is complex" (*For Marx*, 233). Thus, according to Althusser, ideology is precisely so forceful in shaping identity because it creates the illusion of being overt and uncomplicated— in his view it is anything but.

If we combine Althusser's understanding of the dissemination of ideology and the formative role of education therein with Michel Foucault's more sophisticated assessment of discourse and the diffusion of power through fluid networks of distribution (rather than the controlling and pivotal role of the State), the picture that emerges is one in which the academy as an institution plays a prominent role in both the production and dissemination of dominant discourse/ideology. It is intriguing that Althusser and Foucault (who was Althusser's student), as well as other critics of dominant discursive structures such as Roland Barthes (1915–1980), Gilles Deleuze (1925–1995), and Jacques Derrida (1930–2004) did not themselves belong to the academic establishment in France. As the French sociologist Pierre Bourdieu points out, scholars such as these "appear like religious heretics, or, in other words rather like free-lance intellectuals installed within the university system itself, or at least, to venture a Derridean pun, encamped on the margins or in the marginalia of an academic empire threatened on all sides by barbarian invasions (that is, of course, as seen by the dominant fraction)" (xix). Bourdieu makes this observation in the preface to the English translation of his book *Homo Academicus* (1988), in which he offers a sociological analysis of the mechanisms at work in the French academic world. As his analysis makes clear, a structural relation is noted between the work of thinkers such as Althusser and Foucault and their position in the academic field. Although Bourdieu's analysis focuses on the situation in France around 1968, many of his observations and concepts prove useful for analyzing similar power structures operative in the academy elsewhere, including, we would argue, the field of Biblical Studies.

Bourdieu distinguishes two categories in the university field: the academic and the scholar or researcher, both of whom have a specific type of power related to their position. The academic, on the one hand, possesses academic capital, which is, as Bourdieu frames it, "obtained and maintained by holding a position enabling domination of other positions and their holders, such as all the institutions entrusted with controlling access to the" educational system and its guilds (and now one would extend this to include the work-force, especially in the United States context) (84). The researcher, on the other hand, has social power in the form of symbolic capital of renown, for instance through scientific recognition and connections with the media. With this distinction between academic and researcher one also finds a corresponding difference in time-economy, insofar as the first group invests a large amount of time and energy in the accumulation and management of academic capital in the form of institutional power, while the second group gives priority to the accumulation of symbolic capital, such as fame in their field and public recognition with respect to their presence in the media. Of course, there can also be cross-over individuals, those who inhabit a degree of both spheres, as they hold positions of power, but are also involved in the accumulation of symbolic capital. One might think here of Averil Cameron herself for instance.

Within this larger framework, Bourdieu observes that the academic establishment largely regulates access to the system in terms of the requirements for admission and success, and it thus holds power over educational and degree reproduction. Although Bourdieu does not pay explicit attention to facets of gender, sex, and sexuality at work in these structures, two observations he makes in this respect are relevant. His first point relates to the patriarchal authority held by the "doctor's father," a position of control over the process of knowledge production. The second observation relates to the different roles of the academic and scholar, which he compares with that of the clergy and the prophet, two religious but also male gendered and sexed metaphors. These insights are germane to our point, even if they are also somewhat dated, because they reflect the fact that the academy is, at heart, a largely male dominated institution, which has that identity at the core of its system of meaning. Rather than the number of males that actually inhabit these institutions, however, it is the guiding patriarchal metaphors and androcentric institutional structures that shape the ideologies and mechanisms for the reproduction of phallogocentrism in these contexts.

In this respect, the significant advances made by first-wave feminism, in helping more women to reach positions of power (including in academic institutions), in and of itself did not actually change the foundational ideologies and technologies of power within these institutions. This situation means that without systemic attention to the power structures themselves, institutions will not fundamentally change. That said, there is no doubt a dramatic shift in the way that institutions are run since the time that Bourdieu made his observations on the educational structure of the late 1960s. Certainly in the United States (and now being exported to other non-North-American institutions) there is an increasing corporatization of the institutional structure, which has brought with it a market-driven approach to conceptualizing education and to reorganizing labor within the institution.[17] At the same time, while some of the language has changed, the basic hierarchical nature has not, and neither has the distinct androcentric character of educational institutions. The "bosses" look (and perhaps even act) differently, but global market capitalism and educational institutions have also made good companions.

Moreover, the various disciplines that are housed within the larger structure of the institution mimic these structures. In his later work on dominant masculine culture (*Masculine Domination*), Bourdieu explicitly draws attention to the gendered nature of academic disciplines, which are divided into "hard" ones such as the Natural Sciences and "soft" ones such as the Humanities (90–91). He also draws attention to the gendered and sexed character of labor division in society at large, with women being better represented in those jobs that are considered to be an extension of the family, such as, for instance, pre-college education (57–62, 87–88). This extension of the private sphere into the public in acceptable and legitimate ways is critical for how the private "female" sphere continues to play a subordinating role in the guild. It is not difficult to see how this traditional division also applies to institutional power positions. This situation has consequences for the rules and regulations that apply to those who seek access to academic institutions, including their accommodation to and acceptance of the structures at work in the academy with respect to the production of knowledge, such as methods that discipline the scholar in specific kinds of gendered and sexed (and perhaps sexualized as well) reading and writing practices. Women are, for instance, better represented in Women's Studies and Gender Studies departments than say in the so-called *~wHe~* hard sciences, thus providing evidence of a gendering and sexing of the disciplines.

Further, access to scholarly activities such as publishing is easier to manage than access to academic power in the center of the academy, where dissident readings are often literally marginalized and as a result do not affect the more tightly controlled frameworks for the production of knowledge. Despite, for instance, all the feminist and ideological criticisms of historical-critical approaches to the biblical materials, the vast majority of scholarly inquiry in the field goes on as if the former had never existed. In addition, producing readings counter to the dominant discourse may also make it more difficult for those scholars employing such approaches to secure academic posts situated more squarely within the "establishment," those institutions that determine and define "the center" and "the norm." As a result, these scholars have less access to institutional power and thus fewer opportunities to change the system from within. Critical voices are thus often either neutralized by being incorporated within the dominant mode of research or by being ignored by the same. Since Biblical Studies, as a traditionally canonical discipline, combines the ideological function of both Church and School (functioning as ideological state apparatuses in Althusser's framework), it is not surprising that this field is particularly resistant to change, as it often supports the ruling ideology and status quo (both academically and religiously). Even (if not especially) so-called liberal institutions enact the same dynamics, although the manner in which it is done often better masks the power structures at work than is possible in more conservative and authoritarian institutions.

 Critical for our understanding, then, is the way that power is played out in *all* institutional, guild, and disciplinary contexts relative to social, political, and economic values. Moreover, as Bourdieu observes in his work on *Reproduction in Education, Society and Culture*, originally published in 1970, "the apparently purely academic cult of hierarchy always contributes to the defense and legitimation of social hierarchies, because academic hierarchies, whether of degrees and diplomas or establishments and disciplines, always owe something to the social hierarchies which they tend to re-produce (in both senses)" (152).

It would therefore be naïve to ignore the social status and cultural reification that a discipline such as Biblical Studies engages in. As a traditional discipline, it tends to conserve societal tradents and trends that are frequently challenged in more liberal circles and contexts. The societal conservation is bound up in both the discourse of the field (particularly its methods) and in the general guilding practices of its scholars. Different from other disciplines in educational institutions, Biblical Studies also carries with it embedded religious (and theological) values (even if these are often considered to be eradicated by the "objectivity" of the scholar and the "progressive" nature of the field).

While criticism of the academy in general, and of Biblical Studies in particular, often focuses on the mechanisms of exclusion of those who aspire to be included in the system, those aspirations are already informed, as Bourdieu points out, by someone's earlier exposure to this form of cultural capital. It is, for instance, unlikely that someone, who grows up in a social milieu where there exists a disdain for intellectuals, will aspire to become one. As a result, the system is likely to attract those who would already "fit in." The whole notion of "equal opportunity" therefore tends to conceal the already existing inequity in the distribution of cultural capital over different social groups in society. Moreover, specific fields (or even sub-disciplines) tend to attract (and also regulate) particular kinds of interpreters. African American studies tends to draw in African Americans, for instance. There is an expectation that certain fields will more naturally attract scholars predisposed to the particular formulations of knowledge, methodologies, and identities already established in those fields, including the (often unstated) assumption that disciplines that are either racially, ethnically, or gendered in terms of their explicit orientation should attract "one of their own." The educational system at large to which the academy belongs thus serves the established social order of which it is itself a product. One would note here as well that even in the guild, certain fields (such as Gender Studies, African-American studies, LGBTI studies) can be seen to function like ghettos (even if those on the "inside" are themselves indifferent to their marginalized status), which mimic those similar impulses operative in society as a whole. Difference is tolerated, but there is a continued regulation of difference (on all sides of the equation).

In his work, Bourdieu focuses on the role class plays in the access one has to particular forms of education, but a similar analysis is also possible with respect to gender, sex, and sexuality. Biblical Studies is no different from other disciplines in that respect. In order to gain academic credibility, it aspires to the same standards of scientific qualification and uses the same mechanisms of evaluation, such as exams. It thus participates in and re-produces the same power structures present in the academy at large, and does so along "scientific" lines, representing the "hard" line of scholarly inquiry. Criticism of the field also largely remains on the discursive level, and thus within academically confined boundaries, as it is not in the interest of those who owe their position/power to the system to question/undermine its very structures, because the authority of their words depends on the institution that legitimates their power.[18]

In terms of a gender-critical analysis of guilding practices, then, several observations arise out of this discussion. To begin with, given the structure we have outlined earlier, it is worth pointing out how the guild functions by delineating private and public spheres, much like society as a whole (which it mimics on a micro-level). The modern "public/private" distinction offers a regulatory effect by excluding certain individuals from the public sphere and also regulating those who are included. In her book *The Return of the Political* (2005), Chantal Mouffe, following political scientist Carole Pateman, notes how the modern category of the individual has been constructed in a manner that postulates a universalist, homogeneous 'public' that relegates all particularity and difference to the 'private,' and that this has very negative consequences for women (81). We can extend the social and political argument here by applying it also to the discourses of the discipline itself. Thus, for instance, "newer" methods that draw more on personal experience actually become effeminized within the larger sphere of male scientific approaches to the subject matter (which frequently take the form of "historical" discourse in Biblical Studies). There is both a space opened up for "alternative" methods— methods that admit to their own ideological and individual biases—and also a regulation and exclusion of those same methods. The private here has both been given a "voice" within the larger field, but it has nonetheless also been designated as a "private" and "personal" sphere of interaction and analysis.

As a result, alternative, non-hegemonic methods bear a distinctive essentializing "feminine" core, which thereby reifies in many ways the dominant masculine discourse and methods of the field, affirming them to be objective by virtue of the positing of a "feminine" (irrational) opposite.[19] Thus, the appeal to an "objective" "scientific" approach to biblical material in effect constitutes (and constructs) a male heterosexual, white European subject, regardless of whether it is a female or male employing such discourses, irrespective even of whether the individual scholar happens to be white, heterosexual, or European in origin. Just as the center will project gendered, sexed, and sexual identities onto the "other" and the "margins," so it is important for a gender-critical approach to expose that projection, as well as reveal the gendered, sexed, and sexual nature of the center (and how that is linked with class and race). Anyone with even rudimentary knowledge of the field could perceive the complex ways in which these factors are played out. For instance, at times feminist scholars (who sought a political agenda through scholarship) were "forced" to couch their analysis in a scientific, unbiased form. As a result, the formal character of their work exhibits the modalities of the "male" structures of knowledge production in the guild. Failure to adhere to these rules of investigation marginalizes the results of inquiry for a wider public. At the same time, the results so conceived function to legitimate the masculine lines of knowing.[20]

One might also note here the diverse ways in which the public character of male performance is intricately tied to the legitimacy of particular viewpoints vis-à-vis the centers of power. One could well compare the functionally similar queering work of Stephen Moore and Dale Martin, observing the major differences in the form and the formal public reception of their respective work.[21] Martin is located at the center of the power structures (at Yale University), and his historically deconstructive work is much more cautious and conventionally articulated than Moore's.[22] Public comportment (and especially how their own ethos/character is portrayed in their work) also factors in here as well, especially in terms of the expectations of how a scholar from Yale University versus one from Drew University might perform in the public sphere. At the center, a historically scientific modality must exist (even if there is a particular queering function that is passing as the dominant discourse); at the margins, by contrast, there is more freedom to "play" and "deconstruct." In other words, regardless of a specific scholar's own personal predilections, the guild maintains a strong line of male-identified scholarly assessment and production that centers the practices and discursive constructs of the guild, while the "fetish" function is often performed by the excluded "other," which is granted access to the formal structure as a beneficent gesture.

One might think here of someone working on Asian Biblical Hermeneutics, or employing a feminist agenda or a queer approach, for in all cases the assumption is that we will have, respectively, an "Asian," a "female," and a "gay" or a "queer" scholar (or at least individuals who are perceived as such by the dominant structure) promoting the marginalized work. Thus, there is a correlation between the type of nonnormative work undertaken and an essentialized (even as it is otherized) identity. There is often even an over-determination of the difference of the "other" in this respect (whether that "other" is a specific method or content), while the center appears to lack the cultural, racial, and ideological bases that defines the "other." Thus, the absence of these facets from the center defines the center of the discipline—here historical studies—as neutral. Moreover, while the "Asian-American" critic or the "female feminist" can point out the perceived ideological nature of the dominant "male" perspective, the normative "male" center—consisting of those who perform as white, heterosexual males—are expected to maintain the fundamental guild structures. And thus the gendered, sexed, and sexual character (and one could add other factors here too, such as race/ethnicity, class, disability) of the guild structure is highly essentialist in its ways of knowing and the methods used.

Thus, much like Cameron both admitting to a "personal perspective" but also using Anaïs Nin as the gendered, sexed, and sexually objectified trope by which to make a strong point about gendered and sexed identity as being critical to scholarly endeavors (thus functioning as a displacement [or stand in?] for Cameron's own identity), so biblical scholars too tend to project these identities onto the often marginalized Other while normativizing and sanitizing their own standpoint. Again, the "other" here is overdetermined, while the center is represented by absence and lack of specificity. The center thus passes as "normative" and consequently its power is masked. Rather than providing challenges to the larger structures of the guild, then, these other perspectives enable the center to solidify its hold. Therefore, alleged political and ethical work undertaken by scholars claiming to be enacting such often paradoxically sustains hegemony rather than dismantling it as intended. While much is made of the shift in biblical scholarship towards recognizing personal and cultural biases and social locations of interpretation, and while these "movements" and shifts in scholarship are touted as offering a challenge to the hegemonic tradition of "objective" and "scientific" analysis, in principle these two seeming polar opposite positions are not in conflict with each other. In a way, the dominant male-centered guild, particularly in its current social and cultural context, actually requires this dissent in order to maintain its center of power. Thus, for instance, while the Society of Biblical Literature has spaces for alternative scholarship (and also venues for assessing current equity issues such as a committee on the status of women in the academy), it still sustains a male-centered structure. Therefore, the difference that is tolerated does not challenge the phallogocentric and colonial structures of the guild. The illusion of inclusion is essential, particularly in a guild that fully endorses modern liberal discourses of individual freedom and tolerance. Yet, while it is often assumed that the guild has a fractured identity, with say feminist and postcolonial theorists raising ideological questions that seem to be ignored by traditional and conventional scholarship, if we take seriously the structure of the guild as outlined here, then the two spheres are rather working in tandem to sustain a larger normativity related to identity and subjectivity, particularly as those intersect with politics, culture, and society in this period of global capitalism (and capitalist globalism).

Conclusion

Our goal in this chapter has been to outline both the interconnection of race and gender in the formation of biblical scholarship, as well as to detail some contours of the modern gendered and sexed context for Biblical Studies. In the final analysis, we by no means want to suggest that traditional methods should be rejected as a result of these attendant racial and gender biases. They need, however, to be scrutinized in terms of their ideological underpinnings. Critical reflection and analysis are necessary in order to determine which insights are still valid and which ones should either be rejected or redefined. Thus, as Kelley suggests, reconstructions of early Christianity that work with the idea of a pristine origin that was later corrupted should be discarded, because "the primordial/inauthentic antithesis is thoroughly racialized" (*Racializing Jesus*, 214). Similarly, interpretations that dissociate Jesus from his Jewish contemporaries/context are to be rejected. Other insights are, however, still valuable. Baur's historical-critical approach to early Christian writings, for instance, recognizes both the "biased" nature of these sources as well as their historical character, set over against a (church-oriented) dogmatic approach to these sources that essentially left the ideologies unchallenged. While we criticize Baur's ideology, we are also fully aware that he himself was attentive to ideology in his historical reconstructions. Thus, while recognizing the limitations and flaws of his reconstruction of early Christian history, one can still appreciate elements of his basic approach.

Overall, then, our contention is that no time period and no person can ever escape the historical and cultural grip of biases, assumptions, and values that shape the way we think about and perceive the world. Quite contrary to the conventional approach to studying early Christianity, we believe there is no objective standpoint from which to view the past and by which one can interpret historical data. Thus, examining the social constructions that shape our ways of seeing and perceiving is a major first (and critical) step in the gender-critical approach we are outlining here. Obviously, gender, sex, and sexuality are only one part of the larger equation, as class, economics, politics, and religion (among other features) operate together in conjunction with our gendered, sexed, and sexual selves and contexts. One cannot separate out these other components. Indeed, that is one of the primary reasons why we have sought to link race and gender together in the preceding discussion: this connection offers one example of a much more multifaceted and complex configuration of our value systems and prejudices. Further, the attempt to examine and then to disrupt prevailing discourses is an unending task, as the dominant center continually reconstitutes itself, both as it responds to the challenges and transformations brought about by the changes in society more generally. Thus, as we have argued earlier, even though we may no longer have the prejudices and biases of an earlier period (at least in the same form), we must nonetheless still grapple with the way our current scholarly agenda is gendered and sexed (often in problematic ways), including, we might add, bringing criticism to bear on gender-critical approaches themselves (since they are not value neutral).

Part of the challenge, of course, is that society and culture are constantly shifting. Thus, as far as Biblical Studies is concerned, one can perceive a shift from an earlier homosocial guilding formation, when women were fully relegated to the private sphere or a special "ladies program" at conferences, to the current situation wherein the private has become public and women have entered the workforce (the advances brought about by the feminism of the 1960s were key in this respect). The guild has had to adapt to these changes, but the presence of women in the discipline of Biblical Studies, as we noted earlier, probably affected the structures less than most people may have hoped, as patriarchalism, misogyny, and colonialism (with its attendant racism) have simply reappeared in newer and perhaps more subtle guises. By analyzing such shifts, however, a gender-critical perspective can open up spaces for engaging the dominant center through exposing the economic and contingent political and social mechanisms that have shaped the gendered, sexed, and sexual relations and discourses in the guild, which in turn discipline the subjectivities of individual members in the production of biblical scholarly knowledge. At present, one can observe this phenomenon most clearly in the emergence of globalization. While we may well argue that creating global communities and appreciating difference represents a laudable development, there is also a darker side to this process, insofar as these differences are often reduced to products for (affluent society's) consumption. Similarly while the increasing interest in "other" hermeneutical practices—for example, Asian, African, Latino, Scandanavian—can on the one hand be understood as a reflection of openness to difference in the Biblical Studies guild, on the other it can also be seen as a way of incorporating those practices into the dominant discourse. We may see herein a mimicry in the guild of the larger global market economy: just as the world's neocolonial (American/European) markets are open(ed) to the "exotic," so too is the field of Biblical Studies. Following Rosemary Hennessy's approach in *Profit and Pleasure: Sexual Identities in Late Capitalism* (2000), we may also want to examine the way in which Biblical Studies in its institutional and disciplinary forms reconfigures its gendering, sexing, and sexualizing practices and identities in concert with changing economic relations in our society (offering new modes of commodification of both scholarship and individual identity, but also providing alternative points of resistance in the same moment).

For this reason, as we have noted earlier in the book, a gender-critical approach, in its focus on challenging both the binary system of knowledge formation and the masking of ideologies in all methodologies (including its own!), posits a political axis as essential for all interpretive work. Here we agree with Elisabeth Schüssler Fiorenza, who stresses the importance of understanding "the bible and biblical interpretation as a site of struggle over authority, values, and meaning" (*Power of the Word*, 253–54). This understanding is inextricably linked to the "public character and political responsibility" (254) of our interpretive agenda. In this respect, a gender-critical reading of both early Christian texts *and* the history of the interpretation of those same texts is not only invested in offering alternative readings, but also in providing interpretations that disrupt dominant modes of discourse and understanding, both ancient and modern. A gender-critical mode of analysis thus seeks to cultivate textual interpretation as precisely a "site of struggle," wherein the most critical issues for engagement are, ultimately, our own in this present world.

Notes

1 For a more updated version of this approach, focusing in particular on the upper class designation of characters such as Thecla, see Andrew Jacobs, "A Family Affair: Marriage, Class, and Ethics in the Apocryphal Acts of the Apostles" (*Journal of Early Christian Studies* 7 [1999]: 105–38), who argues that the Christian denigration of the upper class family system served to enhance the status of their own alternative social network of kinship.

2 See especially H. Glenn Penny and Matti Bunzl, eds, *Worldly Provincialism: German Anthropology in the Age of Empire* (Social History, Popular Culture, and Politics in Germany; Ann Arbor:

University of Michigan Press, 2003); Andrew Zimmerman, *Anthropology and Antihumanism in Imperial Germany* (Chicago: University of Chicago Press, 2001); and H. Glenn Penny, *Objects of Culture: Enthnology and Ethnographic Museums in Imperial Germany* (Chapel Hill: University of North Carolina Press, 2002).

3 George Steinmetz, *The Devil's Handwriting: Precoloniality and the German Colonial State in Qingdao, Samoa, and Southwest Africa* (Chicago Studies in Practices of Meaning; Chicago: Univeristy of Chicago Press, 2007), explores the complexity that such colonialism could manifest. In this richly detailed study, he analyzes German colonial rule in three different regions and shows that there is not one uniform "colonial formation," but multiple forms of colonial rule, depending on the region and the people/cultures.

4 For an extensive discussion of the debates in Germany surrounding this issue, see Jonathan M. Hess, *Germans, Jews and the Claims of Modernity* (New Haven: Yale University Press, 2002), who rejects the model of assimilation as being prevalent for the Jewish experience in Germany.

5 See further Todd Penner, "*Die Judenfrage* and the Construction of Ancient Judaism: Toward a Foregrounding of the Backgrounds Approach to Early Christianity," in *Scripture and Traditions: Essays on Early Judaism and Christianity [in Honour of Carl Holladay]* (ed. P. Gray and G. O'Day; Novum Testamentum Supplements 129; Leiden: Brill, 2008), 429–55.

6 In this respect, compare the following comments by Genevieve Lloyd: "Past ideals of Reason, far from transcending sexual difference, have helped to constitute it. That ideas of maleness have developed under the guise of supposedly neutral ideals of Reason has been to the disadvantage of women and men alike" (*Man of Reason*, 107–8).

7 That an alternative view and approach to the origins of Christianity was possible and also operative at that time is well documented by Susannah Heschel in her book *Abraham Geiger and the Jewish Jesus* (Chicago: University of Chicago Press, 1998). Abraham Geiger (1810–1874) was a German rabbi and scholar, who, living in the same time period as Baur, challenged the Christian tendency to dissociate Jesus from his Jewish context. For the legacy of the latter mode of biblical interpretation, see Heschel's most recent book, *The Aryan Jesus: Christian Theologians and the Bible in Nazi Germany* (Princeton: Princeton University Press, 2008).

8 See our more detailed discussion in Caroline Vander Stichele and Todd Penner, "Mastering the Tools or Retooling the Masters? The Legacy of Historical-Critical Discourse," in *Her Master's Tools? Feminist and Post-Colonial Engagements of Historical-Critical Discourse* (ed. C. Vander Stichele and T. Penner; Global Perspectives on the Bible 9; Atlanta: Society of Biblical Literature, 2005), 1-29.

9 The recent "turn to religion" in Continental philosophy—particularly in the work of Giorgio Agamben (*The Time that Remains: A Commentary on the Letter to the Romans* [Meridian: Crossing Aesthetics; trans. P. Dailey; Stanford: Stanford University Press, 2005]), Alain Badiou (*Saint Paul: The Foundation of Universalism* [Cultural Memory in the Present; trans. R. Brassier; Stanford: Stanford University Press, 2003]), Slavoj Žižek (*The Puppet and the Dwarf: The Perverse Core of Christianity* [Cambridge, MA: The MIT Press, 2003]), and Jacob Taubes (*The Political Theology of Paul* [Cultural Memory in the Present; trans. D. Hollander; Stanford: Stanford University Press, 2003])—wherein Paul's theological language is read (in varying ways) through an atheistic framework and in which Paul's conceptions of freedom are refracted through a political lens (emphasizing the freedom of the individual and resistance to the tyranny of the dominant order),

in some ways reproduce this older framework in Heidegger. Thus, the criticisms of the work of Bultmann and Heidegger may well apply to these new materialist readings of Paul as well.

10 Gillian Townsley, in her forthcoming essay "The Straight Mind in Corinth: Problematising Categories of Sex in 1 Cor 11.2–16" (in *Bible Trouble: Queer Reading at the Boundaries of Biblical Scholarship* [ed. K. Stone and H. Toensing; Semeia Studies; Atlanta: Society of Biblical Literature]), details more fully the ways in which Engel's understanding of the development of the modern family connects with patterns of reading the biblical text.

11 Science, then, is not, as is often believed, the result of unbiased, detached, objective descriptions of reality, but rather the assessment of observable phenomena in light of particular historical sociocultural concerns and models that regulate the manner in which results are classified and interpreted. The manner in which we currently think about the differences between the sexes—based largely, even if often implicitly, on the capacity to reproduce—is related not in small part to debates from the past two hundred years, which dramatically shaped the way we think today. Although the manner in which we conceptualize sex differentiation is often perceived as a "natural" and "given" component of life, this assumed standpoint overlooks the fact that sex differentiation based on biological classification is also conditioned by sociocultural processes, and that the two—biology and society—are intricately interrelated. For further details beyond the material in Domurat Dreger's and Laqueur's studies, see especially Anne-Fausto Sterling, *Sexing the Body: Gender Politics and the Construction of Sexuality* (New York: Basic Books, 2000); Jonathan Ned Katz, *The Invention of Heterosexuality* (Chicago: University of Chicago Press, 2007); and especially Arnold I. Davidson, *The Emergence of Sexuality: Historical Epistemology and the Formation of Concepts* (Cambridge, MA: Harvard University Press, 2004). For further observations related to the destabilizing of absolute scientific frames of reference, see Sandra Harding, *Is Science Multi-Cultural? Postcolonialisms, Feminisms, and Epistemologies* (Race, Gender, and Science; Bloomington: Indiana University Press, 1998); Stanley Aronowitz, *Science as Power: Discourse and Ideology in Modern Society* (Minneapolis: University of Minnesota Press, 1988); and especially the nuanced study by Lorraine Daston and Peter Galison, *Objectivity* (New York: Zone Books, 2007).

12 A significant amount of (proto)feminist biblical criticism existed in this same time period. For discussion, see the collection of essays by Christiana de Groot and Marion Ann Taylor, eds, , *Recovering Nineteenth-Century Women Interpreters of the Bible* (Atlanta: Society of Biblical Literature, 2007); as well as the original sources in Marly J. Selvidge, *Notorious Voices: Feminist Biblical Interpretation 1500–1920* (London: SCM, 1996); and Marion Ann Taylor and Heather E. Weir, eds, *Let Her Speak for Herself: Nineteenth-Century Women Writing on Women in Genesis* (Waco: Baylor University Press, 2006).

13 Also see Dolores Williams, "The Color of Feminism: Or Speaking the Black Woman's Tongue," in *Journal of Religious Thought* 43 (1986): 42–58. On the larger issue of racism in feminist biblical discourse, see further Kwok Pui-lan, "Racism and Ethnocentrism in Feminist Biblical Interpretation," in *Searching the Scriptures: A Feminist Introduction* (ed. E. Schüssler Fiorenza; London: SCM, 1994), 101–16.

14 For a fuller discussion of the interpretation of Judaism as an antithesis to early Christianity in feminist analysis of religion, see Katharina von Kellenbach, *Anti-Judaism in Feminist Religious Writings* (Atlanta: Scholars Press, 1994), esp. pp. 57–74.

15 These few examples demonstrate that awareness of one issue does not safeguard one from other forms of prejudice and discrimination related to one's own theoretical position and social location. Although every form of situatedness in time and space brings with it certain limitations in the perspective one brings to the texts, it is possible to become at least partially conscious of those limitations and engage them. A way of doing so is suggested by Plaskow ("Anti-Judaism"), who distinguishes five different ways in which anti-Judaism can be addressed instead of being reproduced by feminist Christian interpreters. Her strategy can, moreover, be used to address other -isms. The first step that she proposes is becoming aware of the problem in question by informing oneself about it (for instance, by reading about the matter). A second step is for one to integrate this new awareness of the problem into one's own critical analysis of the texts, in this case the relationship between conceptions of gender, sex, and sexuality and anti-Judaism in ancient and modern Christian writings. Third, one should address the problem as it appears in the sources themselves. This move includes informing oneself about what is not directly present in one's sources, such as the history of women in Judaism. But, fourth, in the case of anti-Judaism, it is important to read the New Testament not in opposition to Judaism, but itself as a source of information about Jewish women. Finally, the fifth step, which is an inclusive approach, requires an attitude of openness towards the concerns of the excluded other, in this case those matters of importance to Jewish feminists.

16 Russell T. McCutcheon offers a sound articulation of the issues involved in studying religion amidst the recognition of the relativity of one's analysis. See his *The Discipline of Religion: Structure, Meaning, Rhetoric* (London: Routledge, 2003), 15–37.

17 See especially Sheila Slaughter and Gary Rhoades, *Academic Capitalism and the New Economy: Markets, State, and Higher Education* (Baltimore: Johns Hopkins University Press, 2004); David Kirp, *Shakespeare, Einstein, and the Bottom Line: The Marketing of Higher Education* (Cambridge, MA: Harvard University Press, 2004); Christopher Newfield, *Unmaking the Public University: The Forty-Year Assault on the Middle Class* (Cambridge, MA: Harvard University Press, 2008); Marc Bousquet, *How the University Works: Higher Education and the Low-Wage Nation* (Cultural Front; New York: New York University Press, 2008); and Stanley Aronowitz, *The Knowledge Factory: Dismantling the Corporate University and Creating True Higher Learning* (Boston: Beacon, 2000).

18 See further Bourdieu's essay "Authorized Language: The Social Conditions for the Effectiveness of Ritual Discourse," in *Language and Symbolic Power* (Cambridge: Polity Press, 1992), 107–16.

19 An interesting example is provided by Max Horkheimer in his book *Eclipse of Reason* (London: Continuum, 2004 [originally published 1947). At one point in his bemoaning of the dominance of modern, post-Enlightenment understanding of Reason, Horkheimer comments: "The more the concept of reason becomes emasculated the more easily it lends itself to ideological manipulation and to propagation of even the most blatant lies" (17). Here Horkheimer refers to the "emasculation" of reason, by which he means its being undermined as a masculine principle. Although obviously not intentional, the explicit opposite of "manly reason" is an openness to manipulation and espousal of lies, which is essentially an effeminization of the principle of non-rationality.

20 Elizabeth Schüssler Fiorenza, for instance, was one of the first scholars to call for the guild of Biblical Studies to explore the politics of its own scholarship (see especially her *Rhetoric and Ethic: The Politics of Biblical Studies* [Minneapolis: Fortress Press, 1999]); and most recently *The Power of*

the Word (2007). Also see Joseph Marchal's challenging analysis of graduate biblical education in the United States, "Giving an Account of a Desirable Subject: Critically Queering Graduate Biblical Education," forthcoming in *Transforming Graduate Biblical Education: Ethos and Discipline* (ed. E. Schüssler Fiorenza and K. Richards; Semeia Studies; Atlanta: Society of Biblical Literature).

21 For instance, one might contrast Stephen Moore's *God's Gym: Divine Male Bodies of the Bible* (London: Routledge, 1996) or his *God's Beauty Parlor: Queer Spaces in and around the Bible* (Contraversions; Stanford: Stanford University Press, 2001) with Dale Martin's recent *Sex and the Single Savior: Gender and Sexuality in Biblical Interpretation* (Louisville: Westminster John Knox, 2006). While both authors address issues of sex, sexuality, and gender in the interpretation of early Christian texts, both of them do so in quite different ways, employing significantly divergent discourses in the process. Martin's discourse is by far the more conventional of the two in terms of his use of the more traditional methods of biblical scholarship. This observation is not a criticism. Rather, we simply recognize the performative aspect of being a scholar in the discipline and its less than random nature.

22 An excellent example of an implicit deconstruction of historical criticism is Dale Martin's essay "Paul and the Judaism/Hellenism Dichotomy: Toward a Social History of the Question," in *Paul beyond the Judaism/Hellenism Divide* (ed. T. Engberg-Pedersen; Louisville: Westminster John Knox, 2001), 29–61. Martin does not employ any unconventional discourses with respect to his historical critical engagement of "Hellenism," and yet he functionally decenters the traditional binary in the construction of this category in normative scholarship. He does so by cautiously deconstructing the inherent contradictions, problems, and inconsistencies in the term "Hellenism" as it has been used by modern scholars.

Bibliography

Althusser, Louis. "Ideology and Ideological State Apparatuses." Pp. 1–60 in *Essays on Ideology*. Translated by B. Brewster. London: Verso, 1984.

—*For Marx*. Translated by B. Brewster. London: Verso, 2005.

Baur, Ferdinand Christian. *Symbolik und Mythologie oder die Naturreligion des Altertums*. Part 1. Stuttgart: Metzler, 1824.

Bourdieu, Pierre. *Homo Academicus*. Translated by P. Collier. Stanford: Stanford University Press, 1988.

—*Masculine Domination*. Translated by R. Nice. Stanford: Stanford University Press, 2001.

Bourdieu, Pierre, and Jean-Claude Passeron. *Reproduction in Education, Society and Culture*. Theory, Culture, Society. Second edn. London: Sage Publications, 1990.

Brown, Wendy. *Regulating Aversion: Tolerance in the Age of Identity and Empire*. Princeton: Princeton University Press, 2006.

Burrus, Virginia. "Chastity as Autonomy: Women in the Stories of the Apocryphal Acts." *Semeia* 38 (1986): 101–17.

—*Chastity as Autonomy: Women in the Stories of the Apocryphal Acts*. Studies in Women and Religion 23. Lewiston: Edwin Mellen Press, 1987.

—"Mimicking Virgins: Colonial Ambivalence and the Ancient Romance." *Arethusa* 38 (2005): 49–88.

— "Response." *Semeia* 38 (1986): 133–35.

Cameron, Averil. "Sacred and Profane Love: Thoughts on Byzantine Gender." Pp. 1–23 in *Women, Men and Eunuchs: Gender in Byzantium*. Edited by L. James. London: Routledge, 1997.

Chakrabarty, Dipesh. *Provincializing Europe: Postcolonial Thought and Historical Difference*. Princeton Studies in Culture/Power/History. Princeton: Princeton University Press, 2000.

Clifford, Michael. *Political Genealogy after Foucault: Savage Identities*. London: Routledge, 2001.

Darwin, Charles. *The Descent of Man and Selection in Relation to Sex*. Princeton: Princeton University Press, 1981 (1871).

Dreger, Alice Domurat. *Hermaphrodites and the Medical Invention of Sex*. Cambridge, MA: Harvard University Press, 2000.

Engels, Friedrich. *The Origin of the Family, Private Property and the State: In the Light of the Researches of Lewis H. Morgan*. Edited by E. Burke Leacock. New York: International Publishers, 1973 (1884).

Goldberg, David Theo. *Racist Culture: Philosophy and the Politics of Meaning*. Oxford: Blackwell, 1993.

Hegel, Georg Wilhelm Friedrich. *Introduction to "The Philosophy of History."* Translated by L. Rauch. Indianapolis: Hackett, 1988.

Hegel *Phenomenology of Spirit*. Translated by A. V. Miller, Oxford: Oxford University Press, 1977 (1807).

Heidegger, Martin. *Being and Time (Sein und Zeit)*. Translated by J. Macquarrie and E. Robinson. Oxford: Blackwell, 1973 (1927).

Hennessy, Rosemary. *Profit and Pleasure: Sexual Identities in Late Capitalism*. London: Routledge, 2000.

hooks, bell. *Ain't I A Woman? Black Women and Feminism*. Boston: South End Press, 1981.

Kaestli, Jean-Daniel. "Response." *Semeia* 38 (1986): 119–31.

Kelley, Shawn. *Racializing Jesus: Race, Ideology and the Formation of Modern Biblical Scholarship*. London: Routledge, 2002.

Laqueur, Thomas. *Making Sex: Body and Gender from the Greeks to Freud*. Cambridge, MA: Harvard University Press, 1990.

Lloyd, Genevieve. *The Man of Reason: "Male" and "Female" in Western Philosophy*. London: Methuen, 1984.

Mouffe, Chantal. *The Return of the Political*. London: Verso, 2005.

Parvey, Constance. "The Theology and Leadership of Women in the New Testament." Pp. 112–49 in *Religion and Sexism: Images of Woman in the Jewish and Christian Traditions*. Edited by R. Radford Ruether. New York: Simon and Schuster, 1974.

Plaskow, Judith. "Anti-Judaism in Feminist Christian Interpretation." Pp. 117–29 in *Searching the Scriptures: A Feminist Introduction*. Edited by E. Schüssler Fiorenza. London: SCM, 1994.

Rousseau, Jean-Jacques. *Émile: Or Treatise on Education*. Translated by W. H. Payne. Amherst: Prometheus Books, 2003 (1762).

Schüssler Fiorenza, Elisabeth. *The Power of the Word: Scripture and the Rhetoric of Empire*. Minneapolis: Fortress Press, 2007.

Stanton, Elisabeth Cady, ed. *The Woman's Bible*. Reprint edn. Salem: Ayer Company, 1986 (1895–1898).

Reading (for) Gender

Thecla longed for Paul and searched for him, sending people around everywhere. And it was disclosed to her that he was in Myra. Girding her loins, gathering together her under and upper clothing as men normally do,[1] she left for Myra, taking young men and women with her. And she found Paul as he was speaking the word of God and she stood with him. But he was astonished to see her and the crowd that was with her, wondering if perhaps another temptation had come over her. She, however, reading his thoughts, told him: "Paul, I have received the bath [i.e., baptism],[2] for he who collaborated with you for the gospel has also collaborated with me for bathing."

—*Acts of Paul and Thecla* 3.40

This epigraph from the *Acts of Paul and Thecla* represents one of the more famous passages in this apocryphal text. Here Thecla undertakes a second search for Paul, while adopting (or desiring to adopt) masculine identity markers. The first time, when Thecla finds Paul in the new tomb, he rebukes her for her desire to cut her hair (*Acts of Paul and Thecla* 3.25). In this second instance, Thecla dresses like a man prior to meeting Paul. Paul initially reacts to the sight of Thecla in male garb, wondering what this new appearance might mean. She discloses to him that she has been baptized, but she does not tell him how that came about or that she in fact baptized herself in the arena. As she believed that she too was about to die after the lioness had been killed, Thecla had thrown herself into a large pool, saying "In the name of Jesus Christ, I baptize myself on the last day" (3.34). However, thanks to divine intervention she survived, was released, and headed off in search for Paul.

In retrospect, a double shift can be discerned in Thecla's behavior throughout the story: she moves from female to male identification and simultaneously from the domestic to the public sphere. In both cases, moreover, a crossing of boundaries occurs, marked by shifting roles, spaces, loyalties, and identities. These are the moments that the *Acts of Paul and Thecla* seems to relish flirting with: the bride-to-be who readily becomes the follower of a "magician," the devoted virgin and chaste ascetic who longs to meet up with her beloved apostle (serving as surrogate husband?). So, which role then represents the "real" Thecla? At what point is "she" not "he" or "he" not "she," and at what point is she neither, thereby opening up a "third" space of gender identity? This textual indecisiveness is further enhanced by the fact that Thecla is portrayed as a virgin, a woman in a liminal state, not yet incorporated into the marriage bond.

There are different ways of reading the relative status of Thecla in this critical moment of the text. Is she really liberated? Is she now simply defined by her absorption into male identification?[3] Is she a proto-feminist character? Does she represent a transgendered type of individual? In the previous chapters we delineated some of the varying scholarly positions related to Thecla's emerging identity in the text. We noted earlier that some interpreters see in her representation a trace of a real historical liberation for females in the ancient world, even perceiving here a story written by females for female communities.[4] We also pointed out that other critics observe in such instances an act of male power-brokering, with females like Thecla being deployed to secure Christian male identity over against pagan counterparts.[5] In sum, there are multiple ways in which to read the same text, and the fate of gender, sex, and sexuality in the interpretation of the Thecla narrative is wedded to the specific reading strategy employed and the value system held by the interpreter. We come back to this point later in this chapter.

For the moment, we take our point of departure from situating our gender-critical approach within the broader context of interpretive choices one can

make when reading for gender. We begin with a presentation of our methodological assumptions, which summarizes and synthesizes key points of the discussion from earlier chapters, followed by a delineation of our own reading
strategies, which we ground in the sociocultural environment of late antiquity.
Next, we situate our approach in the context of other frames of analysis that
engage issues of gender. We conclude this chapter by illustrating our own
approach with three examples, one taken from Paul's letters, another from the
Acts of the Apostles, and a third from the *Acts of Paul and Thecla*.

Gender-critical reading assumptions and strategies

The gender-critical approach that we employ operates with a variety of overt
assumptions and reading strategies that are used to analyze the construction of
arguments related to gender, sex, and sexuality in early Christian texts. These
categories can either be the major focus of a text (i.e., that which is actually
under discussion) or more implicitly involved in the discussion/argument of
something else. As far as our reading assumptions are concerned, we underscore again that the gender-critical approach that we have been framing in this
book brings ideology to the fore. We do so because our epistemological
position is that all systems of meaning establish methodologies for interpretation, and that these methodologies are effectively related to a specific
system in which they were formulated. In traditional modern theological
frames of reference, there was only one, absolute truth, and thus there was little
room for relativity in meaning. In some respects, historical criticism has
secularized and historicized this modern theological principle, in that there is
only one, true meaning to be discerned in a text, which is identified as the
original meaning.[6] In a system of interpretation that prizes unity and precision, multiplicity is often excluded. A presumed objective frame of reference
arises in the process, the ideological bias of which goes unacknowledged.
Consequently, the fact that such a frame of reference comes into existence
within a larger sociocultural system of meaning is ignored. Or, if the presence
of modern ideologies among interpreters is acknowledged, these ideologies are
considered to be identifiable and functionally suppressible, or at the very least
they can be bracketed (and thereby in some sense also dismissed as trivial).

In the view we take here, however, there is neither an absolute system of
meaning nor a fixed methodology for determining meaning in texts, and, as

a result, there is no one right way of studying the past. Rather, each method comes to formation within a system of meaning, and therefore is self-referential to that system, and, consequently, it is limited in terms of the perspective on the past that it provides. In short, any system and its concomitant methods offer *a specific way but not the only way of "seeing"* phenomena. That means that if one uses a historical-critical method to interpret early Christian texts, this method will elucidate specific aspects of those texts, but will simultaneously obscure others. We might elaborate on this principle by noting that even within one particular system of meaning, one is still forced to select certain data to the exclusion of other data that one could employ for analysis. Often times biases within the system of meaning and the viewpoint of the interpreter account for differences in this selection process. The history of interpretation of the Bible amply attests to this point. 1 Corinthians 11.10 ("for this reason a woman ought to have authority on her head, because of the angels") offers a specific example, as this obscure verse has given rise to a great variety of interpretations, most within the confines of a historical-critical framework. Differences in interpretation in this instance are often (although not always) a result of the interplay of interpretation and application, insofar as interpreters often read the text in line with the role they believe women *should* play in the church assembly. Thus, even within a closed, so-called objective system of meaning, multiplicity is always present even if it is not recognized.[7]

In our gender-critical approach we integrate a variety of methods (e.g., literary/rhetorical and historical studies) and make use of a number of other ideology-critical approaches (informed by gender studies, postcolonial studies, and critical theory) to study an ancient text. The methods and approaches so employed result in a different (and unique) perspective on the same text. Within this framework, a gender-critical approach is not touted as *the* sole approach to the study of the past, but it does allow one to observe and interpret particular phenomena in an ancient text in a way that other approaches might not. As we have already outlined in the earlier chapters, a gender-critical approach highlights those features of a text that relate to gender, sex, and sexuality. Moreover, a gender-critical approach fronts its politics and ethics, seeks to expose the same in ancient texts, and engages the embedded politics and ideologies (even though these are often masked) operative in both contemporary methods and interpreters. Thus, not only does a gender-critical approach aim at breaking down a binary system of meaning-making (which many other methods reify and affirm), but it also challenges, at a basic level, the idea of normativity and stability in ancient and modern systems of meaning.

The gender-critical approach we develop in this book focuses on gender as it is constructed in ancient texts, employing a variety of different methods in order to achieve that aim. Our focus on textual constructions rather than on historical realities already indicates a certain *choice*. In other words, our approach is only one possible formulation of what gender criticism might look like. We have, for instance, limited our approach by focusing on texts (rather than say archaeological remains of households, which would provide a context for a different sort of gender/ed reading), and then specific kinds of texts at that (early Christian, and within that we have largely limited ourselves to Paul, the book of Acts, and the *Acts of Paul and Thecla*). These are all selections we have made, and they narrow our approach in quite specific ways. These choices are, moreover, influenced by our own collective and individual ideologies, which shape the way we conceptualize and employ our gender-critical approach. Thus, another gender-critical approach could opt for an alternative politics and ethics.

In what follows, then, we briefly lay out several key elements that we consider to be quintessential for *our* reading strategies, with a special emphasis on the interconnected roles of ideology and rhetoric. As we have made apparent throughout this book, the fronting of multiple ideologies that arise in the act of interpretation is critical for our approach. And this emphasis goes not just for modern ideologies, but for ancient ones as well. The ancient texts we are studying are also contextualized within a complex web of power relations, with interrelated but also competing frames of reference, as people (individually and collectively) often have multiple loyalties to institutional frameworks or commitments even to competing sets of social roles and ideas. For instance, in the third chapter we noted that, depending on where one was situated within the social hierarchy in antiquity, the operative ideology would vary (e.g., a slave and a slave-holder may share some sociocultural perspectives on the world, but they will also differ in their perceptions given their experiences relative to their social position). Interpretive differences and multiplicity are therefore essential in our gender-critical approach, since the perspective on gender, sex, and sexuality we adopt calls for a deconstruction of unitary and unified meanings in texts.

As is clear from our discussion in previous chapters, then, we favor a more complex reading of the evidence, highlighting specific features (historical, textual, cultural, social, etc.) in the act of interpretation, while at the same time allowing for a significant degree of ambiguity in terms of what those features *must* mean for our understanding of antiquity. Finally, the meaning of any concept in the ancient world will be determined, at least in part, by our understanding of that same entity in our own world and the specific location (social, cultural, political, and economic) from which we interpret this evidence.[8] We thus tend to interpret ancient images and concepts based on meanings we are familiar with, that is, in terms of what makes sense to us. In this way, not only do we tend to configure ancient meanings in light of our modern ones, but we also blend various concepts from the ancient world with our own, creating in the process a hybrid mixture of ancient and modern categories.

Despite these acknowledged hermeneutical limitations, we nevertheless choose to highlight texts as socially and culturally constructed products and performances. As we explain in more detail later in this chapter, our interest lies less in reconstructing the history behind the text and more in focusing on the text as a socialcultural entity, in part because we do not believe that one can take for granted that the voice of the text is determinative for what has actually happened or that there is an easy link to be made between the rhetoric of the text and the "real" historical circumstances that produced the text (or that the text itself points to). Moreover, texts often obscure their social conditions of production, thus reinforcing their rhetorical agenda by appearing to provide an absolute perspective on the world. We therefore affirm *historical* analysis in our gender-critical approach, but at the same time we understand by "historical" the sociocultural context of the text itself, rather than the people and places mentioned in the text. For instance, in the second and third chapters of this book we articulated views as they relate to gender, sex, and sexuality at the intersection with empire. In our minds, this thematic intersection represents a historical approach to the language and thought of early Christians, but it also attempts to steer away from historical reconstructions, such as, for instance, focusing on Thecla as an actual historical female.

In light of the earlier mentioned theoretical considerations, then, we opt for analyzing the rhetorical nature of texts in order to assess the arguments made by early Christians. Moreover, in our gender-critical approach we choose to wed ideology and rhetoric, with a focus on how gendered, sexed, and sexual paradigms both promote and sustain particular ideologies. Since texts are multifunctional, they can promote explicit ideologies (e.g., those related to specific ideas about Jesus, the church, or outsiders), while implying (often unconsciously) other ideological elements in the process (gender roles, social hierarchies, etc.). In addition, authors also have varied (and sometimes contradictory)

goals in persuasion. Thus, one reading (or even multiple readings) will never exhaust the possible interpretations of a text. We also employ an ideology-critical suspicion in our reading strategies, in that we do not take for granted the text's explicit representation or argument. These choices—that is, our understanding of the relationship of power and discourse, and our prioritizing of rhetoric for determining meaning in texts—characterize and shape our gender-critical approach in specific ways.

Regardless of the type of ideology that is supported therein, in all cases our approach focuses on the *instrumentality* of arguments and argumentation. In other words, in order to to get to the heart of the gendered, sexed, and sexual nature of, in this case ancient, texts one needs to examine the ways in which texts operate in and through structures of power even as they appear not to be doing so. Thus, a text such as Galatians 3.28 that seems to argue for the obliteration of differences between Jew and Greek, slave and free, male and female, may well reinforce those very differences rather than promote equality as is often presumed. The fact that this equality is established "in Christ" has often been understood to exclude the social realm of "this world," thereby effectively affirming (rather than negating) these supposedly "eradicated" differences in practice. Again, we come back here to the identification of the ideology-critical nature of our interpretive practices as being crucial for our gender-critical approach (in ways that it might not be necessary, say, for a purely historical or anthropological approach to the same text).

Also, since, in our view, all texts embed ideology in rhetoric, distinction between early Christian literary genres is of less importance for our rhetorical analysis, even as different genres of texts may require divergent literary approaches. Thus, it is true that Paul's writings foreground his argument (at least its explicit character), while narratives like we find in the book of Acts or the *Acts of Paul and Thecla* only do so mostly in direct speech or narrator asides. Still, much of the rhetorical force of a narrative is embedded in the narrative itself—its literary features, structures, and tropes—which means that the interpreter must analyze this material as well. In the end, we would argue that the gap between a narrative in the book of Acts and an argument in Paul's letters, especially in terms of the use of rhetoric, is not as wide as one may initially believe, as both texts are saturated with ideology.[9] Given this emphasis, then, our approach is situated in conversation with ancient rhetorical practices, since it is this sociocultural context that frames the strategies we employ in our gender-critical approach. In other words, the focus of our analysis is on rhetoric, and specifically on key features of rhetorical practice and thinking in antiquity. At this juncture, our interpretive assumptions readily give way to our reading strategies. The two—assumptions and strategies—are interrelated precisely because our decidedly modern accent on rhetoric finds a resonant echo in the ancient world's focus on the practice of persuasion.

Since we conceptualize rhetoric in early Christian texts as more than simply the result of unconscious literary activity, but, in part at least, as the product of deliberate intellectual endeavors, we need to account for the influence of the practice (or "art") of persuasion.[10] Ancient writers were inculcated in particular patterns of thinking and writing that related to specific aims of persuasion, which included instruction on how to construct and elaborate arguments. One set of materials to be taken into account in this respect are the *progymnasmata*, which were elementary rhetorical training manuals, a prelude to the more advanced rhetorical training that an educated Greek or Roman male might later study.[11] While all communication (verbal and nonverbal) is effectively rhetorical, ancient writers were taught to be even more explicit than many modern writers are about rhetorical technique, function, and aim. Thus, the ancient world was imbued with a rhetorical spirit, which offers a uniquely intentional framework for understanding ancient rhetorical use.[12] Indeed, as Wilhelm Wuellner once adroitly noted, "there is more rhetoric to be experienced in one hour in the marketplace (or even the nursery) than in one day in the academy" ("Biblical Exegesis," 500). Wuellner's point was not to diminish the formal rhetorical training of the orators, because that was a critical element in the political and social life of the ancient city. Rather, he intended to highlight the broad pattern of rhetorical thinking and acting that was a constituent part of everyday life, so that the orators are not seen as anomalies, but rather as specialists who refine and codify what are more widespread ways of thinking and acting in the ancient world. Ancient rhetorical theory (and practice) provided a reservoir for the construction of arguments, with an emphasis on configuring social and cultural tropes of discourse and communication for the purpose of effectively persuading an audience, while also reflecting the (upstanding) character of the speaker, shaping the values and perception of the audience in the process.

It is important to note here as well that rhetoric and rhetorical training were not restricted to the Greeks and Romans. As we noted earlier in chapter three, there was a widespread rhetorical environment in antiquity, and various groups adopted, cultivated, and adapted rhetorical tropes and techniques differently. Early Christians, for instance, were quite adept at reconfiguring the tropes of the dominant culture, often inverting the inner logic of the trope to a newer, sometimes more potent form of argumentation, undermining in the process the normative dominant cultural understanding of that same trope.[13] We noted earlier how the discourse of martyrdom was shaped in this manner: what was originally considered a sign of weakness (being put to death as a common criminal) was cleverly inverted into a trope of manly comportment, which depicted the Christian movement as exhibiting a superior form of self-mastery and manliness.[14]

Jewish writers in the same time period were making similar rhetorical moves. Not unlike the early Christian use of the martyrdom trope, and quite likely a prototype for it, the book of 4 Maccabees offers an especially powerful display of self-mastery of both male Jews and their mother, all of whom show more "manliness" than the tyrant who is taunting them to abandon their Jewish practice. In quite a different vein, Philo of Alexandria reinterpreted the stories of the Pentateuch in light of a long-standing Greek tradition of allegorical reading, which provided for a philosophical interpretation of narratives. Philo's reading strategy reflected his Greek educational training, and also demonstrated his ability to make use of learned techniques to advocate for Judaism among his Greco-Roman contemporaries. In the later first century CE, Josephus likewise evidences indebtedness to a rhetorical device known from the *progymnasmata*: the rewriting of pre-existing narratives, which, in this case, involved reinterpreting the biblical text (e.g., as he does in his *Jewish Antiquities*, in which he rewrites the narratives of the Hebrew Bible and grafts more recent Jewish history onto the biblical story). In fact, most of Josephus's works offer extensive (although often also subtle) revisions of the biblical narrative in an attempt to portray (as Philo did before him) Judaism in a positive light to the Greeks and Romans.

In line with much of what we have argued in this book so far, then, for different writers and communities such training and practice will have come from a variety of sources and in diverse ways. How rhetorical training may have had an impact on early Christian writers and the extent to which it did are difficult questions to answer, in part because we do not know who these writers were and where they were situated socially, geographically, and so on. Still, the fact that we possess early Christian literature at all, and that there is significant attestation of numerous rhetorical techniques in these texts, allows us to presume at least a basic level of education on the part of these writers. Thus, paying close attention to the rhetorical construction of argumentation is not only required based on how language functions more generally as communication, it is also demanded by virtue of early Christian texts having been written (often) overtly with rhetorical tropes and patterns in view.

The foregoing discussion of rhetorical practice in the ancient world is thus not just important for creating an impression of the general ambient sphere of early Christian literary production. In fact, our purpose is much more restricted, in that we use this discussion as a starting point for making general observations about our approach in terms of reading (for) gender in ancient texts. For instance, that ancient writers and readers were often invested in the construction of plausible and ideal narratives and arguments rather than real and actual ones is difficult for modern interpreters to appreciate fully, since it runs so contrary to how we read narratives and understand arguments today. We tend to presume that ancient writers were interested in achieving accuracy (by which we mean an objective historicity) in their representation of details in line with what modern historiography claims to do.[15] Ancient writers, however, were much more invested in constructing narratives and arguments that would fit with the sociocultural expectations of their communities. The progymnastic manuals are full of examples where the student is instructed to conceptualize a theme or narrative in plausible terms in the service of an argument, rather than asking the question "what really happened."

As we noted in chapter one, this reorientation does not imply that people who are mentioned in these texts did not exist or that we cannot glean anything of historical value about them from the material we study. It does mean, however, that recovering real historical characters from any representation in narrative or other literary forms is a difficult task. Moreover, we are only able to approximate reconstructions, if we can even legitimately entertain "reconstruction" as a goal of historical inquiry at all. It is therefore more meaningful for us to examine the facets of politics, ideology, economics, sexuality, and so forth that constitute the characters in the narrative, because that is the "real" historical world of our texts. In other words, our understanding of a gender-critical approach, particularly because it is indebted in our minds to an ideology-critical enterprise, aims to delineate the sociocultural materials that go into producing the characters, plots, and narratives we encounter in the ancient world, and to explore how these elements serve to solidify the ideology of the text and its distribution and configuration of power structures through discourse.

It is also for this reason that our gender-critical approach pays so much attention to the *literary* dimensions of a text, whether that text is narrative or epistle in genre. We generally focus on the literary portrait of the characters in either genres, which, in our view, offers us a substantive perspective on the gendered, sexed, and sexual ideologies *in* the text. The complexity of this conceptual interplay in the text is such that not all of the various relations need to represent a conscious construction on the part of the author. This feature can be perceived, for instance, in the manner in which ancient characters often embody types of virtue and vice, and are therefore "ideal" portraits rather than representing "real" people as such (in terms of how modern people conceptualize historical phenomena). As we noted in chapter two with respect to the physiognomic portrayal of Paul in the *Acts of Paul and Thecla*, his representation in the text offers an analytic tool for exploring the gendered, sexed, and sexual nature of his portrayal. Descriptions form only a small part of the larger interest here, as actions and interactions in the text are frequently coded as well, particularly in terms of sociocultural expectations related to gender, sex, and sexuality. In the book of Acts, for instance, we observe the bold speech of the apostles before the Sanhedrin (5.17–42); Stephen confounding his opponents with his superior rhetoric (7.1–53); Paul walking away from a stoning (14.1–7), a shipwreck (27.14–43), or snakebite (28.1–6); Paul appealing to Caesar for a judicial hearing (25.10–12); all of which portray the apostles in highly idealized masculine ways. That is, they appear prominently in public forums, they comport themselves masterfully and with aplomb, they enact "bold speech," they are courageous in the face of adversity, and they evidence self-mastery/control of their passions.

Conversely, in the same texts, we also see the Jewish opponents of Stephen failing to do justice and to exhibit self-mastery as they drag him out to be stoned (7.53–60); Simon Magus seeking payment for the gift of the holy spirit (8.14–24); Herod praising himself as a god (12.20–23); the sons of Sceva being beaten by a demon possessed man (19.13–20); and Roman appointed leaders in Jerusalem unable to issue a just verdict for Paul (chapters 24–26) or willing to accept a bribe from him (24:26). All of these actions suggest that the opponents' characters are flawed: they are greedy, unable to control their passions, arrogant, or simply weak and ineffectual. These same actions are also gendered and sexed, in that they depict these male characters in less than ideal terms related to the gendered and sexed expectations in the ancient world: they are not moderate and they do not exhibit (let alone possess the ability for) self-mastery. The relationship of various characters is thus often of major importance for understanding the gendered and sexed dynamics of the text.

In a similar vein, Mary Rose D'Angelo has persuasively demonstrated that the way in which male and female characters are paired and interact in Luke-Acts provides a foil for one character over against another ("Women in Luke-Acts"). That is, frequently the male characters are heightened in status and stature by being offset by their pairing with a female counterpart. Moreover, throughout the book of Acts, one also notes a different manner of pairing, mostly between opposing male characters and groups. Thus, Paul and Elymas are paired in a showdown before the proconsul Sergius Paulus (13.6–12); the sons of Sceva are paired in their failure with the successes of Paul with respect to the performance of miracles (19.13–20); the Pharisees and Sadducees are paired in their respective reactions to Paul's proclamation of the resurrection (23.6–10); and the Stoics and Epicureans are paired in their reaction to Paul's discussion of the resurrection in Athens (17.16–34). These pairings are often intended to provide a foil for the main characters on display, heightening their own power and authority in contrast to their negative counterparts, embodied by the "others" in the narrative. Of course, we also find more positive parallels, such as between the Jesus of the Gospel of Luke and the apostles in the book of Acts, as well as between Peter and Paul in Acts. These comparative literary strategies could thus function in a variety of directions, both negative and positive (see Plutarch's *Parallel Lives* for an extensive and more complex example of the pairing of characters). Moreover, gendered, sexed, and sexual dynamics are formulated through such comparisons, even if sometimes subtly. The ideal character (from the perspective of the text/author) is shown to be superior by virtue of not displaying the negative aspects attributed to others. Foils are therefore critical for developing implied counter-assertions and creating a context for praising (or denigrating) particular individuals, communities, people-groups, and so on. The creation of alterity and abjection, then, form critical components in the representation of the ideal body and its normative performance in early Christian literature.

While this emphasis on characterization in literary perspective operates most overtly in narrative texts, there are clear convergences with epistolary argumentation as well. Too often literary approaches are limited strictly to narrative genres, without recognition that the patterns of persuasion apply across genres, even though the manifestation of those patterns may be different. For instance, Paul's writings are full of similar examples of rhetorical argumentation using comparison. Paul begins his first letter to the Corinthians noting the ministries of other early Christian leaders (Apollos, Cephas), over against which he cleverly juxtaposes his own mission (1 Cor. 3). Later, in his second letter to the Corinthians, Paul will contrast his "weakness in Christ" to the "super apostles," demonstrating, again, his actual superiority in the process (2 Cor. 10–12). In the epistle to the Galatians, Paul compares himself and his mission to that of the Jerusalem apostles (Gal. 2.1–10). In his letter to the Romans, Paul even uses a fictional debate partner (an interlocutor), in dialogue with whom he constructs his theological arguments (Rom. 6–7). Moreover, throughout his writings, Paul also draws implicit comparisons between himself and Christ, evidencing how much he has suffered for the cause of his "beloved Savior."[16] Such implicit comparisons serve to heighten Paul's relative status in the text, but, more importantly, such status enhancement functions to persuade his audience both to accept his leadership and to act in the way that he dictates. In short, then, the strategies of characterization and comparison that we draw from ancient rhetorical practice are not limited to narrative, but reflect a broad mindset operative among ancient writers. Moreover, it is precisely in and through such comparison that the gendered, sexed, and sexual nature of the discourse comes into focus. It is the identification of virtue and "true" character through the abjectifying of another that most visibly highlights the gendered, sexed, and sexual performance of the "chosen" individual in the text. The creation of alterity and otherness, then, allows the mimetic (imitative) features of a text to emerge more clearly.

Further along these lines, we also find it helpful in our gender-critical approach to pay attention to focalization in the text, in order to determine from whose perspective(s) a story is told.[17] Moreover, the ideology of the text is frequently bound up with both the presence and absence of characters.[18] Along these same lines, the location of characters and the spaces they inhabit are also essential to our analysis, since locations and spaces relate in specific ways to the gendered, sexed, and sexual nature of the ideology embodied in the narrative. For instance, the empire plays a central role in the book of Acts, and, as we have already noted, imperial space is gendered, sexed, and sexualized, constituting a male realm, but one in which images of female domesticity are critically important. Thus, the location of characters both with respect to the reader and with respect to the narrative (the relationship to other characters, places, and spaces) helps us to better assess the sociocultural rhetoric of the text. That is, we understand more fully how ancient tropes of gendered discourse are interwoven throughout a text, highlighting in specific ways the affirmation, reconfiguration, or overturning of dominant discourses and values. Further, we are also in a better position to interpret the relationship of these discourses to the larger ideologies represented in a text and to appreciate the complexity of the balance (and dissemination) of power through the various texts under study.

Keeping in view this larger intersection of ideology and rhetoric, we also pay close attention to the *ethos* of the author, or, stated in another way, the way in which the writer constructs his or her own identity in and through a text. In ancient rhetorical training, one of the most critical elements for orators (and by extension also writers) was that their own character and virtue were on display in their narrative compositions. The ancient world attests to numerous examples of ridicule that one could encounter when one's narrative was considered to be weak, effeminate, too exotic, overly dramatic, structurally imbalanced, or practically irrelevant. The appropriate narrative, to the contrary, would reflect well on the author, and would construct "his" identity as superior in an ancient context in which, as we noted in an earlier chapter, bodies were continually on display, contested, and in flux. Narrative comportment (meeting the standards of "good" narrative composition) reflected on the gendered, sexed, and sexual character of orators or writers, who were to be embodied consciously in their speech or text. Thus, narratives evidence the character of their author, and even the representation of other individuals in the narrative had much to communicate about the character of the author (e.g., are the portraits of individuals excessive? If so, then the author has revealed her– or himself as also being excessive, showing that they are not in control of their narrative and, by extension, themselves).

Moreover, in line with our comments in chapter one on gender performance, we also note that writing and textual composition are performative acts. That is, authors are embodied in the text, and the literary product becomes a representation of their own gendered, sexed, and sexual identities (at the intersection of other facets of identity). Thus, in his arguments in 1 Corinthians 11 regarding the proper relationship and public comportment of men and women, Paul similarly constructs not only his own complex identity as an authority and leader of the community, but, perhaps even more so, his own gendered, sexed, and sexual identity as well, which is embodied in that same moment of persuasion. That is, the performance of "leader" and "authority" are gendered, sexed, and sexual acts, and Paul's own sense of "who he is" is also reified through his construction of "self" in his exhortation.

Just as important, the reader and community that consume these texts are also constructed in light of them. The mimetic (or imitative) function of textual representation thus needs to be engaged in order to appreciate how representation transforms individuals and communities, making them "like" the discourses produced in and through the text. Indeed, we may even think here in terms of the creation of desire for the embodied ideologies of the text, which naturally plays into the communication and reception of the gendered, sexed, and sexual dynamics inherent in the discourses present in the text. Paul's rhetoric in 1 Corinthians 11, for example, constructs a specific kind of community comportment, which, while it may ultimately reflect back on his own identity, nonetheless also establishes the Corinthian community as an entity with a strong and "hard" masculine character. Powerful, prophesying women are not only present in the community, but they are also circumscribed within a pattern of male authority. This framing of the community stakes a claim about its own character in light of the social-cultural values of antiquity. In a similar, even if more implicit, vein, a narrative shapes not only the perception of the reader related to the events and characters described, but it also configures the identity of the reader/community in the process. The *ethos* (or "character") of the reader is thus constructed by the text, and this feature of literary production provides one of the more significant ways by which the ideology of the text is communicated to and absorbed by the reader. Thus, ideologies present in narrative are reproduced in often subtle ways.

In line with the theme of this book, we would also note that, alongside many other aspects of these ideological reproductions, one cannot ignore the gendered, sexed, and sexual lines that are reproduced in the process. In the book of Acts, for instance, seeing the apostles continually performing ideal masculinity in the public forum shapes the reader's identity in the direction of ideal masculine comportment in the ancient world—this representation offers a life worthy of imitation, a "reality" that is to be desired (for both male and female readers, albeit in differing ways). Thus, the community in front of the text is shaped in this particular gendered, sexed, and sexual direction. Further, since so many Greek, Jewish, and Roman characters in the narrative are depicted as performing less than ideal masculinity, the reader is being led all the more to the conclusion that true masculinity is embodied solely in the Christian community.

So far we have explained some of the assumptions and basic strategies behind the gender-critical approach we have been developing in this book. We have done so in order to elucidate how we "see" and arrange the historical data related to early Christianity. Further, fronting our assumptions and reading strategies also allows for a more open dialogue to take place between varying approaches and, most important, it creates a space for a meaningful discussion of methodology and analysis in the study of early Christian texts.

Reading (for) gender and the worlds of the text

Having discussed the reading assumptions and strategies of our own gender-critical approach, we now seek to situate them in the context of other ways of reading that foreground concepts of gender, sex, and sexuality in early

Christian texts. In order to do so, we follow David L. Barr (*New Testament Story*) in making a distinction between three different worlds that one deals with when reading a text: the world in front of, the world behind, and the world in a text. The "world in front of" the text is our own contemporary context, which, in the case of early Christian writings, is situated at quite a distance from the original time of production. As a result, numerous interpretations through the centuries stand between our own context for reading and the text itself, and this reception history influences the way we read the text in the first place. This is the case, for instance, with Paul's letters, such as 1 Corinthians 14.34–35, where women are told to be silent, which has been used for centuries to legitimate the subordination of women in society and church. As we already noted in previous chapters, the way we read a text is also informed by the presuppositions and ideas present in our own culture. Thus, Paul's argument that it is "natural" for men to have short hair and for women to have long hair (1 Cor. 11.14) may sound absurd to us, but it evidently made sense to him.

The second world that Barr mentions is the "world behind the text," which refers to the sociohistorical context in which a text was composed. This world is often quite different from our own, and a historical approach is necessary here in order to access the situation in which the text was written and to gain information about its original author(s) as well as audience(s). So, if one is interested in discovering why Paul wrote his letters to the Corinthians, and what the circumstances in Corinth might have been that provided the catalyst for his interventions, then one is moving behind the text in order to construct a plausible historical situation as a basis for subsequent interpretation.

Finally, the "world in the text" is the literary world created by the text itself. A literary approach is appropriate in this instance, since it pays attention to the genres and rhetorical features of a text in order to understand how and what it communicates. Assessing the storyline, plot developments, recurring tropes, intertextual connections, character representation, and so forth offers one an entry into the world generated by the text. Here a literary approach makes it possible to map out the structure of a story, while a rhetorical analysis aids in the reconstruction of its underlying arguments.

That Barr lists these three worlds in this particular order, starting with "in front of" and from there to "behind" and "in" the text, is far from accidental. As he explains, his goal "is to hear these documents in something like their original key: to try to understand what they may have meant to the people who first heard them" (*New Testament Story*, 15). Barr's interest, therefore, is clearly oriented towards the past, with an emphasis on going back to a supposed original meaning (in its sociocultural and historical contexts) or at least as close as possible as we can reasonably get. His project then is one of historical reconstruction, and the cultural biases that influence modern understandings of ancient texts are thus identified so they can be bracketed in the interpretive process. As already noted, our interest lies elsewhere, but Barr's distinction between the different worlds of the text provides a helpful tool by which to enter into a methodological discussion of how and why our own approach differs. Moreover, the distinction between these three worlds can be related to different ways of interpreting biblical texts. The first approach, with its focus on contemporary culture, explores the impact of the reader on the process of interpretation, and thus engages the reception of the text (including the ethics of interpretation). The second approach emphasizes more squarely the creation of the text by a particular author at a specific historical moment in time, and is therefore oriented towards the pastness of the text. Finally, the third approach concentrates on the text itself and what it communicates to the ancient and contemporary reader.

Since we use Barr's distinction here in order to situate our own approach, in what follows we discuss these three worlds, although in a slightly different order. We start with the world behind the text and move from there to the world in the text and end with the world in front of the text. As will become clear, this separating of worlds is an artificial exercise, because all three intersect in the act of interpretation, and the same is the case with the respective approaches related to the study of those worlds. As a result, interpreters often address more than one world of the text in their analysis (often without realizing it), even as one or another world is usually foregrounded in the act of reading and interpreting.

The world behind the text

In order to recover the world behind the text, a historical reconstruction of both the text and the historical circumstances in which it was written is required. This move is the main focus of the historical-critical method that originated in the modern period. As already noted in the previous chapter, F. C. Baur and the Tübingen school played a major role in its development. This method is oriented towards the original text, as well as to the authors and audiences of the early Christian writings, and seeks to reconstruct the situation addressed *by* the author of the text, but often also the situation described *in* the text. The results of such reconstructive work, however, vary widely.

For instance, in the case of 1 Corinthians 11.2–16, which contains Paul's argument regarding how women should pray and prophecy in the Christian assembly, the activities of the women Paul has in view have been interpreted negatively as well as positively. In the first case, Paul's attitude is seen as justified because the behavior of the women in question cannot be tolerated. They are often depicted as (proto)feminists, whom Paul "rightly" puts in their proper place. Thus, for instance, James B. Hurley notes that "the Corinthian women no doubt saw the loosing of their hair as a sign that they possessed authority equal to that of the men. Paul pointed out that their action was in fact a rejection of the order of God and of the role of women; loosed hair was a sign of rebellion and disgrace" (*Man and Woman in Biblical Perspective*, 177).

A significantly different interpretation is put forward by Antoinette Clark Wire, who understands the women to be prominent female prophets in Corinth whom Paul seeks to control. She argues that "Paul's forceful move against opposition can only be seen as an effort to restrict her [i.e., the female prophet's] role in the community. Therefore it provides a measure of her considerable social power" (*Corinthian Women Prophets*, 130). In both cases, an effort is made to uncover the historical situation Paul addresses in his first letter to the Corinthians, but the results of that reconstruction are quite different. Of further note here is that Clark Wire arrives at her reconstruction through an analysis of Paul's rhetorical strategies, an approach that clearly relates to the world in the text. Her method thus combines a literary approach with historical investigation. In her reading of the text, she counters the Pauline discourse, providing a "mirror" construction of the positions of the women mentioned in (but really behind) the text. Herein, she offers a positive interpretation of their religious activity and posits a more negative evaluation of Paul's rhetorical moves. In other words, she does not accept Paul as the norm, but rather sees him as representing a dominant male perspective (patriarchal in orientation) as he suppresses women's voices and experiences (in this case their prophetic activity) in the local Corinthian community.

The world in the text

Although every approach deals with the world in the text in one way or another, a literary approach focuses more squarely on the characteristics and structures embedded in the text itself. Literary approaches will, however, differ depending on the genre of the text in question. A narrative approach, for instance, is more appropriate for analyzing a story rather than a poem or an argument in one of Paul's letters. Moreover, the world behind the text also plays a role in one's understanding of the world in the text. For instance, as Barr points out, in the case of Paul's epistles one needs to take into account that letters were a particular literary genre in antiquity and that the use of rhetorical techniques was a common practice. Further, as already noted earlier in this chapter, we also find the study of ancient rhetoric to be a helpful tool for grasping more fully the ways in which Paul shapes the argumentation in his letters. It is clear, then, that our understanding of the ancient world informs how we approach the material in a text, and it becomes almost impossible to read the text without having a significant reconstruction of the world behind it in mind.

This point can be further substantiated by a brief look at various interpreters who have employed a rhetorical analysis to understand 1 Corinthians 11.2–16. In his essay "Veiled Exhortations Regarding the Veil," Troy Martin uses the concept of *ethos* as it appears in the ancient rhetorical handbooks and in Aristotle's treatise *On Rhetoric* to interpret this difficult passage. The term *ethos* here refers to the way in which the speaker presents himself—his character—to the audience he addresses in his speech. It thus relates to his own self-construction and self-fashioning, that is, the image and character he creates of himself in order to be convincing. Martin argues that the appeal Paul makes to custom in 11.16 ("we have no such custom, nor do the churches of God") has to be interpreted in light of Paul's own authoritative *ethos*. Martin notes, "unless the Corinthian readers accept the *ethos* of Paul and the churches of God, the exhortations and the supporting rationale lack persuasive force" (272). Here again, elements of the world behind the text (e.g. the study of ancient rhetoric) are used to understand the world in the text.

Elisabeth Schüssler Fiorenza provides another example of a rhetorical approach to 1 Corinthians, particularly in her *Rhetoric and Ethic* (1999) and, more recently, *The Power of the Word* (2007), where she understands the letter to evidence deliberative rhetoric. This rhetorical classification means that a speaker's main purpose is to contribute to the process of decision-making by seeking to convince the audience that a particular course of action is either desirable or not. If that is indeed Paul's intent, then he is addressing a certain group of people in the community, more specifically those with a higher social status like himself, who are in a position to make such decisions. But, Schüssler Fiorenza notes, "His 'veiled hostility' and appeal to authority in the so-called women's passages indicates . . . that he does not include women of high social and educational status in this appeal" (*Rhetoric and Ethic*, 122).

1 Corinthians 11.16 should therefore be read as "an authoritative assertion of the will of Paul" (117) placed at the end of an argument that itself lacks persuasion. In her reading of the text, Schüssler Fiorenza clearly foregrounds a rhetorical analysis of 1 Corinthians, but she does so with the historical situation in mind, and thus she moves from the world in the text to the world behind it. However, she also addresses the world in front of the text by paying attention to the way the text has been interpreted by later readers. Thus, she notes that Paul is a "skilled rhetorician, who throughout the centuries has reached his goal of persuading his audience that he is right and the 'others' are wrong" (111). This remark foregrounds subsequent readers of the text, both past and present, illustrating that the world in front of the text is always operative in terms of the choices one makes in reading gendered, sexed, and sexual ideologies with respect to the world in the text.

The world in front of the text

The cultural context in which a given text is experienced and interpreted by the reader (of any time period) is the world in front of the text. It is here that the contemporary reader of a text is to be situated. In the case of a text from the past, however, a tradition of interpretation is often situated between the text and its subsequent readers. This framework is also referred to as the "reception history" of a text. It not only includes scholarly interpretations, but also artistic and popular renderings that are part of a larger cultural reservoir of texts, images, and meanings. While there are innumerable ways of pursuing this discussion, we choose here to examine more closely feminist resistance to male dominated readings as a means to explore broader issues in confronting the "world in front of the text." We note, for instance, that the reader of the text is most often presumed to be male, but, as Jonathan Culler queries in his book *On Deconstruction* (1982), "suppose the informed reader of a work of literature is a woman" (43), might this not make a difference for how one reads a text? Culler is thinking here of feminist literary criticism as it developed in the second half of the twentieth century, and his assertion is reminiscent of the conversation between Burrus and Kaestli that we highlighted at the beginning of the fourth chapter. Indeed, as we argue in what follows, his analysis can also be applied to feminist approaches within Biblical Studies. Although the categories used can at times seem essentialist in their formulation, we consider them to offer a helpful and strategic heuristic tool for breaking down normative structures of meaning. By viewing interpretive moves through the lens of the

repressed "other," we are in a position to expose the illusory nature of the normative, stable, and dominant center that has been the axis of meaning for most
interpretations of early Christian literature.

Culler distinguishes more specifically between three modes of reading in
his discussion of feminist literary criticism. The first mode of reading is
thematic in terms of its emphasis on the female characters in a work. This
focus is at odds with an uncritical identification of male readers with the male
characters in a text. Moreover, it draws on the experience of female readers as
a source of authority for their own reading, an assertion that Culler believes
stands on its own. The second mode of reading, to the contrary, problematizes
the idea that it is enough to be a female in order to read as a woman. This
distinction is necessary, in Culler's view, in order to explain why women have
not always been reading as women over the years. Instead, they have often
identified with male characters and interests. "Reading as a woman," then, is
not a given, it is something one has to learn, a principle reminiscent of Simone
de Beauvoir's famous line "one is not born, but, rather, *becomes* a woman."
In other words, one does not read "as a woman" just because one identifies
"as a woman." Thus, this principle could also be expanded to include all
readers, male and female alike, as this framework is about reading through the
lens of the repressed "other." In the same moment, we also become more fully
aware of the presence of the dominant center—the normative, hegemonic
principles of reading that have passed as universal and therefore stand uncon-
tested. One therefore has to become a "resisting reader," one who reads against
the ideological grain of a text.[19]

In the third mode, Culler goes even further by investigating the underlying
ideology that associates male/masculinity with rationality and privileges intel-
lectuality over sensuality (which is identified as its "female" counterpart). This
third mode represents an alternative option: to read from a situation or experience of marginality with respect to dominant discourses. To that effect, different strategies are used. *One strategy* is the development of a feminine discourse
as an alternative to dominant male discourse (a practice called *écriture feminine,* which literally means "women's writing"), a convention that is represented
by French feminist theorists such as Julia Kristeva (1941–), Helene Cixous
(1937–), and Luce Irigaray (1932–). This approach offers a strategy of resistance against the reduction of the Other to the One and the Same, meaning
that a dominant (male), universal subject becomes the norm for all others.
Thus, all other subjects have to conform to *that* one (male) type, reducing
diversity and alterity to phenomena that merely relate to dominant male

identity. Luce Irigaray, for instance, sought to create a discursive space for the "female feminine" to express a different mode of subjectivity. Far from being a given, this practice is a mode of intentional thought that needs to be constructed and that becomes performative through repeated enactment (it is, in short, a discipline). For Irigaray herself, the place to start was with the body as a libidinal space of female pleasure (*jouissance*). A *second strategy* is to criticize and challenge from the margins the phallogocentric nature of dominant discourse itself, phallogocentrism being the ideology that identifies masculinity (*phallus*) with rationality (*logos*).

As Culler notes, in all three feminist modes of reading some appeal is made to the experience of the reader, but this experience is increasingly understood as a complex category that is presumed, produced, and configured in the process of reading. Thus, Culler points out, reading as a woman is "not to repeat an identity or an experience that is given but to play a role she constructs with reference to her identity as a woman, which is also a construct" (*On Deconstruction*, 64). Both what it means to "be a woman" and what it means to "read as a woman" are therefore constructs. That is, they are formulations of identities and subjectivities that shape the way we read and they will vary depending on who is using the strategy and in which context it is employed. This focus brings us back to our discussion of bodies in the first chapter, particularly the fluidity and instability of the categories we use to construct modern gendered, sexed, and sexual identities. One could thus be a "man" reading "as a woman" or, conversely, a "female" can choose to read as a "male" (without necessarily adopting the phallogocentric discourse). For Culler, it is the engagement of these categories—understanding their relative nature—that empowers readers of texts. Moreover, in the process of adopting these reading strategies, we are also disciplining our own bodies and forming new subjectivities for ourselves and our communities, even as we may also be crossing boundaries, moving between various chosen identities.

As already noted, Culler's analysis of feminist literary criticism can be applied to similar developments within the field of Biblical Studies, which were often informed by literary criticism, including Culler's own deconstructionist approach. The first mode of reading in this case corresponds to those interpretations of the Bible in which biblical women are reclaimed. In this case, female experience and images are recovered from the biblical text and revalued as sources of inspiration and empowerment for women today. This process of recovery has a political and ethical function in that it offers positive models for identification with biblical women of the past and legitimates women's struggles in the present, while also giving voice to women's repressed identities in the past. Thus, the prophetic activity of women mentioned in 1 Corinthians 11 has been reclaimed by female interpreters. Such a reclamation is found in the *Study Bible for Women: The New Testament* (1995), where female prophets are seen as "proof that God calls and equips women for religious leadership" (124) and where God is understood as "an *equal opportunity employer*" (125).

Culler's second mode is represented by a feminist hermeneutics of the Bible that claims it is not enough to read as a woman, but that one rather has to be a feminist reader, who consciously resists the rhetorical tactics and ideological games of the biblical text. Needed, therefore, is an approach that questions the depiction of women in the text, rather than taking those representations at face value and as "real." Thus, in *A Feminist Introduction to Paul* (2005), Sandra Hack Polaski notes that 1 Corinthians 11.2–16 "betrays an underlying suspicion of women's dangerous sexuality, a suspicion that seems to be grounded in a fear of difference" (56).[20] In other words, the rhetoric of the text easily seduces (perhaps even coerces in some respects) the reader into taking the text's perspective (reading with the text). However, this perspective suppresses in the process female alterity or otherness, particularly with respect to sexuality, and aligns the female subject with the pattern of the male norm (in which sexuality needs to be controlled, repressed, and situated outside of dominant male discourse).[21] It is therefore not by accident that women become a site for sexualized discourse and repression in the first place, as the male norm displaces that "dangerous pleasure" onto the female "other." There is thus both displacement onto the female and then an attempt to control the female, often in the same moment. The resisting reader, in Culler's view, is able to circumvent this process by being aware of how the text itself functions to sustain these complex moments of projection and displacement, thereby recovering the alterity of the female subject in the text.

Culler's third mode is reflected, on the one hand, in the use in biblical interpretation of insights from the French feminist theorists and, on the other, in the feminist criticism (from the margins) of both dominant discourses in the field of Biblical Studies and the latter's inherent phallogocentric value-system. An example of the former strategy can be found in Jorunn Økland's essay "Feminist Reception of the New Testament." Here she reads 1 Corinthians 11 through the interpretive lens of Luce Irigaray's *Speculum of the Other Woman* (1985), in which Irigaray suggests that within a phallogocentric paradigm woman is non-representable or, as Økland frames the point, "the word 'woman' only functions within this discourse as an empty category with changing content" (151). In other words, "woman" is a word that is constantly filled with male meaning. It is not about women, then; rather, it is about men, and women become a trope for the construction and maintenance of male identity. When applied to Paul's discussion in 1 Corinthians 11.2–16, this approach entails that the term "woman" in this text represents nothing but "a category of otherness in relation to the male" (151). As a result, the text no longer provides access to the history of women behind the text. For Økland, then, rather than trying to reconstruct that history, a more fruitful way forward is to demonstrate the instability that notions of gender, sex, and sexuality have had through time.

An example of the second strategy in Culler's third mode of reading can be found in the work of Elisabeth Schüssler Fiorenza. We refer here more specifically to her essay "Defending the Center, Trivializing the Margins" and the first part of her book *Rhetoric and Ethic,* in which she insists on the necessity of a paradigm shift in the self-understanding of biblical scholars. She states, "biblical studies must be decentered in such a way that the voices from the margins of the discipline who raise the issue of power, access and legitimation can participate on equal terms in fashioning a multi-voiced center that is perpetually decentering itself" ("Defending the Center," 30). As far as the strategies for such decentering are concerned, the place to begin, in her view, is with a hermeneutics of experience and social location. The experience in question is that of "wo/men," symbolically split in two, to denote both the term's ambiguity and its inclusive character. The category of "experience" is problematized here as well, insofar as it does not simply refer to someone's individual or personal experience, but rather to how one's experience is shaped by one's sociopolitical location. Thus, the question becomes "how wo/men's social, cultural, and religious location has shaped their experience with and reaction to a particular biblical text or story" (*Rhetoric and Ethic,* 49), such as, for instance, 1 Corinthians 14 (or 1 Cor. 11 for that matter). This approach not only exemplifies the second strategy mentioned by Culler (feminist criticism), it also shows that one and the same interpreter can use different approaches to the text, depending on the particular agenda she or he has in mind. Thus, Schüssler Fiorenza herself uses a rhetorical approach to analyze the world in the text and a mode of reading from the margins to address issues related to the world in front of the text.

On a final note, we observe, as Culler also does, that in all three modes of reading an (sometimes veiled) appeal is made to experience. Thus, the world in front of the text is always present. This appeal to experience is not so surprising when one realizes that, when he wrote his book, Culler was indebted to the insights of the feminist movement beginning with Simone de Beauvoir's *The Second Sex* (1953) and developing through the 1980s. Only later in the twentieth century did the major issues regarding this feminist interpretation arise: that in the process of reclaiming a female reader's position, the male-female binary was not only confirmed but also naturalized. It is precisely this point that Schüssler Fiorenza addresses in her later work by fragmenting the word "wo/men." Moreover, interpretive strategies emerged that sought to queer both the text and its readers. Such methods further destabilized hegemonic heterosexual identities. Essentialist and unitary notions of gendered, sexed, and sexual identity were thus replaced by fragmentary and multiple conceptualizations and, as a result, identity as a stable signifier was further undermined. In the process, then, masculinity and maleness as static categories of meaning became destabilized as well (see chapter one for more detail).

Summary

In order to contextualize the three examples that follow, we draw a few links with the preceding discussion that help situate our own approach in the following pages. To begin with, rather than focusing on one world, our gender-critical approach to a text aims at addressing all three worlds of the text as well as the multiple intersections between them. As already noted, as far as the world *behind* the text is concerned, we are not invested in reconstructing some reality that lies *behind*, but rather in addressing issues related to the socio-historical context of the text that help us understand the facets evident *in* the text, such as the gendered, sexed, and sexual tropes of ancient religious discourses and the sociopolitical context of empire. This agenda fits better with the overall focus of our approach than do reconstructions of actual historical readers and communities, even as we also acknowledge the tentative and relative nature of our own results.

The world *in* the text thus comes into focus when we address its rhetorical character and ideological texture, exploring both the way it promotes particular ideologies and how it assumes and implies other ideological elements in the process. Our emphasis is therefore on how gendered, sexed, and sexual paradigms reflect and promote or resist the ideologies in question. As far as the world *in front of* the text is concerned, our gender-critical approach has most in common with Culler's third mode of reading, in that it has *both* an overt political agenda in terms of interpreting past and present constructions of gender, sex, and sexuality *and* a commitment to destabilizing the dominant phallogocentric subject (which we understand to be normatively and universally gendered, sexed, and sexualized) and the latter's inherent association with rationality (including also the attendant principle of the female subject's inherent connection to sensuality). This approach also addresses the history of interpretation in engaging other readings (often exposing the way in which subsequent interpretations tend to mimic earlier ones), but seeks to go a step further in widening the scope beyond the male-female, heterosexual dichotomy/binary to include a more complex understanding of constructions of gender, sex, and sexuality.[22] Ideology-critical interpretive strategies thus come to the forefront, as we explore how rhetoric sustains both power structures and dominant discourses while at the same time also masking the visibility and reality of these same dynamics.

In summary, then, just as it is important to delineate the various assumptions and reading strategies for our gender-critical approach, we consider it as crucial to be aware of the various worlds in, in front of, and behind the text, which we are continually engaging. The three are consistently intertwined in any act of reading and interpretation, and for that reason it is critical to be conscious of the moves and shifts we make between these worlds of the text. As we noted at the end of the previous section, not only is such an awareness important for helping one assess his or her own analysis of a given text, it is also useful for analyzing and engaging other, often divergent, approaches to the same text.

Three examples of reading (for) gender

The following examples are offered in order to illustrate the preceding discussion of our gender-critical approach. The first example is taken from Paul's letters. Here we analyze a particular argument in 1 Corinthians 11, which we have also used as an illustration throughout this book. The second example comes from the Acts of the Apostles, and demonstrates how a narrative text can be analyzed. The third example is drawn from the *Acts of Paul and Thecla*, and provides a noncanonical illustration of our approach. In the following discussion, we are interested in how the three worlds of the text (behind, in, and in front of) are intertwined, and also how they are engaged in our gender-critical reading strategy, all with the aim of assessing more clearly the gendered, sexed, and sexual lines of context, rhetoric, and interpretation, and the interweaving of these elements in the text.

1 Corinthians 11.2–16

As we noted earlier, our gender-critical approach addresses all three worlds of a text but, with respect to the first two worlds, it focuses primarily on the historical context that gives shape to the world *in* the text rather than on the history *behind* the text. Moreover, our specific point of interest is the construction of gender, sex, and sexuality operative in these three levels of reading. In 1 Corinthians 11.2–16, as in Paul's letters as whole, the argument is foregrounded and therefore a rhetorical method is an appropriate tool with which to analyze the world in the text. We further broaden this perspective on the historical context of the text by examining some parallel passages from Epictetus (50–ca. 130 CE) and Plutarch (46–ca. 120 CE). To conclude, we shift the focus from the world in and of the text to the world in front of the text, by looking at the implications of our observations for the interpretive tradition of this passage.[23]

Our main interest in analyzing Paul's argumentation is how issues related to the proper comportment of men and women, which are at stake in this passage, are being negotiated with the use of ancient rhetorical tools. Thus, rather than focusing on the question of what exactly was going on in Corinth and what the issue under discussion in this passage was all about (veiling, headcovering, hairstyle, or some other practice), we rather emphasize how the issue is presented and argued. Critical for our interpretation is 11.5b, where two different situations are compared and identified with each other: the states of being uncovered and of being shaved. The purpose for this juxtaposition is to transfer the scandalous character of being shaved to that of being uncovered. This move is achieved by the underlying logic that goes as follows: it is shameful for a woman to cut or shave her hair (11.6b); to have her head uncovered is the same as being shaved (11.5b); therefore it is shameful to be uncovered (11.5a). By making this move, Paul seeks to convince his audience of a particular point, arguing that "uncovering," which is the issue under discussion, is as disgraceful as shaving, a position with which he believes his audience will agree. The logic of the passage hinges on a presumed shared cultural value, which is one of the critical elements in any rhetorical argument.

As a result, the issue at stake is identified with a conviction that is undisputed, and the former (being "uncovered") should therefore (in his view) be rejected by his audience as well. Paul further strengthens his argument in 11.13

with an appeal to what is "proper" behavior: "Judge for yourselves: is it proper for a woman to pray to God uncovered?" It is clear that the answer to this rhetorical question that Paul presumes to hear from his audience is a resounding "No!" Of interest to us, however, is that this appeal, and also the argument in 11.5–6, relates to cultural values and assumptions regarding the nature of proper gendered and sexed behavior, in this case for women (but with an implied converse for men). These arguments from culture are followed by a reference to nature in 11.14–15 that does not really sound convincing to modern ears: "Does not nature itself teach you that if a man wears long hair, it is degrading to him, but if a woman has long hair, it is her glory? For hair is given to her for a wrapper." Once again Paul confronts his audience with a question, but this time the answer is supposed to be "Yes." Nature, Paul argues, indicates that there is a clear gendered and sexed distinction when it comes to long hair: it is a woman's glory, but dishonorable for a man. Paul invokes nature as a teacher to make this point, which has the functional status of a normative, universal standard, as nature is understood to offer the pattern for human behavior.

Here then we arrive at a second element in our gender-critical approach: the historical context of the text, which includes paying attention both to ancient religious discourses as well as to the sociopolitical context of empire. In what follows, we will focus on similar arguments that are made regarding hair in Greco-Roman moral discourse, more specifically in Epictetus and Plutarch. In his *Discourses*, Epictetus offers a comment that bears striking similarities with the appeal to nature made by Paul:

> Come, let us leave the chief works of **nature**, and consider merely what she does in passing. Can anything be more useless than the hairs on a chin? Well, what then? Has not **nature** used even these in the most suitable way possible? Has she not by these means distinguished between the male and the female? . . . Wherefore, we ought to preserve the signs which God has given; we ought not to throw them away; we ought not, so far as in us lies, to confuse the sexes which have been distinguished in this fashion. (1.16.9–12, 14)

With respect to the parallels in the arguments of both Epictetus and Paul, nature appears personified, it is "she" who distinguishes between men and women. In the case of Epictetus, this argument is accomplished by way of highlighting the presence of hair on men's chins (and its absence on women), in the case of Paul, by way of noting the respective difference in length of hair on the head of men and women. Yet these elements of gender and sex difference are also normative, in that they indicate what the appropriate behavior of both men and women is to be, as well as pointing out that the distinctions between the sexes should not be eradicated or confused.

This need for distinction becomes even clearer in another passage from Epictetus, where he discusses the presence or absence of hair on the body and ridicules men who remove that hair. He states:

> Woman is born smooth and dainty **by nature**, and if she is very hairy, she is a prodigy, and is exhibited at Rome among the prodigies. But for a man not to be hairy is the same thing, and if **by nature** he has no hair he is a prodigy, but if he cuts it out and plucks it out of himself, what shall we make of him?... Man, what reason have you to complain against your **nature**? . . . Make a clean sweep of the whole matter; eradicate your—what shall I call it?—the cause of your hairiness; make yourself a woman all over, so as not to deceive us, half-man and half-woman. (3.1.27–31)

Again, Epictetus fulminates against the blurring of sexual difference, especially by men, and appeals to nature to argue in favor of a clear distinction between women and men. As with Paul, hair is an important "natural" indicator of sex difference, a difference that needs to be respected and reflected in human behavior and appearance. The appeal both writers make to nature should be understood against the background of popular Greek ideas, also shared by Hellenistic Jewish writers such as Josephus (37-ca. 100 CE) and Philo (20 BCE-50 CE). It is based on the distinction between nature and convention or custom, a conceptual relation that comes close to, but is not entirely identical with, the distinction modern people make between nature and culture.

However, as the following example from Plutarch makes clear, the appeal to either nature or custom was also determined by the argumentative end in question. In a context related to a discussion of funeral rites, Plutarch refers to the way that men and women should appear and act:

> Why do sons cover their head when they escort their parents to the grave, while daughters go with uncovered heads and hair unbound? Is it because fathers should be honoured as gods by their male offspring, but mourned as dead by their daughters, that **custom** has assigned to each sex its proper part and has produced a fitting result from both? Or is it that the unusual is proper in mourning, and it is more usual for women to go forth in public with their heads covered and men with their heads uncovered? So in Greece, whenever any misfortune comes, the women cut off their hair and the men let it grow, for it is usual for men to have their hair cut and for women to let it grow. (*Moralia* 267A–B)

When compared with Paul, we note again some remarkable similarities. Both Plutarch and Paul establish a connection between covering the head and the length of hair, using similar terminology to do so. Both also agree that long hair and a headcovering are typical for women, but unusual for men. A remarkable difference, however, is that Plutarch considers this practice to be a matter of custom, while both Paul and Epictetus appeal to nature when they discuss this matter. This difference in approach may well be related to the fact that Plutarch seeks to explain a practice that he does not consider problematic per se, while Paul and Epictetus have a vested interest in the argument they are making. Thus, their appeal to nature is intended to serve their rhetorical end, in that they seek to convince their audience of the normative character of the behavior they are advocating (or discouraging). They are thus *pre*scribing a certain practice, while Plutarch is merely *de*scribing one. This observation not only throws some light on Paul's use of "nature," but also on the role this use plays in the context of his larger argument.

These examples from Epictetus and Plutarch bring us back to the issue of Paul's rhetoric in 1 Corinthians 11. As the comparison with Epictetus and Plutarch makes clear, Paul's rhetoric reflects the sociocultural discursive conventions of his time, as well as its gendered, sexed, and sexual politics of identity formation. However, his rhetoric also reflects back on him, in that it establishes his own *ethos*/character in the process. After all, his own gendered, sexed, and sexual identity is at stake in all of his argumentation. That Paul has a vested interest in what he argues often goes unnoticed by modern readers, and, as a result, subsequent interpretations tend to reinscribe Paul's "hairy" rhetoric and the multidimensional identity politics embedded therein. Part of that larger gendered, sexed, and sexual identity politics includes the display of both *virtus* and *imperium* on the part of the male orator. His self-mastery should be evident in his own rhetorical performance. Insofar as the Corinthian community is a manifestation of Paul's own *ethos* as its founder, not only the character of the community but also his own image and character is at stake in his rhetorical performance in the text.[24] Indeed, the two are inextricably linked: the comportment of the community reflects Paul's own standing, because he is their "founder" and "father," while Paul's status characterizes the community he has founded. These ideas are reflected in his rhetoric, as he seeks to control the bodies in Corinth using his power of persuasion. Through this rhetoric the bodies of the women in Corinth are constructed as most in need of such control (and men, by implication, are those who are to exhibit that control). These women are perceived to be threatening order and transgressing the gendered and sexed boundaries of the community. This facet of his argument further demonstrates that Paul's rhetoric not only reflects but also reinscribes the normative male/patriarchal gendered, sexed , and sexual identity of his cultural context and time.

Insofar as interpretations of this and other Pauline texts focus on content but are oblivious to the thoroughly gendered, sexed, and sexual nature of Paul's rhetoric itself, they run the risk of reading with the text and of reproducing Paul's androcentric and phallogocentric rhetoric. Indeed, it is the overlay of male gendered and sexed rhetoric that helps sustain the androcentric reading patterns that scholars have frequently followed. This reinscription often occurs as a result of focusing on Paul's theology as the true essence that can be abstracted from the particularities of historical time and place. For instance, Francis Watson, in his discussion of this passage, notes that Paul wants women to cover their heads in order to "ward off the erotically charged male look from the face of the woman who prays or prophecies, in order that nothing might detract from the authority of her voice" ("Authority of the Voice," 535).[25] Paul may not have convinced the Corinthians with this argument, but still "the original symbolism of the veil retains its theological value" (536), in that it signals the possibility of a relationship between men and women that is no longer based on eros (sexual desire) but on agape (Christian love). While Watson's reading attempts both to retain Pauline authority and to reinterpret the text so as to make it appear less harmful to women in the assembly, it also simultaneously attests to the impact that Paul's own rhetoric continues to have on the history of interpretation of this text. Thus, Paul's authority is retained in reading *with* Paul's rhetoric rather than *against* it. It is perhaps not surprising, then, that the traditional reading of Paul (reflected here in Watson's interpretation) is frequently embraced by male scholars.

Acts 18.1–18

The second example for illustrating our gender-critical approach to an early Christian text is a short passage dealing with Paul's stopover in Corinth as part of his "missionary journey," which appears in the book of Acts. At the outset of the narrative, Luke notes that the two Jews whom Paul meets, Priscilla and Aquila, have recently arrived from Italy, which they left as a result of the expulsion of Jews by the Emperor Claudius (18.1–3). Luke thus explains their presence in Corinth as the result of a decision made by Roman imperial powers. Luke further notes that Paul stays with them and that he visits the synagogue "every Sabbath" (18.3–4). As a result, Paul appears first and foremost within the local Jewish community, a point Luke makes clear before he mentions that Paul's audience actually consists of both Jews and Greeks (18.4). A conflict with the Jews arises, however, and this leads to Paul's decision to turn his missionary attention solely to the Gentiles (18.6). He leaves the synagogue and goes to the house next door, which belongs to a man who is introduced as Titius Justus and is described as "a worshipper of God" (18.7). Presumably this individual is a Gentile, probably a Roman, but the designation "worshipper of God" also relates him to the Jewish community, since he worships the "Jewish" deity. Next, the leader of the synagogue, Crispus, and his household, as well as many Corinthians, become believers and are baptized (18.8). But when the proconsul Gallio arrives on the scene (18.12), problems arise from within the Jewish community again, and they bring Paul before the court of the Roman proconsul. Gallio, however, promptly dismisses the Jewish complaint as an internal affair and, as such, it is a matter that no longer concerns him (18.14–15). The scene ends with an ambiguous group of individuals (Jews, Greeks, and/or Romans?) turning on Sosthenes, the (new) leader of the synagogue. This group beats him in front of Gallio, who simply ignores their actions. As a result of the proconsul's indifference Paul goes free and continues his teaching (18:18a).

Some intriguing elements arise from this brief story for a broader discursive analysis of Luke's mapping of space as well as his distinctive gendered and sexed point of view. More generally, we note that Luke consistently focalizes on spaces and places in his accounts, moving between public and private domains. Further, alongside the broader movement from Athens to Corinth to Ephesus (on a spectrum of movement toward Jerusalem and Rome), in this story in particular Paul moves from inside the Jewish community, symbolized by the synagogue, to the household next door, which belongs to a Gentile "god-fearing" man. Moreover, Paul's shift from the public male stage of the synagogue to the domestic sphere of a house that is identified as belonging to a male (Titius Justus), reenacts on a small scale what unfolds in Acts on a grander scheme. That is, the heroes in the book of Acts are shown claiming spaces and places for Christ, while progressively moving the focus of missionary activity from the Jews to the Gentiles. Furthermore, as Paul repeatedly shifts from domestic to public spaces in empire, and from public to domestic, he also mimics that movement in this particular locale. In all of this spatial movement, his proclamation and authority reigns supreme, to the extent that "many of those Corinthians hearing [Paul] believed and were baptized" (18.8). Here, then, the power displayed in both domestic and public spaces at Corinth yields dramatic results in terms of the numbers of people converted to the emergent faith, which further remaps authority in social and political space. Also, in stark contrast to the lack of control exhibited by his Jewish opponents in Corinth and the indifference in terms of judicial oversight shown by the Roman authority, Paul evidences a superior display of *imperium* (authority/power) and *virtus* (manliness), critical elements of male comportment in the ancient world, traditionally embodied in ideal form in the emperor himself.[26] Romanness may appear to be the vanishing point in this narrative, but in fact it resurfaces in Paul's own narrative comportment. That is, Paul is the one who embodies what it means to be a "true" male, and the Romans, alongside the Jews, provide a foil for Paul's superior display in word and action.

The response of some of the prominent Jews, such as Crispus, as well as others in Corinth, affirm that Paul is a convincing speaker. His power of speech is apparent throughout this brief narrative. Thus, in a variety of different ways, Luke, the writer of Acts, has shaped Paul as an ideal masculine type. This is not the only direction in which Paul's character has been configured, and, using another model of interpretation, one could read these elements in a non-gendered way as well. But in a gender-critical approach it is precisely the gendered, sexed, and sexual (or potentially so) nature of the portrayal that is foregrounded in the analysis, allowing one to interpret these elements in the portrait of Paul as being significant in terms of his depiction as an ideal male.

One might also look at other elements in the narrative in a similarly gendered and sexed manner. For instance, the religious remapping that accompanies the shaping of the story cannot be ignored. Greek religion does not play a role in this story; rather, it is the Jewish law that becomes the center of the charge brought before the Roman proconsul Gallio. This religious and cultural issue—the two are clearly fused here—represents a critical component in the narrative argument. The Jewish law becomes the trope around which the spatial movement (and conflict) takes place. Indeed, in Luke's presentation of this story, the final affront to the Jews is Paul's statement (18.6; cf. 13.46; 28.28) that he will take his message that "Jesus is the Messiah" to the Gentiles.

At this point in the Corinthian episode a highly symbolic shift takes place, as the conceptual images related to the chosenness of the people of Israel and salvation by the hand of the Lord run deep in Jewish epic, and Luke explicitly remaps these elements in this instance onto the Gentiles. He thus reconfigures the present by shifting the focus of the past Jewish story. This move is perhaps symbolized in the fact that Paul continues to preach after the incident before Gallio (18.18) while Sosthenes is beaten before the Roman colonial authority (not to forget as well that Crispus, the former leader of the synagogue, has already come to believe in Paul's gospel, providing a positive contrast to Sosthenes). Again, there are a variety of ways to interpret this point of Luke's short narrative. From a gender-critical perspective, however, Paul and Sosthenes could be viewed as two rival "males" contesting for authority and respect in the public forum (certainly they are both representative in the narrative of two groups of Jews vying for Roman [or readerly] recognition). Much like the actual showdown between Paul and Elymas before the proconsul Sergius Paulus in Acts 13, the question again is which individual will "win" favor with the Roman authority. We are, of course, not surprised to see that Paul triumphs. The contest for masculine identity played out between synagogue (public space) and house (domestic sphere), and between the leader of the synagogue and Paul, in the end all comes down to Paul showing himself, and thereby also the nascent communities identified with him, to be the "true" male performer in the narrative. He is the one who comes out "on top" and, in the process, the cultural and religious identities represented by the Jewish opponents is remapped onto the heroes in Luke's narrative, which not surprisingly embodies (mimics) something of Rome's own imperial aspirations.

Moving next from the world in the text to fleshing out facets of the world behind the text, we turn briefly to the geographical mappings of Pausanias in the second century CE. In his *Description of Greece,* Pausanias offers a discussion of Corinth in which the earlier period of the city dominates his presentation. Although Pausanias details elements of contemporary Corinth for his readers, he is more preoccupied with the one destroyed in 146 BCE (by the Roman commander Mummius), rather than the Roman colony established by Caesar in 44 BCE. Greek history and culture and the glory of the Golden Age thus emerge as essential themes throughout his treatment. This reconfiguration serves to decenter Roman authority and control, celebrating instead an earlier era of alternative power structures. Indeed, Pausanius relates his "story" in such a way that the Romans are consistently "written out" as the new founders, over and against the "original" (Greek) Corinthians whose history, culture, and traditions are distinguished throughout.[27] Although in Acts 18 Luke is not concerned with the earlier period of Corinth per se, he is likewise invested in reconfiguring Jewish (past and present) and Roman spaces so as to celebrate his narrative heroes as well as to demonstrate their superiority. Like Pausanias, Luke is devoted to remapping spaces and places in empire, and he does so in order to ground emergent Christian identity through the construction of an idealistic founding narrative.

Still looking at the way in which the broader sociocultural context of the world behind the text might be useful for understanding the world in the text, we further note that Luke connects places with social identity (a trend attested elsewhere in Acts as well). It is thus not by accident that Luke uses Corinth as a setting for the unfolding action in this passage. Corinth was an especially important colonial city in the ancient world, since, although the Romans colonized the city from early on, it maintained a strong Greek character, one that was a model for imitation by those invested in cultivating Greek values and civic virtue.[28] Paul's appeal to the Corinthians (and their positive response) in the Acts narrative therefore says much about his reputation among those who are thought to embody traditional virtue and culture. Like he does in Athens, Paul here receives a hearing among the more cultured elites of the empire. Moreover, it is also in this narrative about Corinth that Paul, alongside Priscilla and Aquila, is first identified as a tradesman, a tent-maker to be precise (18.3), which provides a social identity for Paul in Corinth, and thereby contributes to Luke's emergent portrait of Paul as an ideal, self-sufficient philosopher.[29] Through all of this, Paul also appears in the presence of seemingly important individuals, which says much about Paul himself—after all, one is the company they keep. The production of nascent "Christian" identity in this text is thus intricately linked to place—place in empire, place in social hierarchy, place in the renowned city of Corinth itself.

While the Corinth narrative represents a small episode in Luke's overall literary scheme, it serves as a prism for some larger aspects of his ideology. The geographic, spatial, and also religious movement that takes place in the narrative creates the impression that Paul is taking the empire by storm. A new power is on the scene, and it has reconfigured Jewish, Greek, and Roman identities in Corinth and beyond, with Paul embodying all three of them throughout Acts. When we think of the emergence of nascent "Christian" identity in the ancient world, we should therefore take seriously the influence that the (re)mappings we have investigated here could potentially have had in this larger process. Of course, as we noted earlier in this chapter, Luke's own character has also been placed on display in his narrative. The story he tells, and particularly the way in which he shapes the narrative material, embodies his person and virtue. This story is as much about him as it is about the people he describes. And the attributed male identity that permeates the narrative also underscores Luke's own identity (even as that facet is largely concealed from the reader's view).

With Luke's character/*ethos* on display, we have already implicitly moved from the world in the text to the world in front of the text. But more explicitly, the reader/interpreter of Acts is also transformed in this same moment, insofar as this text produces distinctive gendered/sexed/sexual conceptions in relation to cultural/social/political/religious identities, which the reader then engages (and enacts) in encountering the narrative. Luke has explicitly invoked the "reader" at the outset of his two-volume work (Lk. 1.1–4), and *his* own performance has quite intentionally been one that seeks to shape the reader's perceptions vis-à-vis the explicit character or *ethos* of the emergent community in the narrative. In a culture of imitation and replication, the reader is inscribed within this new terrain mapped here by Luke through the broader narrative poetics unfolding in Acts. Insofar as Luke fronts a colonizing edge in his narrative, as well as displays an ideal masculine identity in the text, the reader is also shaped in this same direction. Not only does the reader come to see the ideology of Acts as correct and true, the reader is encouraged to enact and embody these same values and virtues, as well as the elements of imperial masculine identity, which, in turn, also creates desire for empire. Thinking of the world in front of the text now as being less about our own shaping of Acts, and more about its shaping of us, we might recall that Eusebius of Alexandria, whom we mentioned in the third chapter, wrote his magisterial *Ecclesiastical History* heavily influenced by the book of Acts, to which he repeatedly pays homage throughout. It is telling, in this respect, that the desire for imperial rule that surfaces in front of the text is readily imitated in Eusebius's triumphal heralding of Constantine as the new "Christian" Roman emperor, and the masculine lines that the book of Acts draws out are reified even further in Eusebius's embracing of the stable, authoritative traditions of the "founding fathers of the faith."[30]

The *Acts of Paul and Thecla*

In the previous two examples, we focused our attention on the worlds *behind* and *in* the text. In this last example, picking up on various comments we have already made throughout each chapter related to the characters in the *Acts of Paul and Thecla*, we turn here to an interpretation of the world *in front* of that text. At the beginning of this chapter, we already cited the portion of the narrative that detailed Thecla's immediate actions after her baptism in the arena and upon her release. In the interpretation that follows, we are specifically interested in two issues: 1) how the multiple crossings of Thecla are interpreted by ancient and modern readers, and 2) what the significance of this text might be in its relation to the canonical New Testament texts, especially the Acts of the Apostles and the epistles of Paul.

Since the declaration by Tertullian that the *Acts of Paul and Thecla* was problematic because it inspired women to follow in the ("unorthodox") footsteps of Thecla (*On Baptism* 17), it has been argued that the *Acts of Paul and Thecla* represents a "heretical" text, even if only in terms of its praxis (i.e., it portrays a female in an active role, preaching and baptizing, which, as we noted in the third chapter, was an activity that early Christian "fathers" such as Tertullian limited to men).[31] Modern attempts to recover the story's significance more specifically suggest that this text offers a different perspective on the history and development of earlier Christianity, and that it challenges the status quo of patriarchal structures in particular. In his book *Lost Christianities* (2003), Bart Ehrman, for instance, follows Tertullian's assessment that the *Acts of Paul and Thecla* is a forgery, written by a presbyter in Asia Minor. Ehrman further suggests that it is most likely, in light of what we know about forgeries in antiquity, that the presbyter in question claimed he had discovered a document that he actually wrote himself, in order to give it credibility. Ehrman is quick to add, however, that just because it is a forgery does not therefore mean that the presbyter invented this story. Rather, in his view, the presbyter most likely relied on preexisting stories and oral sources in order to compose his own narrative of Paul and Thecla. In Ehrman's view, the presbyter wrote his story for the purpose of entertainment, and thus modeled his narrative after the Greek novels. The content, however, differed substantially from these novels, as the Christian message it endorsed was one of asceticism rather than marriage (which is one of the predominant values promoted in the Greek novels). According to Ehrman, this "ascetic ideal went hand in glove with what we, in hindsight, might think of as the 'liberated' form of ancient Christianity, which stressed the equality of women in Christ" (46).

The *Acts of Paul and Thecla*, in this view, reflects a strand in early Christianity that was suppressed by the dominant tradition of which Tertullian is representative, and, as a result, this tradition "was lost, only to be rediscovered in modern times" (*Lost Christianities*, 46). Ehrman's appreciation of the *Acts of Paul and Thecla* is remarkably ambivalent. On the one hand, he accepts Tertullian's claim that the *Acts of Paul and Thecla* is a forgery, although he admits in a footnote (262, note 7) that, as some suspect, Tertullian himself may have made up the forgery claim in order to discredit this text. On the other hand, at the end of the chapter, Ehrman blames "powerful pro-orthodox leaders and writers like Tertullian" (46) for suppressing Thecla's liberating story. A similar ambiguity can be noted with respect to the role of the presbyter who, according to Tertullian and Ehrman, wrote the story. Ehrman considers him to be its author, but he is also quick to note that the presbyter relied on traditions for composing the text. In thus foregrounding the presbyter, Ehrman distances himself from the work of Burrus (*Chastity as Autonomy*), Steven Davies, and Dennis MacDonald (see chapter one), all of whom consider the *Acts of Paul and Thecla* to be more directly related to women's traditions (Ehrman labels their studies "intriguing," 262 note 8). Although Ehrman does not exclude the possibility that women in the Pauline churches are behind the traditions about Thecla, in the end the discussion about the role of women in Ehrman's interpretation is one between males, be it Jesus, Paul, the presbyter who wrote the *Acts of Paul and Thecla*, the writer of 1 Timothy, or Tertullian. They all express their views on what women could or should not do. Thus, even the alternative, liberating strand within early Christianity is based on male authority figures, such as the presbyter, and, as a result, this position mimics the dominant tradition in the way it considers women as others that either need to be kept in check or liberated.

From this brief foray into the interpretive history of the Thecla story, it becomes apparent that it is rather tempting for modern scholars to reinscribe mimetically the oppositional structures of this textual body and the unique comportment of its bodies on display in the narrative. Frequently, in their modern renderings of the story's sociohistorical context and its import, scholars see the challenge that Thecla offers to the social values of the ancient city and seek to reinscribe that contestation, at least in part, as a social challenge to orthodox Christian structures of patriarchy. Yet, as we have noted in our analysis throughout the book, the various crossings in Thecla's performance, thinking broadly of her transgendering acts as well as her transgressive cultural actions, offer a more complex rendering of border and boundary crossing than a simple binary structure will accommodate. While the conventional approach is to query what kind of readers would be invoked by such images—ascetic women? Christian male power-brokers?—we suggest that this approach may be too simplistic. In line with Virginia Burrus's argument in her later work on the *Acts of Paul and Thecla* ("Mimicking Virgins"), which we discussed at the beginning of chapter four, we should rather ask what broader identities could be produced by these images offered for adulation, imitation, and disruption.

Both ancient and modern readers of *the Acts of Paul and Thecla* might well find themselves enamored with the crossings and passings that Thecla initiates and embodies. There is a fluidity here that has attestation elsewhere, even in so-called orthodox Christian literature, both on individual and corporate levels in terms of the production of identities—shifting, morphing, crossing, passing, transcending. Such identities reflect a network of interrelated and complex public and private performances. Our modern scholarly impulse to correlate text and context—aligning one type of narrative with one type of reader and one specific situation or life context—often excludes these more complex dynamics. And the fact that early Christian identities, individual and communal, are being produced and disciplined within this multifaceted process, also raises further complications for the interpretation of the meaning of Thecla's many crossings. For instance, we see in the *Acts of Paul and Thecla* that social class and cultural position, particularly among the elite in the Greek eastern cities of the Roman Empire, are still to be regulated and negotiated. In fact, the Thecla story (perhaps like the Acts of the Apostles and even some of Paul's letters) seems to court the elites of empire or at the very least fantasize that the elite strata of society are invested in engaging Christians. So what does Thecla's crossing of the social and cultural borders mean for the text? Is it as liberative as Ehrman implies? Is it as dangerous as Tertullian suggests? In line with the emphasis on the world "in front of the text," it is fairly easy to see that there is no "right" answer to this question. So much depends on the interpreter's social location and their cultural value system. Thus, Tertullian's and Erhman's appreciation of Thecla is divergent precisely because of their respective historical and theological locations. Still, coming back to the text for a moment, we suggest that social status in empire is not to be equated necessarily with the same in early Christian social mapping. Early Christians (at times) developed their own (diverse) frameworks for social hierarchies that reshaped and resituated the constructs of the broader culture. We catch a glimpse of that in the *Acts of Paul and Thecla*, but tracing out lines to the world "behind the text" simply ends in conjecture.

Pursuing this argument further, if we take seriously the structural dynamic of Thecla's multiple crossings (and her returns), we also need to acknowledge that in some respects the *Acts of Paul and Thecla* reproduces some of the critical features of the Acts of the Apostles and the Pauline letters. As we noted earlier in the book, when we find transgressive border crossings, we also have to recognize that there are *boundaries* to transgress in the first place. Contrasting the *Acts of Paul and Thecla* with canonical literature may fail to catch the nuance of the act of crossing itself. There is a correlative enterprise of identity formation enacted and embodied in both corpuses, as well as a shared concern for control and authority, with the body being the thing to be harnessed as a source of power, and those who control the body are the ones possessing ultimate authority and control.

Here we may begin to rethink how narratives are rhetorically constructing (rather than just reflecting) larger communities or at least processes of social formation, which brings us back to the discussion of canonical boundaries in chapter three, where we noted that early Christian texts discipline individuals and communities in ways of thinking and acting. Bodies of texts influence the bodies of individuals, and, while the morphing and shifting nature of Thecla's character in the text may denote many different types of historical possibilities as to the "reality" behind the text, at the very least we can say that the text opens up a significant space for "transgression" and "crossing," however we may conceptualize those concepts (for Tertullian it was negative, for Ehrman, positive). As spatiality theorist Henri Lefebvre once noted, in order to change life, one must first change space (*Production of Space*, 190). While all early Christian writings illustrate the potency of that observation, the story of Thecla embodies more than most the power that comes from changing space and place, and with it the possibility is raised for "new life."

These observations may also help us understand more fully how it is that one body of literature became canonized while another one was not, or, more precisely, help us rethink the act of canonization itself as a social operation. In other words, when thinking about the canonical process, we may also gain some appreciation for why, despite their similarities at some levels, the Acts of the Apostles might have been canonized for normative purposes while the *Acts of Paul and Thecla* was not. In this light, the differences seem to have been more important than the similarities. As we noted earlier, such a premise would suggest that canonical formation may have partially been a process directed by the texts themselves. In the end, then, it may not have been so much the particular theo-ideological proclivities of this text over another that marked it for inclusion or exclusion within the body of authoritative texts, but rather how these were constructed and read based on the bodies that were displayed within them, especially in terms of the possibilities that were opened for boundary-crossing itself (and the problems that such entailed for emergent "orthodox" leaders). In this way, particular texts cohered rather well together, cementing between them a boundaried system, while marginalizing the traces of more transgressive aspects within those same texts.

Finally, then, postulating either a univocal "female" or "male" use of this text hardly does justice to the complexities that this text evokes, and any simple delineation of the *Acts of Paul and Thecla* as a challenge to patriarchal, canonical, "normative" Christian bodies (of literature, of church hierarchy, of social patriarchy) does not fully appreciate the ways in which the story of Thecla both simultaneously affirms and transgresses those other textual and social bodies. Modern interest in this story seems at least in part to be based on its ability to provide a space, in Fredrick Jameson's words, for "narrative heterogeneity and freedom" (*Political Unconscious*, 104) from the domination of normative modes of being in the contemporary world. Seeking and seeing the complex and multivalent social mappings that Thecla inscribes throughout the narrative, then, one may well wonder, in the end, if thinking *of* Thecla is really all that much different than thinking *with* Thecla. What matters rather is the use to which she is put (and our awareness and intentionality of that use). Therein, we would argue, lies the politics and ethics of scholarship. In our view, a gender-critical reading should serve the purpose of raising a different set of historical questions, in order to move us *beyond* Thecla, into a fuller appreciation of the complexity of human experience, both ancient and modern. Perhaps we can also catch a glimpse herein of a complexity, heterogeneity, and even hybridity based in everyday life—shifting, morphing, crossing, and then coming back again. These are not the kinds of subjectivities that scholars usually explore in the ancient world. And this limitation in our reading may be a problem that also confronts and confounds our interpretations of the *Acts of Paul and Thecla*. While there is no doubt an effective edge to the rhetorical constructions of the story of Thecla, wherein life is shaped and disciplined by rhetoric, there may also be something here of the reflective edge as well, wherein rhetoric may imitate life.

Conclusion

In this chapter we have sought to lay out a variety of features related to how we understand and employ our gender-critical approach to early Christian literature. Obviously, the discussion in this chapter is suggestive, rather than exhaustive, providing some broad outlines of the types of questions we are interested in with respect to gender, sex, and sexuality in early Christian writings, as well as the various components that go into framing our gender-critical approach. In the earlier chapters we laid out the elements of our assumptions related to the construction of gender, sex, and sexuality in the ancient world. In this chapter we were more interested in laying out our textual and interpretive assumptions and reading strategies in order to highlight how we connect the earlier observations in this book with actual readings of early Christian texts. For this reason, we not only laid out a variety of assumptions and reading strategies, but also delineated the three worlds of the text, all with the aim of demonstrating how interpretations attentive to gender, sex, and sexuality shape and determine the kind of meaning that is derived from texts.

As we noted throughout this discussion, our major focus has been on highlighting the choices and selections that we have made for our own gender-critical approach. Different assumptions and reading strategies, alongside alternative approaches to the three worlds of the text, including variations in the way those worlds are specifically understood, constructed, correlated, and interwoven by the interpreter, will ultimately result in another hermeneutical framework for a gender-critical reading of early Christian texts. In light of this diversity and multiplicity in interpretation, our main emphasis is to encourage readers to be upfront about their own choices and selections, as well as the embedded values and ideologies operative in their approaches to texts. As we have noted throughout this chapter, we do not claim that our gender-critical approach is value-neutral or nonideological. Quite the opposite is the case. Thus, being clear about one's assumptions and reading strategies, and developing clarity about the various worlds of the texts (and especially one's understanding of how those are constructed and interrelated), will prove not only to nurture intentional reading and interpretive habits, but also, we believe, to foster more open dialogue between various approaches (gender-critical and others) to early Christian texts.

Notes

1   The gist of this phrase is that Thecla takes on male identification through dress. One could translate it more literally as "girding herself and taking (or sewing) together the under garment with the upper garment according to the way (of clothing) of a man."

2   The text does not have the Greek word for "baptism" (*baptismos*) here, but *loutros,* which literally means "bath," but baptism is clearly in view since this initiation ritual took the form of an immersion in water.

3   Scholars such as Willi Braun ("Body, Character and the Problem of Femaleness in Early Christian Discourse," *Religion and Theology* 9 [2002]: 108–17) and Johannes Vorster ("The Blood of the Female Martyrs as the Sperm of the Early Church," *Religion and Theology* 10 [2002]: 66–99) have identified this transformation as representing a thoroughly male/androcentric discourse, resting on an extreme form of patriarchalism in early Christianity. That is, the male body becomes the ultimate marker of full human and spiritual existence. Both scholars are suspicious of the liberating potential

for females in this framework. In this reading, then, Thecla is not liberated by adopting this "male identity," but is in fact further subjugated to androcentric inscription and identification.

4 Stevan L. Davies, *The Revolt of the Widows: The Social World of the Apocryphal Acts* (Carbondale/ Edwardsville: Southern Illinois University Press, 1980); and Virginia Burrus, *Chastity as Autonomy: Women in the Stories of Apocryphal Acts* (Studies in Women and Religion 23; Lewiston: Edwin Mellen Press, 1987).

5 Kate Cooper, *The Virgin and the Bride: Idealized Womanhood in Late Antiquity* (Cambridge, MA: Harvard University Press, 1999).

6 In this context it is noteworthy that historical criticism originated in Protestant traditions, often as a way of juxtaposing historical interpretations that could (even if implicitly) undermine Catholic theological principles (for further discussion, see Jonathan Z. Smith, *Drudgery Divine: on the Comparison of Early Christianities and the Religions of Late Antiquity* [Chicago: University of Chicago Press, 1990]).

7 Jacques Berlinerblau develops a similar argument in *The Secular Bible. Why Nonbelievers Must Take Religion Seriously* (Cambridge: Cambridge University Press, 2005).

8 In a similar vein, Dale B. Martin, in his book *Sex and the Single Savior: Gender and Sexuality in Biblical Interpretation* (Louisville: Westminster John Knox, 2006), helpfully illuminates how modern ideologies related to homosexuality influence the way scholars reconstruct the position of the early Christians on homosexuality. Also see the two volume collection of essays that highlights the difference that social location makes for interpretation: Fernando Segovia and Mary Ann Tolbert, eds, *Reading from This Place* (2 vols; Minneapolis: Fortress Press, 1995).

9 We use "rhetoric" here in a general sense. We do not solely focus on the ancient forms and techniques of rhetoric, but, even more so, emphasize ancient rhetoric as embedded in broader sociocultural communicative practices. Vernon Robbins's work on rhetoric has been helpful in this respect. See especially *The Tapestry of Early Christian Discourse: Rhetoric, Society, and Ideology* (London: Routledge, 1996); and, most recently, *The Invention of Christian Discourse* (Rhetoric of Religious Antiquity; Blandford Forum, UK: DEO Publishing, 2009). George A. Kennedy's *New Testament Interpretation through Rhetorical Criticism* (Chapel Hill: University of North Carolina Press, 1984) was one of the first studies to open up this field of inquiry, demonstrating that one could move beyond the strictly technical works of Quintilian and Cicero to analyze the impact of rhetoric more generally on early Christian writings.

10 On rhetorical education in the Greco-Roman world, see especially Teresa Morgan, *Literate Education in the Hellenistic and Roman Worlds* (Cambridge Classical Studies; Cambridge: Cambridge University Press, 1998); and Raffaella Cribiore, *Gymnastics of the Mind: Greek Education in Hellenistic and Roman Egypt* (Princeton: Princeton University Press, 2001).

11 For more on these rhetorical manuals, see the introduction and compilation of texts in George A. Kennedy, ed., *Progymnasmata: Greek Textbooks of Prose Composition and Rhetoric* (Writings from the Greco-Roman World 10; Atlanta: Society of Biblical Literature, 2003).

12 See further Todd Penner, "Reconfiguring the Rhetorical Study of Acts: Reflections on the Method in and Learning of a Progymnastic Poetics," *Perspectives in Religious Studies* 30 (2003): 425–39.

13 For a more detailed analysis of this phenomenon, see Todd Penner and Caroline Vander Stichele, "Rhetorical Practice and Performance in Early Christianity," in *The Cambridge Companion to Ancient Rhetoric* (ed. E. Gunderson; Cambridge: Cambridge University Press, 2009).

14 See further the discussion and references in Elizabeth Castelli, *Martyrdom and Memory: Early Christian Culture Making* (Gender, Theory, and Religion; New York: Columbia University Press, 2004); as well as Virginia Burrus, *Saving Shame: Martyrs, Saints, and Other Abject Subjects* (Divinations; Philadelphia: University of Pennsylvania Press, 2008).

15 For details on the ensuing assertions related to the construction and intention of ancient narrative, see Todd Penner, *In Praise of Christian Origins: Stephen and the Hellenists in Lukan Apologetic Historiography* (Emory Studies in Early Christianity 10; T & T Clark International, 2004); and a shorter presentation in Todd Penner, "Early Christian Heroes and Lukan Narrative: Stephen and the Hellenists in Ancient Historiographical Perspective," in *Rhetoric and Reality in Early Christianities* (ed. W. Braun; Studies in Christianity and Judaism 16; Waterloo, ON, Canada: Wilfrid Laurier University Press, 2005), 75–97.

16 For an exploration of some elements of this theme, see Stephen D. Moore, *God's Beauty Parlor: Queering Spaces in and around the Bible* (Contraversions; Stanford: Stanford University Press, 2001), 133–72.

17 See further Mieke Bal, *Narratology: Introduction to the Theory of Narrative* (Toronto: University of Toronto Press, 1985).

18 One should also pay close attention to the absence of characters that one would otherwise expect to be present in the narrative. Absence however, does not necessarily mean unimportance. The character of God is frequently absent in texts, even though often times this absence is overdetermined and thereby actually indicates a significant presence. The same could be said for the role of the emperor in Acts, who is generally invisible throughout the text and yet in many respects is everywhere by virtue of being represented by his appointed figures. In this way, absence often obscures the larger ideology of the text, including some of the gendered and sexed interplays (e.g., God's envoys continually triumph over the emperor's appointed leaders, demonstrating their true *virtus*/manliness).

19 The expression refers to the title of Judith Fetterly's book, *The Resisting Reader: A Feminist Approach to American Fiction* (Bloomington: Indiana University Press, 1978).

20 For more details on these and related themes, see Dale Martin, *The Corinthian Body* (New Haven: Yale University Press, 1999).

21 Critical here is the lack of choice or awareness in this identification. There are, of course, females who choose male/masculine identities (see, e.g., Judith Halberstam, *Female Masculinity* [Durham: Duke University Press, 1998]). We are not contending with that position at all. Ours is a theoretical point about the tendency in Western philosophy for phallogocentric discourse to be dominant, masking its constructed and relative nature, and passing itself off as a universal, normative subject.

22 At this juncture a gender-critical approach easily intersects with queer readings of texts, since a queer approach also seeks to deconstruct the normative framework of meaning and identity in a text. The queer approach proceeds by taking an element in the dominant discourse and exposing its logic and its inherent structures of meaning so as to make the agreed on normative element seem strange and out of place to the dominant perspective, thereby queering the hegemonic

perspective from *within* its own system of meaning. For an excellent example of a queer approach to early Christian texts, see Stephen Moore, *God's Beauty Parlor*.

23 For a more extensive version of our analysis, see C. Vander Stichele and Todd Penner, "Paul and the Rhetoric of Gender," in *Her Master's Tools? Feminist and Postcolonial Engagements of Historical-Critical Discourse* (ed. C. Vander Stichele and T. Penner; Global Perspectives on the Bible 9; Atlanta: Society of Biblical Literature, 2005), 287–310.

24 For a more thorough discussion of Paul's ethos in this passage, see Todd Penner and C. Vander Stichele, "Unveiling Paul: Gendering Ethos in 1 Corinthians 11:2–16," in *Rhetoric, Ethic, and Moral Persuasion in Biblical Discourse* (ed. T. H. Olbricht and A. Erikson; Emory Studies in Early Christianity; New York: T&T Clark, 2005), 214–37. In earlier portions of 1 Corinthians, Paul has already been highly invested in "father" imagery, which stands alongside the representation of himself as the "founder." The two concepts appear to go hand in hand for him, as he reconfigures the social and political (and public) connotation of "founder" by blending it with the domestic image of "father."

25 Also see Francis Watson, *Agape, Eros, Gender: Towards a Pauline Sexual Ethic* (Cambridge: Cambridge University Press, 2000), 1–89.

26 For further assessment of some of these elements in other parts of Acts, see our more detailed evaluation in Todd Penner and Caroline Vander Stichele, "Gendering Violence: Patterns of Power and Constructs of Masculinity in the Acts of the Apostles," in *A Feminist Companion to Acts* (ed. A.-J. Levine and M. Blickenstaff; New York: T&T Clark International and Cleveland: Pilgrim, 2004), 193–209; and idem, "'All the World's a Stage': The Rhetoric of Gender in Acts," in *Luke and His Readers: Festschrift A. Denaux* (ed. R. Bieringer, G. Van Belle, and J. Verheyden; Bibliotheca Ephemeridum Theologicarum Lovaniensium 182; Leuven: Leuven University Press, 2005), 373–96.

27 We have developed these themes further in Todd Penner and Caroline Vander Stichele, "Script(ur)ing Gender in Acts: The Past and Present Power of *Imperium*," in *Mapping Gender in Ancient Religious Discourses* (ed. T. Penner and C. Vander Stichele; Biblical Interpretation Series 84; Leiden: Brill, 2007), 231–66.

28 Tim Whitmarsh, for instance, notes the accent in ancient literature on Corinth being both a "traditionally Greek" but also "mimetically Greek" (i.e., imitating a conception of Greekness) city (*Greek Literature and the Roman Empire: The Politics of Imitation* [New York: Oxford University Press, 2001], 121). Also see the discussion by Luca Graverini, "Corinth, Rome, and Africa: A Cultural Background for the Tale of the Ass," in *Space in the Ancient Novel* (ed. M. Paschalis and S. Frangoulidis; Ancient Narrative, Supplementum 1; Groningen: Barkhuis Publishing and the University Library Groningen, 2002), 58–77, especially 60–66.

29 See further the discussion in Ronald F. Hock, *The Social Context of Paul's Ministry: Tentmaking and Apostleship* (Philadelphia: Fortress Press, 1980), 52–59, who connects this "self-sufficiency" motif more specifically to the Cynic tradition.

30 For a helpful discussion of this correlation between the book of Acts and Eusebius's *Ecclesiastical History*, see Ron Cameron, "Alternate Beginnings—Different Ends: Eusebius, Thomas, and the Construction of Christian Origins," in *Religious Propaganda and Missionary Competition in the New Testament World: Essays Honoring Dieter Georgi* (ed. L. Bormann et al.; Supplements to Novum Testamentum 74; Leiden: Brill, 1994), 501–25.

31 We have not dealt with the "after life" of Thecla in early Christianity, but she became a dominant presence in cultic worship and tradition history in the second century and beyond. For further discussion of the cult of Thecla and the literary tradition of her miracles, see Scott Fitzgerald Johnson, *The Life and Miracles of Thekla: A Literary Study* (Center for Hellenic Studies; Cambridge, MA: Harvard University Press, 2006), who offers an extensive literary reading of the *Acts of Paul and Thecla* as well; and Stephen J. Davis, *The Cult of Saint Thecla: A Tradition of Women's Piety in Late Antiquity* (Oxford Early Christian Studies; Oxford: Oxford University Press, 2001).

Bibliography

Aristotle. *On Rhetoric: A Theory of Civic Discourse.* Translated by G. A. Kennedy. New York: Oxford University Press, 1991.

Barr, David L. *New Testament Story: An Introduction.* Belmont, CA: Wadsworth, 1995.

Beauvoir, Simone de. *The Second Sex.* New York: Bantam, 1961.

Burrus, Virginia. "Mimicking Virgins: Colonial Ambivalence and the Ancient Romance." *Arethusa* 38 (2005): 49–88.

Clark Wire, Antoinette. *The Corinthian Women Prophets: A Reconstruction through Paul's Rhetoric.* Minneapolis: Fortress Press, 1990.

Culler, Jonathan. *On Deconstruction: Theory and Criticism after Structuralism.* London: Routledge, 1982.

D'Angelo, Mary Rose. "Women in Luke-Acts: A Redactional View." *Journal of Biblical Literature* 109 (1990): 441–61.

Ehrman, Bart. *Lost Christianities: The Battles for Scripture and the Faiths We Never Knew.* New York: Oxford University Press, 2005.

Epictetus. *Discourses.* Translated by W. A. Oldfather. 2 Vols. Loeb Classical Library. Cambridge, MA: Havard University Press, 1925–28.

Hurley, James B. *Man and Woman in Biblical Perspective.* Grand Rapids: Zondervan, 1981.

Irigaray, Luce. *Speculum of the Other Woman.* Ithaca, NY: Cornell University Press, 1985.

Jameson, Fredrick. *The Political Unconscious.* Ithaca, NY: Cornell University Press, 1982.

Kroeger, Catherine Clark, Mary Evans, and Elaine Storkey, eds. *Study Bible for Women: The New Testament.* Grand Rapids: Baker Books, 1995.

Lefebvre, Henri. *The Production of Space.* Translated by D. Nicholson-Smith. Oxford: Blackwell, 1991.

Martin, Troy. "Veiled Exhortations Regarding the Veil: *Ethos* as the Controlling Proof in Moral Persuasion (1 Cor 11:2–16)." Pp. 255–73 in *Rhetoric, Ethic and Moral Persuasion in Biblical Discourse.* Edited by T. H. Olbricht and A. Eriksson. Emory Studies in Early Christianity. New York: T & T Clark, 2005.

Moore, Stephen. *God's Beauty Parlor and Other Queer Spaces in and around the Bible.* Contraversions. Stanford: Stanford University Press, 2001.

Økland, Jorunn. "Feminist Reception of the New Testament: A Critical Reception." Pp. 131–56 in *The New Testament as Reception*. Edited by M. Müller and H. Tronier. Journal for the Study of the New Testament Supplement Series 230. London: Sheffield Academic Press, 2002.

Pausanius. *Description of Greece*. Translated by W. H. S. Jones et al. 5 Vols. Loeb Classical Library. Cambridge, MA: Harvard University Press, 1918–35.

Plutarch. *Parallel Lives*. Translated by B. Perrin. 11 Vols. Loeb Classical Library. Cambridge, MA: Harvard University Press, 1914–26.

Polaski, Sandra Hack. *A Feminist Introduction to Paul*. St. Louis: Chalice Press, 2005.

Schüssler Fiorenza, Elisabeth. "Defending the Center, Trivializing the Margins." Pp. 29–48 in *Reading the Bible in the Global Village: Helsinki*. Global Perspectives on Biblical Scholarship. Atlanta: Society of Biblical Literature, 2000.

—*The Power of the Word: Scripture and the Rhetoric of Empire*. Minneapolis: Fortress Press, 2007.

— *Rhetoric and Ethic: The Politics of Biblical Studies*. Minneapolis: Fortress Press, 1999.

Watson, Francis. "The Authority of the Voice: A Theological Reading of 1 Cor 11.2–16." *New Testament Studies* 46 (2000): 520–36.

Wuellner, Wilhelm. "Biblical Exegesis in the Light of the History and Historicity of Rhetoric and the Nature of the Rhetoric of Religion." Pp. 492–513 in *Rhetoric and the New Testament: Essays from the 1992 Heidelberg Conference*. Edited by S. E. Porter and T. H. Olbricht. Journal for the Study of the New Testament Supplement Series 90. Sheffield: Sheffield Academic Press, 1993.

(Dis)closure

The exilic intellectual does not respond to the logic of the conventional but
to the audacity of daring, and to representing change, to moving on, not
standing still.

—*Edward Said*, Representations of the Intellectual, *64*

In the end there is no way to detach politics—relations of power, systems of
belief and practice—from knowledge and the processes that produce it . . .

—*Joan Scott*, "Women's History," *61*

Michel Foucault once made the astute observation that "discourse transmits
and produces power; it reinforces it, but also undermines and exposes it,
renders it fragile and makes it possible to thwart it" (*History of Sexuality I*, 101).
In many respects, this statement encapsulates Foucault's main concern in his
History of Sexuality project, alongside the rest of his oeuvre. Indebted to his
intellectual heir, the Nietzsche of the *Genealogy of Morals*, and his doctoral
advisor, Louis Althusser, whose emphasis on the ideological structures of institutions was clearly formative, Foucault understood the complex intersection
of knowledge and power produced in and through discourses. It was only by
tracing out the unspoken and the concealed that power structures could be
revealed. Ultimately, Foucault's project was a democratic one. It was focused
on creating alternative structures of meaning and life that would give people
genuine freedom of choice, that would open up spaces and places for the
disenfranchised, not least by revealing that those most marginalized are
frequently kept so through discursive constructions of the world rather than
by virtue of some inherent deficiency in their humanity. Freedom of choice
was essential for Foucault, and his intellectual endeavors could be read as
advocating for more options in a democratic society that is frequently dominated by the power of institutions.

As we made clear at the outset of this book, Foucault is a major influence on us in terms of our thinking about the task of a gender-critical approach to early Christian writings (and their modern interpreters). As a result, we find it increasingly difficult to look at past discourses without paying close attention to the ways in which we also (re-)produce those discourses in the very act of studying them. We find Foucault's interpretive framework appealing precisely because he employs a deconstructive edge (an interrogation of the character and history of specific discourses) in the service of the construction of a better democratic society. For this reason, throughout our book we have fronted the politics of interpretation. Elizabeth Schüssler Fiorenza's groundbreaking work has provided an exemplary model for such an endeavor (*Rhetoric and Ethic* [1999] and *Power of the Word* [2007]). Indeed, with her we agree that it is not enough simply to provide alternative methods or readings for historical analysis. Rather, it makes a fundamental difference what interpretive choices we employ since these reveal substantive aspects about who we are, who we want to be, and what kind of world we hope to inhabit.

Ultimately, we undertake these scholarly and educational exercises in order to humanize ourselves (and to encourage discourses that make us more humane in thought and action). Examining discourses and their representations of humanity in historical contexts is, finally, about us; it is not an end in itself. And, for that matter, we do not consider this kind of study to be a luxury (or a demand, as it is so often for students in the modern university system). It can be, of course, but our aim is to move beyond such limiting (and banal) constructions of study toward a richer and deeper appreciation of the "mirror" we hold up when we analyze the human subject in its diverse and varied contexts, ancient and modern. In some respects, we see this form of scholarship as an alternative to a so-called "scientific" mode of investigation, which tends to reduce the relevance of scholarship to its immediate subservience to the needs of contemporary society and to the demands of consumerism and the marketplace. Such a modernist approach thinks solely in terms of a linear progression of society, and little substantive attention is given to issues of justice, power, and contingency. The study of the humanities and the humanists who operate therein should offer a counter to these modern trends, and here we believe it is critical to cultivate the humanities as a locus of resistance to dominant paradigms of limited and oppressive conceptuality. Said aptly captures the concern we raise when he observes that "We are bombarded by prepackaged and reified representations of the world that usurp consciousness and preempt democratic critique, and it is to the overturning and dismantling of these alienating objects ... [that] the intellectual humanist's work ought to be devoted" (*Humanism and Democratic Criticism*, 71). A society that forgets its history is in danger of becoming totalist/izing, as knowledge of the past stimulates the development of a critical spirit, helping us to passionately, sensitively, and creatively engage our present world in substantive and formative ways.

We are definitely not thinking here of a nostalgia for the past, for a better time. Rather, by exposing power structures in the ancient and modern worlds we cultivate spaces wherein we might hear and listen to alternative and excluded "other" voices. To this end, then, our gender-critical approach, in line with its genealogy, has an acute political focus: it is not just interested in analysis, it seeks change, especially a shift away from essentialized identities and the methods and discourses that sustain those identities (and the oppressions that essentialized identities frequently entail). One of the commitments in our understanding of a gender-critical approach is therefore to deconstruct the center precisely through challenging the multiple essentialist notions that sustain it. We are, however, not seeking some utopian ideal. As Chantal Mouffe notes, "there will always be a 'constitutive outside,' an exterior to the community that is the very condition of its existence" (*Return of the Political*, 85). Mouffe, particularly arguing here for a feminist political agenda, proffers that the "true" goal of a feminist politics ought to be for struggling "against the multiple forms in which the category 'woman' is constructed in subordination," and that there is in fact no "'true' form of feminist politics" (88), just as there is no "true" category of "female" or "woman," since depending on the discourse (and the end in view) the strategy will necessarily shift.

Taking a cue from feminist and women's movements, the most pragmatic way to proceed may therefore be to form temporary alliances based on common interests, a form of coalition politics, clustered around themes or concerns differing people share. As Linda Nicholson suggests, this focus means "that we think about feminist politics as the coming together of those who want to work around the needs of women where such a concept is not understood as necessarily singular in meaning or commonly agreed upon" ("Interpreting Gender," 62). In the 1980s, for instance, feminists formed alliances with the peace movement in order to take a stand against the arms race. Another coalition established ties with women in more traditional family roles in order to obtain better childcare for single mothers.

In line with such a feminist agenda, then, our gender-critical perspective seeks to challenge essentialist notions of gender, sex, and sexuality, in which individuals and constituent communities find themselves subordinated to a dominant center. This focus has everything to do with helping form a better democratic society, one that nourishes difference and distinction. To quote Mouffe again,

> When we envisage democratic politics from such an anti-essentialist perspective, we can begin to understand that, for democracy to exist, no social agent should be able to claim any mastery of the *foundation* of society. This signifies that the relation between social agents becomes more democratic only as far as they accept the particularity and the limitation of their claims; that is, only in so far as they recognize their mutual relation as one from which power is ineradicable . . . [D]emocratic character can only be given by the fact that no limited social actor can attribute to herself or himself the representation of the totality. (*Democratic Paradox*, 21–22)

We are decidedly not arguing for an illusory utopian ideal for society, but rather for a system that resists those institutions, groups, and people that would seek to limit options and establish their discourses as normative and universal (see especially Rancière, *Hatred of Democracy*). Still, our rhetoric might seem overly theoretical to some readers. One might wonder what *practical* and *real* difference a gender-critical approach to early Christian literature makes in light of these larger issues. That is, while one can discuss the deconstruction of the center and the exposure of the margins, it is still a question of how one actually goes about doing that. Moreover, a further issue is whether or not there is any palpable effect on the world in which we live, for, as we noted, such an impact is a vital component of the agenda of feminist and gender-critical approaches.

Initially, these analytic lenses were intended for the study of modern gendered, sexed, and sexual phenomena, because there was to be a direct cultural and political challenge to the patriarchal and phallogocentric gendered and sexed systems, to *contemporary* norms and structures, that were seen to exclude non-normative positions, identities, and subjectivities. It is thus a legitimate question as to how the study of ancient texts can functionally fulfill the political and cultural agendas inherent within a gender-critical approach. Does it become just another application of gender theory to the past? Just another proffering of an alternative reading of an ancient text? If so, can this application truly be designated "gender-critical" in the sense that we intend by that term? Does pointing out gender, sex, and sexual divergence in the ancient world challenge in fundamental ways the orientation of our own?

One is reminded here of Camille Paglia's scathing criticism of higher education ("M.I.T. Lecture"), where she took on a number of "sacred cows" of the establishment. One such criticism was leveled at the use of theory in the Western academy. In tackling Marxist theorist Terry Eagleton, she stated: "These people are hypocrites! . . . It's all a literary game. There's no authentic self-sacrifice, no direct actual experience of workers or working-class people" (255). More recently, Antonio Negri has made a similar observation regarding postmodern theory (*Porcelain Workshop*, 77–89), where he considers it "weak thought" precisely because it has so little practical value in terms of resistance (he labels it "marginal resistance") to the cultural and political hegemonies. Thus, theoretical discourses on resistance often function as elite performances, displays of cultural and social capital that become ends in their own right without any real aim to change global and local structures of power and domination.

Although one could point to the expanding range of subversive readings that were and are eagerly published (in some forums at least), the question can still be asked to what extent all these subversive readings really challenge dominant discourses. Their presence on the market can easily be explained by that fact that the global market absorbs the "exotic" because it sells. Critical voices do not escape this mechanism or, as Christina Petterson aptly states, "the cultural critics, the contextual critics and the postcolonial critics are also all construc- tions of and supporters of the (imperial) machine, despite all efforts and desires to the contrary" ("Autobiography and the 'Real Readers,'" 5). Academics also profit from this form of consumerism, as it offers them access to the economy of global consumption (of "thought") and the possibility of having their ideas disseminated (and therefore achieving fame and perhaps also financial gain). There is thus a shared interest between market forces and the academy, even if for different reasons.

Of course, not everybody has equal access to such opportunities. The pub- lishing business reflects the power dynamics of culture at large as well as of the guild, and, although the interests of the academy do not necessarily correspond with that of the publishers, they are related. Moreover, the fact that dissident voices have access to the market does not yet mean that they are valued by the guild and have any impact on dominant discourses as a result. In other words, so few postmodern analytic frameworks, like the postcolonial paradigm we have integrated with gender criticism in this book, seem to have any real impact on our world and the various powers—for example, military, economic, political, religious, cultural—that limit and oppress nonnormative identities. In a similar vein, serious engagement of gendered, sexed, and sexual normativ- ities often stays at the discursive level and inhabits academically confined boundaries. So the question remains how a gender-critical approach might actually make a difference and, in the process, challenge the body of the institution and the discipline, in this case Biblical Studies.

In our view, a scholar's task is necessarily related to the communication of one's knowledge. There are two major areas where such communication takes place: as a teacher in the classroom and as a participant in one's guild/discipline. The impact one can have in both areas is not just related to the content of one's work (i.e., what one communicates), but also situated on a more structural level. Practices in both areas can also be revised in light of a gender-critical approach. To begin with, one has to be fully aware of the context in which such a gender-critical engagement is taking place. Our own primary contexts are a public educational institution (University of Amsterdam) and a private one (Austin College). While we understand there to be other contexts in which interpretation is undertaken, we are thinking here primarily of our own in the following comments. In particular, we are invested in fostering the transformative politics of gender-critical readings of early Christianity towards the end of engaging the academy and educational institutions. With respect to the former, those with power in the academy and in the production and dissemination of knowledge are seldom interested in changing the system itself, since they owe their power to this same system and there is little incentive to question its structures. Hector Avalos, in his recent interrogation of the field of Biblical Studies (*End of Biblical Studies*), has raised precisely this issue with respect to biblical critics across the board: they appear to have little investment in challenging traditional paradigms because their jobs and positions are indebted to continuing the illusion of the importance of the material they are studying as an end in itself. In some respects, while biblical scholars frequently tout the significance of the Bible in contemporary culture, one might at least raise the question just how much of that importance is also manufactured by the guild and its current preoccupation (and collaboration) with the media.

In terms of educational institutions, our argument entails that we examine critically our own institutional settings and also the way in which knowledge is disseminated in our own classrooms and among our colleagues. A gender-critical approach, because of its concern to disrupt the binary and expose inequity and masked ideologies, can thus be enacted precisely in and through interaction with our own institutional locations. We view these interactions as constituting one of the critical components of the politics of our method. Whether one is a "professor" or a "student," or, more likely, somewhere in between those two essentializing categories, the vital issue of our time is to foster critical-thinking engagement in our classrooms and institutions. Students are often constructed both institutionally and pedagogically as consumers. We have established an array of delivery mechanisms for education that solidify this positioning. Summarizing remarks by Paulo Freire, Jacqui Alexander notes that the increasing use of corporate-world paradigms for higher education have resulted in a "'banking concept of education,' a mode of teaching in which knowledge is an investment, a set of received concepts that need not be subject to critical engagement or dialogic reflection" (*Pedagogies of Crossing*, 107). But, as Ira Shor challenges us (*Empowering Education* and *When Students Have Power*), the very practice of education, of teaching and learning, can also embody the critical engagement we talk and theorize about. Indeed, as Henry Giroux and others have encouraged, we can also motivate students to think critically about their own education and institutions (*Beyond the Corporate University*). And, aside from mutual collaboration between students and professors (and administrators), it may fall to students to take on this responsibility themselves when academics, educators, administrators, politicians, and cultural institutions fail them.

Extending this observation to our own institutional locations, a gender-critical engagement, here focused on early Christian texts, ideally forces us and our students to question the dominant discourses operative in our (gendered, sexed, and sexualized) institutions and classrooms, which we would identify as androcentric ways of constructing knowledge. The professor herself and himself, then, also becomes part of this enterprise, as authority structures of all types are involved in the production and dissemination of knowledge. We seek to engage these regimes of discourses (and their concomitant real world consequences) from within. A gender-critical approach thus seeks to uncover the gender, sex, and sexual ideologies that operate in our classrooms, in our communities (micro and macro), and in ourselves. The politics of this approach demand that serious consideration be given to our own prejudices, as well as to how we interact with and engage the gender, sex, and sexual identities of students. As the issues of gender, race, colonialism, and anti-Judaism form a substantive part of the biblical cultural legacy, taking this heritage seriously means to engage in cultural criticism from within. Simply outlining early Christian perspectives on gender, sex, and sexuality is only the first-step towards exposing the hidden ideologies operative in our midst.

Similarly, within the larger guild of Biblical Studies, it is important for those who advocate for change to continue challenging the system both from without *and* from within. This dual focus has to happen not only on a discursive level, but also on a structural level. It is, therefore, not enough to produce alternative readings and writings outside or inside of the academy. Also needed are alternative *practices* in the production and dissemination of knowledge, such as experiments in transgressive academic action that have as their goal to subvert the binary oppositions still in place. Here scholarship becomes a form of resistance to the hegemonic paradigms of the guild. Our own guilding practices—our processes of academic social formation—also have to be scrutinized in the process. What are the hidden ideologies present in our practices of association? How do we deal with difference? A gender-critical perspective similarly challenges us to think about our scholarly communities as much as it does about the scholarly production and dissemination of knowledge. Indeed, one way of changing the latter is to form new networks of interaction, which would create, presumably, new modalities for producing, disseminating, and embodying knowledge. Do we engage in the older paradigm of scholarship as a form of homosocial bonding (or hazing)? Or, do we seek to create just and equitable lines of access for junior scholars and for those working on methods that appear more marginal? How open to criticism of our own methods and interpretations are we? Do we embody the values that we tout in our theories and methods and that we claim are represented in our overt ideologies? Is there space for engagement and interaction, or is it all, in the end, simply a "language game"?

Extending this analysis further, there are at least two complementary types of politics needed to address these larger issues. On the one hand, one can engage in a politics of resistance towards the centers of power; on the other, there is the possibility of a coalition politics with allies that coalesces around shared interests, depending on the issue at stake: gender-critical and postcolonial approaches, for instance, can work in tandem when addressing exclusionary politics by the dominant discourse based on gender and ethnicity, while gender-critical, queer, and transgender studies can collaborate to expose oppressive normative views of gender, sex, and sexuality. This strategy takes into account that each of these interest groups has its own agenda, including both common and differing values and goals. In line with the gender-critical approach outlined in earlier chapters, then, this dual type of political engagement allows for migratory and transgressive practices of both disrupting and crossing the multiple boundaries established to keep people, norms, and discourses in place.

This last facet of our larger political agenda brings us back to one of the fundamental aspects of the character of Thecla in the *Acts of Paul and Thecla*, an element we have stressed throughout this book. That is, whatever else Thecla represents for us, she is first and foremost a "boundary-crosser." Thus, *thinking beyond Thecla*, in our view, entails giving serious consideration to the structures and mechanisms of boundary-crossing itself. Here we move to a more proactive accent in our larger agenda. In our assessment, boundary-crossing is primarily an *ethical* task. Boundary-crossing solely for its own sake (and only for self-pleasure) is a completely different enterprise, one that is often abusive. We are thus bound by the social contract in our boundary-crossing— we cannot just do anything we want, and every boundary we cross requires serious evaluation and self-reflection. Of course, there is no such solution as the final eradication of boundaries, just as there is no ultimate social harmony or just society. Every boundary that is crossed, every territory that is reconfigured, therein produces a redrawing of borders and lines, and elicits new patrolling mechanisms. Boundary-crossing is an endless task, one in which we ourselves also ought to be challenged and provoked (and willingly so).

Of course, boundaries are also fluid, they are not stable and static. Boundary-crossers, therefore, have to be attuned to the shifting and redrawing of boundaries in our own times and places, realizing that power comes through the ability to remap and to reconfigure space and place, not simply through the description and analysis of those spaces and places. For example, in her recent book *Terrorist Assemblages* (2007), Jasbir Puar has persuasively argued that American boundaries have been redrawn in the past few years in order to hetero-ize homosexuals in the United States so as to displace a hideously deformed homoerotic image onto the Oriental/terrorist other. Such remappings of our conceptual and social life often go unnoticed, and have all the more power as a result. We therefore need all the analytic tools we can muster in order to identify these shifting boundaries in the hope of challenging them.

In the final analysis, a plea for "boundary-crossing" represents one of the critical components of the gender-critical approach we have developed in this book. Being "out of place," as we noted in the introduction to this volume ("InterseXions"), ultimately offers us a space and place in which to scrutinize our most cherished "convictions" about the world, to expose the ways in which our deepest held beliefs are always and already complicit in the very power structures we are immersed in and so resolutely oppose. To cross boundaries, to live in the interstices between borders, is, finally, to be transformed oneself, to embody the values and ideas of one who has been "on both sides." There is no outside of this situation, since there is, as we noted in our earlier discussion of Foucault, no outside of power.

Our final hope, then, is that readers of this book will take up this challenge, or, at the very least, critically engage the political and ethical facets (and under-pinnings) of the gender-critical approach we have outlined herein. In thinking "beyond Thecla," we consider it imperative that we remember "her" well, and, in that respect, this book is indebted to boundary-crossers like "her," both ancient and modern.

Bibliography

Alexander, M. Jacqui. *Pedagogies of Crossing: Mediations on Feminism, Sexual Politics, Memory, and the Sacred.* Perverse Modernities. Durham: Duke University Press, 2005.

Avalos, Hector. *The End of Biblical Studies.* Amherst, NY: Prometheus Books, 2007.

Foucault, Michel. *History of Sexuality I: Introduction.* New York: Vintage Books, 1978.

Giroux, Henry A., ed. *Beyond the Corporate University: Culture and Pedagogy in the New Millennium.* Lanham: Rowman & Littlefield, 2001.

Mouffe, Chantal. *The Democratic Paradox.* London: Verso, 2000.

—*The Return of the Political.* London: Verso, 2005.

Negri, Antonio. *The Porcelain Workshop: For a New Grammar of Politics.* Translated by N. Wedell. Los Angeles: Semiotext(e), 2008.

Nicholson, Linda. "Interpreting Gender." Pp. 39–67 in *Social Postmodernism: Beyond Identity Politics.* Edited by L. Nicholson and S. Seidman. Cambridge: Cambridge University Press, 1995.

Paglia, Camille. "The M.I.T. Lecture: Crisis in the American Universities." Pp. 249–98 in *Sex, Art, and American Culture.* New York: Vintage Books, 1992.

Petterson, Christina. "Autobiography and the 'Real Readers.'" Paper presented in the "Critical Theory and Biblical Interpretation" Session. International Society of Biblical Literature Annual Meeting. Vienna, Austria, July 2007.

Puar, Jasbir. *Terrorist Assemblages: Homonationalism in Queer Times.* Next Wave: New Directions in Women's Studies. Durham: Duke University Press, 2007.

Rancière, Jacques. *Hatred of Democracy.* Translated by S. Corcoran. New York: Verso, 2006.

Said, Edward W. *Humanism and Democratic Criticism.* New York: Palgrave Macmillan, 2004.

— *Representations of the Intellectual.* New York: Vintage Books, 1994.

Schüssler Fiorenza, Elisabeth. *The Power of the Word: Scripture and the Rhetoric of Empire.* Minneapolis: Fortress Press, 2007.

— *Rhetoric and Ethic: The Politics of Biblical Studies.* Minneapolis: Fortress Press, 1999.

Shor, Ira. *Empowering Education: Critical Teaching for Social Change.* Chicago: University of Chicago Press, 1992.

—*When Students Have Power: Negotiating Authority in a Critical Pedagogy.* Chicago: University of Chicago Press, 1996.

Index of Ancient Writers and Sources

Index of Modern Authors

Subject Index